FIGHTING *the* GOOD FIGHT

America's "Minister of Defense"
Stands Firm on What It Takes
to Win God's Way

Reggie White
with Andrew Peyton Thomas

A
JANET
THOMA
BOOK

THOMAS NELSON PUBLISHERS
Nashville

Published in Nashville, Tennessee, by Thomas Nelson, Inc.

Unless otherwise noted Scripture quotations are from the HOLY BIBLE: NEW INTERNATIONAL VERSION®. Copyright © 1973, 1978, 1984 by International Bible Society. Used by permission of Zondervan Publishing House. All rights reserved.

Scripture quotations noted KJV are from the KING JAMES VERSION.

Library of Congress Cataloging-in-Publication Data

White, Reggie
    Fighting the good fight : America's "minister of defense" stands firm on what it takes to win God's way / Reggie White and Andrew Peyton Thomas.
       p.   cm.
    ISBN 0-7852-6964-9
    1. Christian life—Baptist authors. 2. United States—Moral conditions. I. Thomas, Andrew Peyton. II. Title.
    BV4501.2.W4497   1999
    241'.046—dc21

98-52084
CIP

Printed in the United States of America.

1 2 3 4 5 6 BVG 04 03 02 01 00 99

To Leonard Collier, my stepfather. I wish I would've been more loving and less judgmental.

Contents

Acknowledgments

This book grew out of the speech I gave to the Wisconsin Assembly in March 1998 and the controversy that followed. The people I'm about to thank either stood with me through the fire or paved the way for what I said.

I want to thank, first of all, my wife, Sara, and our children, Jeremy and Jecolia, for all their love and support through the good times and the hard times. My mother, Thelma, my grandmother, Mildred, and the rest of my family were also there for me through it all.

My thanks also go out to Vaso Bjegovich, Pastor Isaiah Williams and Gloria Williams, Pastor Harold Ray and Brenda Ray, David Sitton, Bill and Stacy Horn, Nathan and Donna Johnson, Gary Bauer, Sandra Peters, and Jerry and Janice Upton for their support and prayers.

To the approximately 100,000 people who wrote to me in support of what I said, thank you for letting me know you were with me.

To my teammates and coaches, and the coaches and players around the NFL who expressed their support, thank you for your solidarity. I won't name names so the firestorm will pass you by!

I'd also like to salute three brave women who fought the good fight before me: Anita Bryant, for being a great soldier who lost a lot but gained much more; and Angie and Debbie Winans, for being so bold.

Finally, I'd like to thank the Wisconsin Assembly for asking me to give the speech. Many members of the assembly have written me to express their support. As for the rest, they weren't nearly as unfriendly as the media said they were.

I have fought the good fight,
I have finished the race,
I have kept the faith.
—*2 Timothy 4:7*

Chapter One

I Didn't Make the Rules

In football and in life, there are rules. In football, the rules are simple. They're written in a rule book and known to all the players. Referees enforce them. Everyone knows the penalties for breaking them.

There are rules in life too. They're just as simple as the rules in football. They're written in the Bible and known to all the players. But unlike football, there aren't referees to call a penalty against the people who break these rules—most of these rules, anyway. People are on the honor system. Too many people break these rules because they think they can get away with it. A lot of people would rather see these rules go away altogether. The game is more fun without them—at least while you're winning.

What happens to a society when the rules of life are ignored or mocked? I'm afraid that's what we're seeing in America today. We're a rich and powerful country. Times have never been better in terms of money and careers. But the America I see is losing its soul.

At the age of seventeen, I became a minister of the gospel. A few years later, God blessed me with a career in professional football. Ever since I was a child, I wanted to play football for a living. But I knew that God expected me to do more than cash in on the opportunity for my own gain. I knew God expected me to speak up for Him and to defend His rules. I had to set a moral example, both on and off the field, for the millions of children who view athletes as heroes, whether we athletes like it or not.

Most of all, I had to talk straight with people when I saw them straying from God's rules. Even when it was unpopular. Even when I had to stand alone.

1

The National Football League (NFL) is one of the world's greatest pulpits. My career as a pro football player has allowed me to reach out to millions of people who wouldn't otherwise have heard my message. At times, though, the enemies of that message have distorted what I've said. In our society today, the enemies of that message are many and powerful.

Speech to the Wisconsin Assembly

I found out how powerful these enemies of the truth are in March 1998 after I gave a speech to the Wisconsin Assembly in Madison. When my state legislator invited me to give a speech to the state legislature, I felt honored. My family and I had moved to Green Bay, Wisconsin, in 1993 when I joined the Green Bay Packers. Four years later, the Packers won the Super Bowl and brought home the Vince Lombardi Trophy. During those years, the people of Green Bay and Wisconsin took my family and me into their lives and treated us as their neighbors. The invitation to speak at the legislature was a chance for me to share my beliefs and values with the leaders of my adopted state.

One topic that I intended to bring up was Urban Hope. It's an organization my wife, Sara, and I founded that seeks to empower, both economically and spiritually, the people of the inner city. I've always focused my ministry on the young people of the inner city. I know that many people look upon these kids as hoodlums and hustlers, and I won't deny that some of them are both. But I see a side that others often don't see. I know them as the children of broken homes, battered lives, and hopelessness. The Bible I preach from says that even the most dangerous, hardcore gangsters and criminals aren't beyond redemption.

These kids were on my mind when I walked to the podium before the Wisconsin Assembly. I had no prepared remarks. I planned to share with the legislators what I'd said in many sermons over the years. I felt that a speech about my inner-city ministry couldn't ignore some of the bigger issues in our society. I also thought it was high time somebody stood up and laid it all on the line—about how we're failing our children.

I wanted to challenge the consciences of parents and political leaders so that we might truly put children first. That was my goal. But the result was a whirlwind of angry criticism that I never expected, and that I still can't really understand.

I began my speech by talking about Urban Hope and the problems of the inner city. The breakup of the black family, I said, is a national tragedy that's causing many of our worst social troubles. The heart of the problem is that we don't have enough fathers in our community who take responsibility for raising their kids. Because of this shortage of fathers, we're not able to train our children to live good lives.

Mothers have done the best job they can. But they don't have the resources to do it all by themselves. Besides, children need fathers. It's that simple.

I explained how we're up against a me-first mentality that comes from years of free welfare checks and government entitlement programs for single parents. But this is only one reason for our moral decay. We've also created a culture that glorifies violence and fornication. These days, young men in the inner city judge their manhood by the number of guns and girlfriends they have.

Now, if I'd just stuck to these themes, my speech wouldn't have caused such a fuss. In fact, I bet it wouldn't even have been reported in the media outside Wisconsin. Let's face it: criticizing black folk in the inner city is a popular thing to do these days. If that were all I'd said, all the journalists who attacked me for my speech probably would've just yawned and written about something else.

But I had a lot more to say. The problems that I see threatening America aren't limited to the inner city or to blacks. The problems are moral and spiritual. They're rooted in sin. And sin is an equal opportunity destroyer.

So I went on. I said that we've become a materialistic people. We care more about our careers and money than we do about right and wrong. What's more, we get so caught up in the rat race, we forget about people who haven't fared as well in life. The poor are left to fend for themselves.

Because we're so infatuated with money and possessions, we have no place for compassion in our lives.

We adults have produced a culture that corrupts our children and robs them of their innocence. TV talk shows and programs glorify senseless violence and sex outside marriage, not to mention the other perversions that parade across the TV screen. Turn on the TV at practically any hour of the day, and you'll see "gangsta rappers" encouraging gunplay and promiscuous sex, foul-mouthed teenagers disrespecting their parents on talk shows, and drag queens sexually confusing our children.

Sure, we say we don't want children exposed to these things. But we make no real effort to prevent it from happening. Hollywood producers know they can get away with anything because American parents will let them. We've become so apathetic that anything goes. Besides, how can we control what our children watch when not even one parent is home when the kids return from school?

I also told the legislators that we've come to accept promiscuous teenage sex as normal. We're content with telling our kids to practice "safe sex" so that they don't die from sleeping around. We act as if children have always behaved this way. Well, there was a time when a majority of girls didn't lose their virginity out of wedlock before they turned eighteen. Fornication does have consequences.

Our children yearn to know the truth. They look to us for answers. But when they ask us for bread, we give them stones instead.

We tolerate corruption in our leaders because the economy is growing and we have money in our pockets. Now, I'm no politician. I'm not even a Democrat or a Republican. But I am an American who cares about what I see going on in the halls of power these days. It can't be healthy for our children to see that the leader of our country betrays the vows he made to his wife by having sexual affairs. Is there really any wonder why so many people are disillusioned with our political system? It seems as if there are few heroes in government anymore—mostly just people serving their own interests.

These were some of the themes I brought up in my speech. But you probably never heard about these remarks. That's because two parts of the speech caught the media's attention and overshadowed the rest of what I said.

Homosexuality

One of these two topics was homosexuality. I called it a sin because the Bible says it is. I know many people disagree with that view these days. But remember, I didn't make the rules.

I stressed that I'd have no problem being a friend of a homosexual. Christ walked among the outcasts of His time, including tax collectors and prostitutes. Befriending homosexuals lets us minister to them. That's what we're called to do, and that's what my ministry does.

Although I don't have a problem being the friend of a homosexual, I have a big problem with the gay rights agenda. Homosexuals, like everyone else, have a right to live free of fear and persecution. They enjoy all the other civil rights of Americans too. But that's where it must end. They're not a special class of people who deserve special rights. Let me put it more bluntly. I believe it is offensive and morally wrong to compare the evil of racial discrimination with opposition to homosexuality.

God's rules on homosexuality are clear. He declared in Leviticus 20:13: "If a man lies with a man as one lies with a woman, both of them have done what is detestable." The New Testament confirms this rule in several passages. Islam and orthodox Judaism also reject homosexuality.

Some defenders of homosexual rights have pointed out that Jesus didn't comment directly on homosexuality. That's true. But He didn't need to. God had laid down clear rules on the subject that were already known to everyone in Jesus' audience. When God lays down the rules once, He doesn't have to keep repeating them.

Comparing the gay rights movement to the civil rights movement is wrong. I explained it this way in my speech: "Homosexuality is a decision. It's not a race." Members of all ethnic groups slide into this wrongful lifestyle. Just because homosexuality is popular doesn't make it any less sinful.

Some people believe that homosexuals are born that way. Well, even if that's true, this much is obvious: homosexual intercourse is a choice. It's just as much a choice as fornication, a decision by an unmarried hetero-sexual couple to have sex. Both are sins. The difference is, marriage can sanctify a heterosexual union, but homosexual union is always offensive to God. With homosexuality as with all other sins, it's important for us to remember to love the sinner while rejecting the sin. But God's rules are clear.

"The Complete Image of God"

The other part of the speech that the media focused on was my dis-cussion of race relations. I asked a simple yet important question: "Why did God create us differently?" It's a question that a lot of people must have thought about. These days, though, most people are afraid even to try to answer it. The whole issue of racial diversity has become so touchy that we're expected to ignore the obvious—and glorious—differences among us or risk offending someone.

I thought I'd try to break the silence. As I see it, each race has a unique gift to offer to society. Consider, for example, my people, blacks. Blacks excel at worship and spirituality. Go into any black church in America, and you'll find enthusiasm and energy like you'll rarely see in a white church. People sing, clap, dance, and encourage the preacher with cries of "Amen"—all in joyful celebration of God. These are forms of worship that blacks have followed for centuries, that go all the way back to religious customs in Africa.

I know I'm biased, being a black preacher, but I think blacks have cre-ated the greatest form of worship that man has ever offered up to almighty God. And I think black folk should be proud of that.

Whites have their gifts as well. I think they're gifted at structure and organization. Whites can build businesses and invest money better than any other group. If you don't believe me, look at the list of the richest men in the world and the CEOs of the top corporations. Racism may well play a role in how lopsided this list is. But there's obviously something more to it than that.

Whites have dominated economically ever since Europeans began exploring and colonizing the other continents. We can argue about why such economic inequality persists. Still, it gets us nowhere to deny obvious facts.

Hispanics are gifted in family values. I pointed out in the speech that many Hispanics are comfortable living together in a single house. I don't think that's offensive. It's a gift. It's also a fact because Hispanics have large families. That, too, is something to be proud of, especially in a time when so many families are coming apart.

Besides, the Hispanic experience is really just part of the immigrant experience. Not that long ago, a lot of Irish and Italian immigrants lived together in close quarters. Once they'd saved enough money to buy or rent their own places, they were able to move out on their own. I don't think we should deny or be ashamed of this part of our national heritage.

I also talked about how Asians are creative and gifted at inventing things. Because of these qualities, Asians have been very successful economically. I used the example of Asians turning a television into a watch. I meant that to be humorous, even if the media didn't take it that way. My point is that they're hardworking, intelligent people who have prospered for good reason.

The diversity of the races is, in my opinion, our most beautiful feature as a nation. I explained to the legislators, "When you put all of that together, guess what it makes? It forms the complete image of God."

With respect, I challenge anyone to show me where I was wrong in what I said. It is a fact that the different races excel at different things. I didn't say that these differences are because of genetics, or that individuals don't have their own talents in addition to those gifts. My point was that these gifts of the races form a brilliant mosaic that's pleasing to God.

Why does this bother some people so much? Isn't it possible that racial diversity is just a tribute to the imagination of God? And wouldn't we all be a lot better off if we admitted these differences instead of being ashamed of them? If we look upon these differences as ordained by God, wouldn't we as a people be happier with ourselves and one another?

Blasted by the Media

Looking back, I realize I could have said some of these things more clearly. But the journalists who reported what I said didn't take issue just with the way I made these points. They clearly disagreed with my message, especially about homosexuality. I said the Bible calls homosexuality a sin, and the media said I was a bigot. I paid several compliments to each of the races, and the media said I was using stereotypes.

Reporters described the state lawmakers as "stunned" or "shocked" by my remarks. That was not the case. They gave me a standing ovation at the beginning of my speech and another at the end. However, some legislators seemed to have changed their minds once the media began criticizing me. The media came at me from every direction. I felt like a quarterback being blitzed.

The TV newscasts on the major networks chastised me for being insensitive. ABC's 20/20 devoted a segment to the speech and its aftermath, including an interview of Sara and me. The segment was called "Reggie's Offense." The show's host, Hugh Downs, introduced the segment by saying it would talk about my "fall from grace." Some people might consider that kind of statement offensive, even blasphemous, given the context. But apparently, as long as Christians instead of gay rights activists are on the receiving end of a tough comment, there's no controversy. Those seem to be the rules of today's journalism.

The newspapers were just as rough. The Associated Press said the speech was "laced with ethnic stereotypes." Articles in various newspapers described my speech and beliefs as "extremist and outdated" (*New York Times*), "stereotypical" (*USA Today*), "odious" and "vicious" (*Atlanta Journal and Constitution*), "crass" (*Kansas City Star*), and "reprehensible" (*Baltimore Sun*).

One journalist in the *Houston Chronicle*, James T. Campbell, asked, "What more can we expect from a guy who mugs quarterbacks for a living?" As far as I know, no one questioned whether he was out of line for calling me a professional mugger, with all the racial implications of that comparison.

A columnist for the *Washington Post*, Jennifer Frey, described me as "incredibly arrogant" and "incredibly ignorant." She then added: "White sounded like a bigot, and he sounded like a hypocrite. Mostly, though, he sounded like a fool." She went so far as to argue that my comments were "far, far worse" than Fuzzy Zoeller's comments at the Masters Tournament in 1997, when he joked that Tiger Woods would want fried chicken and collard greens at the next year's champions' dinner. And you know, she's right—that is, if you believe, as she clearly does, that opposition to homosexuality is just as bad as racism or racial insensitivity. I reject that point of view.

Back in Wisconsin, several members of the state legislature spoke out against the speech—members of both political parties, in fact. Yet the same people, after the speech was over, had asked me to pose for pictures and to give them my autograph!

The fallout from the speech spread to my corporate sponsors. I had appeared in commercials for Campbell Soup throughout the previous year. You might have seen the one in which an actress playing my mother, dressed like a cheerleader, asks me if I'd eaten my Chunky Soup. Campbell had been very generous to the poor on my behalf, feeding a million and a half people through the "Tackle Your Hunger" program (Campbell's donations were based on how many sacks and tackles I made during the season).

But after the controversy over the speech erupted, a spokesman for Campbell said that my comments were "not consistent with the principles of Campbell Soup company." A few days after the speech, Campbell Soup let my contract lapse.

I was especially disappointed with CBS. A few months before my speech, CBS bought from the NFL the right to televise games from the

American Football Conference (AFC) during the 1998 season. CBS beat out NBC, which had televised AFC games for as long as I can remember. CBS Sports needed to hire its own team of sportscasters. Like other networks, CBS was interested in signing former players.

In February, CBS approached me about a broadcasting job. At that time, I was seriously considering retiring from football. I had chronic back pain that I thought wouldn't allow me to play another season. About a month before the speech, I flew to New York and met with Sean McManus, the president of CBS Sports. He was a young, energetic guy who really impressed me.

Sean said he wanted me to be the lead studio analyst for the network's AFC broadcasts. The way he described it, I would've had basically the same role that Terry Bradshaw has on Fox's NFC broadcasts. Since I have a background in public speaking as well as football, his proposal seemed like a good fit. It was an exciting offer.

During our meeting, I reminded Sean that I was a Christian minister. I told him point-blank that I didn't intend to stop preaching after I retired from football. I even specifically brought up my beliefs about homosexuality. I knew that the gay rights lobby might make an issue of them. Sean assured me that my ministry wasn't a concern to him. As for homosexuals, he told me that as long as I wasn't advocating killing homosexuals, there would be no problem with CBS.

Over the next few weeks, Sean and my agent spoke on the telephone and ironed out the details. Eventually, we struck a deal. We agreed orally that I would be CBS's main studio analyst for its AFC telecasts. I would receive a five-year contract with a three-year guarantee. We even agreed on salary. All that was left was to draw up the contract and sign.

Everything changed after the speech. I first became concerned about CBS's reaction when I heard the comments of a spokeswoman for CBS Sports, Leslie Ann Wade. "Reggie White is not a CBS employee," she told the reporters who asked for her comments on the speech. "I will say that CBS as a corporation has a hard-and-fast policy against bias of all kinds." She added, "No employee of CBS or any other network, as far as

I know, has survived comments that were insensitive to large numbers of people."

I spoke to Sean on the phone soon after that. "Let's hold off for a while," he said, referring to the contract. "Let's see how things play out." I told him that was fine. I didn't mind riding out the controversy because I thought that I'd be vindicated.

It soon became obvious, though, that CBS had had a change of heart. A few weeks later, I heard that CBS had hired Marcus Allen for its AFC broadcasts. I was extremely happy for Marcus. He's one of the best running backs of all time, and he's contributed a lot to the game of football. But I knew that by hiring Marcus, CBS was sending a message. The network had already hired several other studio analysts, and there really wasn't enough room on the set for both Marcus and me. By signing Marcus, CBS was letting me know that our deal was over.

Once again, I called Sean McManus. I told him I thought that the people at CBS could've handled things better, that they could've at least let me know they'd decided not to hire me. Sean was nice but firm. He told me that he was concerned about being picketed by gay rights activists. He didn't want any distractions. He also brought up my comments regarding the gifts of the races.

"Sean," I said, "come on. Your decision has nothing to do with what I said about the gifts of the races. I've said the same thing countless times in my sermons, and no one's ever complained. It's what I said about homosexuality that's causing all the problems." He didn't deny it.

Then I pointed out that CBS wasn't being consistent. "Sean, CBS has just hired Howard Stern to do a program on Saturday night. How is it that Howard Stern isn't too controversial, but I am?" Sean admitted I had a point. (I found out that after my speech, Howard Stern defended me on his program.)

In the 20/20 segment about my speech, spokespersons at CBS were asked whether they'd ever reached an agreement with me. They responded that they'd "never finalized an agreement." They insisted that their decision was not based "on influences from any special interest groups."

But we had reached an agreement, at least orally. And Sean had admitted to me that his fear of seeing homosexual activists protesting outside CBS had influenced his decision.

Then there were the letters. In the days following the speech, I received a stack of angry, hateful mail—mail that, ironically, accused *me* of hate. A lot of the letters were from homosexuals angry about my criticism of their lifestyle. But as I said on *20/20*, I felt they should take up their complaints with God. I didn't make the rules.

Some of the letters went even farther over the line. Some letters from gay activists called me a "nigger." And that was coming from people who said they wanted to promote tolerance!

If the attacks were supposed to make me back down, my enemies counted wrong. I've learned several valuable lessons for life from my career in football. Football taught me how to discipline myself and how to submit to authority. It also taught me that the only people who make a difference on a football field are the ones who never back down from the battle. No matter how many men are blocking you, no matter what cheap shots they use to try to trip you up or hurt you, the only way to win the battle is to charge ahead.

These lessons guided me in the days after the speech. I refused to apologize. I believed I'd done nothing wrong. I explained to reporters that "I am not politically correct." In response to questions about my comments on homosexuality, I replied, "I'm only stating what the Bible states. You might as well be calling the Bible racist or God a racist." The only apology I offered was for my comments about the gifts of the races—not for the substance of what I said, but for the clumsy way I said it. As for the corporations who might not stand behind me, I told them, "I'm not going to sell out."

What was funny about the media uproar over my comments on homosexuality was that a year before, I'd been criticized by *conservatives* for a speech I gave in Knoxville, Tennessee. In a speech at an inner-city high school there in 1997, I said a lot of the same things I told the Wisconsin Assembly a year later. But what drew flak from conservatives were my accusations against the police. I said that the police sometimes harass inner-city youths for no good reason. I still stand by those remarks, too, because they're based on hard experience.

After my speech in Madison, it was the other way around. Conservatives defended me and liberals scolded me. Christians and believers in traditional morality were some of my strongest allies during that tough time. They rallied around me and really boosted my spirits.

Some of my corporate sponsors also backed me up. Nike didn't cave in. Phil Knight personally told me he'd stay with me regardless of all the hoopla. Edge Shaving Gel also kept its contract with me.

Even many members of the Wisconsin Assembly wrote me to offer words of support.

Most encouraging were the many Packers fans who stood by me through the whole experience. To all the fans who wrote to the newspapers in my defense, who sent me a letter of support, or who stuck up for me in some other way I'll never know about—I want you to know that your support and prayers meant more to me than I can express.

Round Two

A few weeks after my speech in Madison, I needed once again all the support I could get. A fresh round of controversy broke out when I considered retiring from football.

Right after the Super Bowl in January 1998, I talked to my coach, Mike Holmgren, about my future in the NFL. I told him I was going to retire. My back had been causing me a great deal of pain. The fifth lumbar disk in my lower back had slipped out of place. The doctors weren't sure if football or something else caused the condition. All I know is that I had painful back spasms. In fact, when I awoke some mornings, my back was crooked. I reached the point that I thought I just couldn't play football anymore.

Mike and Ron Wolf, general manager of the Packers, counseled me to give it some time and think things over. I decided they were right. I didn't want to let the team down. So I didn't make any announcement about my future.

But in April, on the second day of the NFL draft, I rode my motorcycle down to Packers-headquarters in Green Bay. When I saw Mike there, he asked me if I'd changed my mind about retirement. I told him no. I'd thought about it long enough. I was definitely going to retire.

Mike was supportive of my decision. He did say, however, that if I was sure about retiring, we should let the fans know soon. I was scheduled to give a speech at the University of Wisconsin the weekend of the Packers' minicamp. People would wonder why I wasn't with the team. I gave Mike permission to tell the public about my plans. The Packers scheduled a press conference for a few days later.

The day after my meeting with Mike, I was getting a back massage when something came to me that made me reassess things. I really can't explain what it was. I didn't hear an audible voice, see a burning bush, or experience something spectacular like that. But I believe I heard God speaking to me, in His own way, directly to my heart.

As I lay there, God reminded me of the terms of my contract with the Packers. When I had signed a five-year deal with the Packers the year before, I had agreed to play a minimum of two more years. By retiring, I'd be breaking that agreement. God told me, *Reggie, I want you to be a man of your word. You made a promise, and you should fulfill that promise.*

The truth is, while I told Mike and Ron I'd think about playing another year, my mind had been made up ever since the Super Bowl. So for me to change my mind at that stage was a remarkable thing. As the reporters found out the day after my speech in Madison, I don't change my mind very easily.

I'd convinced myself that I couldn't stand the pain. But the Lord saw things differently. He cut right through the self-pity.

Reggie, He said, *you're just being lazy.* He was right, of course. I knew that if I followed the exercise program my doctors had prescribed, my back spasms could be kept under control. I could still play football if I could find the will and the heart.

At my press conference on April 22, called originally to announce my retirement, I caught the media by surprise — again. I explained to the reporters that I'd decided to play another season. I told them that the Lord had commanded me to honor my contract. I had to honor the promise I made by playing another season — my last season.

Some people seem to think I'm dishonest or crazy for saying that God speaks to me. As I said, I don't hear a voice with my ears. But I would tell my critics that they shouldn't get mad at me just because God, for whatever reason, chooses to speak to me. I don't have a unique relationship with God. I don't know why I hear what I hear. But I do know that it helps to seek Him, and that often we can find His voice in the stern words of conscience. That is, by listening to and living by God's rules.

Once again, though, the media had fun with my announcement. One journalist who seemed to go out of his way to criticize me was Keith Olbermann, a former sportscaster with ESPN who has gone on to anchor the late-evening news at MSNBC. At the end of his show one night, he questioned whether I really could've heard God's voice and why God would even bother to talk to me. Sportscasters on Fox Sports News and other channels had some laughs too.

I had my own suspicions about why the media attacked me so strongly again, this time about my retirement announcement. In an editorial called "Honor Thy Contract," the *Wall Street Journal* confirmed some of what I'd been thinking. The editorial said that I was in "big trouble for having said, 'Homosexuality is a decision, it's not a race.'" The article explained,

> The world of TV and Hollywood likes to think that it defines what the culture values, and so its Furies would be unleashed when a Reggie White declares the long-standing religious view that homosexuality is a "sin" or says something about ethnic groups that even *sounds* critical.

Whether my enemies attacked me out of anger, or whether they were trying to intimidate me, I don't know. This much I do know: I forgive my enemies so that I might be forgiven for my sins. I can say before God that I truly hold no bitterness toward them. But I will also say this. Anyone who thought I would run and hide from these attacks was wrong.

Through God's grace, I was able to come back to play one more season. I was even named the 1998 NFL Defensive Player of the Year. I'm still preaching and speaking out for God's rules. I have no intention of going through "sensitivity training" to satisfy my critics. And I've authored this book.

About *Fighting the Good Fight*

After the speech, I decided the best way to share my message was to write a book about my beliefs and values. The title *Fighting the Good Fight* comes from 2 Timothy 4:7. The verse was written by Paul: "I have fought the good fight, I have finished the race, I have kept the faith." As I end my career in football and prepare for a more full-time ministry, I thought that this verse summed up the transition I'm experiencing. The title also helps to make clear that all the criticism that came my way for my speech didn't break my faith in God and His rules.

Each chapter in this book is devoted to a subject I discussed or touched on in my speech: sin and sexuality, race relations, family values, raising children, sports, and other topics. Like other public figures who've written a book to share their views on society—people as diverse as Booker T. Washington, Hillary Rodham Clinton, and many ministers of the gospel—I've benefited from some assistance in preparing this book. But the beliefs expressed here are my own.

In this book, I rely on some statistics, polls, and other research to support what I'm saying. I do this so you'll know that the points I'm making are more than just the random thoughts of Reggie White. I don't pretend to be a social scientist, economist, or anything more than what I am—a minister of the gospel who's deeply concerned about where our country is headed.

Being a pro football player and a minister, I've worn two very different hats as I've walked through society. But the America I see is the same, whether I'm looking through a football helmet or over a pulpit. I see a nation full of great promise and hope, but also of growing acceptance of selfishness and sin. We have great wealth and power, but weak families and communities. Above all, our children are paying the price for our neglect of their souls.

Heaven knows I'm no Isaiah or Elijah. Through all these recent events, however, I drew strength from their examples. Their lives show that God sometimes chooses unusual people to do His bidding in difficult times. What they had in common is the one thing God demands of all those He calls to serve: that they stand firm to the end.

I believe we owe it to our country and our children to level with ourselves. I see a nation that's become too comfortable with self-centeredness and vice. I see churches that have made their peace with sin. I see politicians and activists and celebrities who benefit from these troubles.

I've learned over the last few months that anyone who stands up and challenges our "comfort level" with sin is ostracized. We can't let that discourage us. There are too many problems in our society, too many people suffering from them, for us to abandon hope. We can remake our society in a better image. But it won't happen until we decide to strap on the armor of God, stand together, and fight the good fight.

It's time for us to end the silence. The truth must be told, no matter how politically incorrect it has become. We need to remind ourselves of God's rules of life. I didn't make the rules, but they're rules worth defending.

I hope you'll join me in considering where America went wrong, and what it will take from all of us to make things right again.

Chapter Two

The New Slavery

Some of my strongest defenders following my speech were people committed to speaking the truth about homosexuality. They had a message of love and hope for homosexuals. They believed that homosexuals could leave their lifestyle behind and find both great joy and lasting heterosexual relationships in God's service.

These ministers and groups had crossed swords with the media too. The media didn't seem very interested in sharing their good news about homosexuality with the public. One good thing to come out of my speech and all the ruckus that followed was that we began to get this message out.

A few months after my speech, some of these ministries got together and ran a newspaper ad with my picture on it. The ad appeared in *USA Today*, the *New York Times*, and the *Washington Post*. It was a full-page ad that said across the top, above my picture, "In Defense of Free Speech."

The ad argued that people should be able to talk openly about the real causes of homosexuality. It pointed out that many ex-homosexuals have found new life as heterosexuals after converting to Christianity. The ad offered the names and numbers of organizations and ministries dedicated to helping homosexuals in this way.

The ad stirred up more controversy. Newspapers reported that NFL officials had scolded me for the ad (in fact, they hadn't). ABC's *World News Tonight* discussed the ad and the controversy, as did newspapers across the country.

My remarks on homosexuality have received more attention than anything else I said. If I've learned one thing from that speech, it's that a lot of powerful people in this country don't want to hear the truth about homosexuality. For example, a few months after my speech, the president and CEO of the *San Francisco Chronicle* refused to run an ad by ex-gay ministries. His explanation? "We didn't want to inflame a segment of our community." At Harvard Law School, members of a Christian student group posted flyers in October 1997 to announce a press conference for National Coming Out of Homosexuality Day. According to the *Boston Globe*, "most [flyers] were ripped down, replaced with duplicates that had a different message. 'For those struggling with Judaism, there is hope in the truth,' they read. 'You can walk away (to the gas chambers).'"

San Francisco and Harvard Law School are supposedly two of the most "tolerant" places in the country. Yet both have offered recent examples of a broad campaign to suppress the truth about homosexuality. The powerful people behind this campaign—including the people who went after me—would prefer for you to think that homosexuality is either an incurable disease or a lifestyle that's as good as any other. To them, homosexuality is a sacred cow. They'll try to destroy anyone or anything that disagrees with them.

I'm not in the habit of backing down from bullies. I'm also not one to stand silent in the face of lies. I know that there's hope for homosexuals. I know that many of them were abused as children—abuse that deformed their spirits and drew them into homosexuality. They deserve our deepest sympathy and love. The only way we can honestly show them both is to stand up to all these lies.

The fact that so many heterosexuals accept homosexuality shows that our society is suffering from a problem much broader than homosexuality. This problem is a new form of slavery. Americans have become slaves to sin. We've concluded that we must be "tolerant" of sin, lest we be considered bigots. We've even defined sin as natural and incurable. We've convinced ourselves that there's no way out. So, the thinking goes, we might as well live it up.

This kind of slavery is really a very old kind of slavery. In fact, it's the oldest kind around. The only difference is that this slavery—slavery to sin—has been dressed up as something new.

These days, so-called experts and professors tell us that all kinds of sinful behavior are the result of things a person can't control. A frequent excuse is, "My genes made me do it." These authorities quote research that supposedly shows that homosexuals were born that way and can't help themselves. We're told that this research means we can't hold homosexuals responsible for their actions.

These authorities say we're slaves to our genes. I say they're wrong.

For one thing, many of the more famous researchers saying this are practicing homosexuals. Their research just happens to reflect what they already believe. How convenient!

Some of these so-called authorities are telling us that people who commit crimes, engage in violence, or abuse alcohol or drugs can't help themselves because they, too, are born that way. Their genes are their masters. It's reached the point that, as *U.S. News & World Report* noted recently, a geneticist who reported finding a possible genetic link to violent crime started receiving calls from criminal defense lawyers on behalf of their clients in prison. Their clients hoped her findings might help them get their convictions overturned.

These theories about genes controlling our behavior are high-sounding nonsense. They're just a fancy way of denying our God-given free will—and of justifying sin.

God makes all of us unique. Each of us is born with certain qualities. Some of these qualities are good; some aren't so good. Some of us are aggressive, some are shy, and some have a quick temper. It's all part of the diversity of life.

God expects us to use the traits He has given us for the good. We're commanded to overcome our more challenging qualities and even channel them into doing good deeds. He doesn't want us to complain about them or use them as an excuse for sin.

Even if you believe that homosexuality is a trait you're born with, that belief gets you only so far. It doesn't mean that homosexuals should be able to indulge in that lifestyle. All it means is that they have to work at denying that impulse. They have to work at it the same way other people have to work at controlling their temper, overcoming envy, or counteracting laziness.

Remember, every wrongful act starts with a choice. Whether our genes make us quicker to be violent, to become alcoholic, or even to be attracted to the same sex, it's still the choice that leads to the behavior. Some say we are what we're made of. I say we are what we make of ourselves.

What if everyone came to believe in the new slavery? What if we could excuse all our sins based on our genes? We could say we're born with a bad temper, so it's okay to yell at people. We're born to a violent father, so it's okay to be violent. We have a "gay gene," so it's okay to lie down with other people of the same sex.

Where does the new slavery end? I'll tell you where it ends, for all of us. For society, it ends in chaos. For individuals, it ends on the road to hell. And I don't just mean in the afterlife. I mean hell on earth, too, because people who practice the new slavery create suffering for themselves and others.

Paul explained in his letter to the Romans how God gives us a choice. Either we can strive to be slaves to righteousness, or we must accept being slaves to sin. There's no middle ground.

We have been "set free from sin," Paul told us. Under God's rules, "sin shall not be your master, because you are not under law, but under grace."

We're not preprogrammed to commit acts that God declares to be sins. We're free to choose our own destiny. Our freedom is one of our most precious gifts.

The Price of Defending God's Rules

Today, anyone who stands up for God's rules on homosexuality risks persecution. Anita Bryant was the first major celebrity to be persecuted for defending these rules. A former Miss America, she became a household name in the 1970s after starring in TV and radio commercials for Florida orange juice. A Christian, Bryant often said that she believed in "something bigger than vitamin C—Christ."

In 1977, Bryant's beliefs led her to speak out against gay rights ordinances in Dade County, Florida. She paid dearly for her stance. Because of pressure from gay rights activists, she lost her lucrative contract with the Florida Citrus Commission. A TV critic with the *Washington Post* called her a "female Archie Bunker." Her marriage crumbled. She became addicted to sleeping pills. At one public event in Iowa, a gay rights activist smashed a pie in her face.

Yet today, she still stands by God's rules. "It's not my position," she recently told a Canadian newspaper reporter. "It's God's position."

Angie and Debbie Winans, young gospel singers, went through the same kind of ordeal a couple of years ago. Their first, self-titled album was critically acclaimed and sold very well. They were nominated for a Grammy.

But in 1997, they sang a song called "Not Natural" that criticized homosexuality. The media turned on them. MTV, VH-1, and The Box all banned their video. Black Entertainment Television (BET) shunned the video, even after Angie and Debbie agreed to cut out a part the BET producers objected to. Angie and Debbie's manager received thirty death threats as a result of the song.

Three months after my speech, Trent Lott, the majority leader of the U.S. Senate, reaped abuse after giving his views on homosexuality. Armstrong Williams, a conservative black radio talk show host, asked Lott on his program whether he thought homosexuality is a sin. Lott said, "Yeah, it is."

Then Lott said basically what I had said: "You should still love that person. You should not try to mistreat them or treat them as outcasts. You should try to show them a way to deal with that problem, just like alcohol . . . or sex addiction . . . or kleptomaniacs." A day later, the House majority leader, Dick Armey, stuck up for Lott, saying, "The Bible is very clear on this."

In response, President Clinton's spokesman, Mike McCurry, chastised Lott. He called his remarks "backward." McCurry said that homosexuality is just "part of defining one's sexuality." I'm not sure what that means. Regardless, the media took McCurry's side in their reporting.

It's time for us to stand up to this intimidation by gay rights activists and their allies in the media. There's just as much hope for homosexuals as for any other children of God. God doesn't condemn anyone to a lifetime of sin. No matter how much grief comes our way, we must start to tell the truth about homosexuality — and help homosexuals find a way out.

Reconsidering Homosexuality

The theory that homosexuality is incurable is like a pretty house built on sand. When the truth rolls in like the tide, the house washes away, leaving nothing behind but the house's angry owners.

I should start this discussion with a point I emphasized in my speech. Even though I reject homosexuality, I love homosexuals. The cliché about "loving the sinner but hating the sin" is truly what God commands. Besides, as I talk about the real causes of homosexuality, I think you'll see why it's not hard to love homosexuals.

Most homosexuals have had a tragic childhood. Almost all of them had poor or nonexistent relations with their fathers. Many were sexually abused. Only the most hard-hearted among us would fail to be moved by their stories. I'm speaking out on homosexuality so that homosexuals might finally learn the truth about their condition, a condition many of them have suffered since childhood.

Not Natural

In talking about homosexuality, I think it's important to begin with the basics. Angie and Debbie Winans were right about something. Their message was tough but undeniable. No matter how we look at it, homosexuality isn't natural.

For the moment, let's set aside all the theories and research about homosexuality. Let's even set aside the moral questions about homosexuality. Let's just focus on whether homosexuality is natural.

Clearly, it's not. Homosexuality offends God's design for men and women. People can't reproduce through homosexual sex. Homosexual sex requires people to do unnatural, unsanitary things. I won't spell out these activities to you. But we must get the general picture, because these unnatural acts are what homosexuality means in practice.

Homosexuality is also impractical for society. What if everyone became a homosexual? The human race would die out. Homosexuality can't be right because, quite simply, it violates the laws of nature.

A belief that people are born as homosexuals doesn't end the discussion. Because homosexuality then becomes, at best, a misfiring of nature.

So even if you don't like the moral view of homosexuality, at least think about the natural side of things. When certain homosexuals mutilate their bodies to try to change their sex, they're doing it for a reason. They realize that their view of sexuality isn't compatible with the bodies God gave them.

Nature penalizes people for engaging in homosexual sex. God doesn't penalize them—nature does. I'm not talking specifically about AIDS, although it's still a fact (obscured by the media) that the vast majority of people with AIDS are homosexuals. Homosexuals also have a high rate of other sexually transmitted diseases, anal warts, and other afflictions.

I don't believe these afflictions represent "God's retribution" against homosexuals. God says that He reserves His justice for the time after death. And so many homosexuals have lived such tragic lives that I have to believe a just God—our God—will take all of these facts into account when He judges them. Yet I do think that through these diseases, *nature* is trying to tell us something. The message, as I see it, is that human beings just aren't made for that kind of intercourse.

The Powerful 1 Percent

Homosexual activists claim that homosexuals are 10 percent of the population. This number came from research conducted by Alfred Kinsey in 1948, research done on prisoners, prostitutes, and pedophiles. In 1993, the Batelle Human Affairs Research Centers found in an extensive report that the number is actually *1 percent* of the population.

Homosexuals may be only 1 percent of the population, but they hold a powerful position in our country. They are disproportionately rich and influential white men. That's the main reason, I believe, that it's so hard to spread the truth about homosexuality.

Is Homosexuality Treatable?

Those who've read or heard that homosexuality isn't treatable should know that a lot of information is being suppressed. Years of studies and experience indicate that there's hope for homosexuals wishing to leave their lifestyle. As with any addiction, clinical and spiritual treatment are available and effective for homosexuals who are open to them.

Clinical Treatment

In 1997, several professors of psychiatry and practicing psychiatrists, including Charles Socarides of the Albert Einstein College of Medicine and Benjamin Kaufman of the University of California-Davis, wrote an article for the *Wall Street Journal*. The article posed the following question:

> Suppose that a young man, seeking help for a psychological condition that was associated with serious health risks and made him desperately unhappy, were to be told by the professional he consulted that no treatment is available, that his condition is permanent and genetically based, and that he must learn to live with it. . . .

> How would this man and his family feel when they discovered years later that numerous therapeutic approaches have been available for his specific problem for more than 60 years? . . . What would this man feel if he discovered that the reason he was not informed that treatment for his condition was available was that certain groups were, for political

reasons, pressuring professionals to deny that effective treatment existed?

The psychiatrists noted that this is what is happening to men who feel a homosexual urge: "It is not surprising that many of these young men fall into depression or despair when they are informed that a normal life with a wife and children is never to be theirs."

These psychiatrists have held fast in their conviction that homosexuality is treatable. Quite a bit of evidence is on their side. Studies have shown that between 25 to 70 percent of homosexuals seeking treatment for their homosexuality experience significant improvement. Some of these studies were conducted decades ago. Others are more recent. The studies I'm about to discuss are cited at the end of the book. I encourage people with doubts about what I say to read these studies for themselves.

Dr. Charles Socarides treated forty-five "overt homosexuals" from 1967 to 1977. Twenty patients, nearly 50 percent of the total, "developed full heterosexual functioning and were able to develop love feelings for their heterosexual partners."

In 1979, Masters and Johnson studied a group of homosexual men who had been treated at their institute. The men had stated that they strongly desired to become heterosexual. The failure rate for their treatment program was only 20.9 percent. In 1984, Schwartz and Masters did a follow-up study and reported that the failure rate had risen to 28.4 percent. That is, more than seven out of ten homosexuals succeeded in leaving their lifestyle.

A 1998 study by the National Association for Research and Therapy of Homosexuality gave homosexuals further reason for hope. The survey was conducted among more than 850 individuals and 200 therapists and counselors (statisticians at Brigham Young University tabulated the results). Before counseling or therapy, 68 percent of the participants said they were "exclusively or almost entirely homosexual." Another 22 percent said they were "more homosexual than heterosexual."

After treatment, only 13 percent said they were "exclusively or almost entirely homosexual." Thirty-three percent said they were "either exclusively or almost entirely heterosexual." Thirty percent had had homosexual sex "very often" before treatment. This number fell to 1 percent after treatment. Ninety-nine percent said they now believe treatment to change homosexuality can be effective and valuable.

Researchers and psychiatrists who've worked with homosexuals have found that men struggling with same-sex attractions and behavior have many things in common. A large majority of homosexual men say they lacked a father who was loving and engaged in their lives. Dr. Joseph Nicolosi described fathers of homosexuals as "emotionally avoidant." In the vast majority of cases, the fathers were distant and uninvolved in the upbringing of their sons. Another study by Dr. William L. Dreikorn in 1998 reported that every homosexual he examined reported a poor relationship with his father.

The ex-gay ministries mentioned in my "In Defense of Free Speech" ad feature many ex-gay members who tell similar stories of failed relationships with their fathers. George Morales, age thirty-two, of Norcross, Georgia, says that his father often called him "stupid" and said that he ran "like a faggot." Morales says his troubled relationship with his father caused him to look for affection from other men. "It was subconsciously, 'If you can't give me that love, I'm going to go to a man to get that love.'"

John Paulk is chairman of Exodus North America, a network of ministries assisting homosexuals who want to become straight. He and his wife, Anne, were on the cover of *Newsweek* in 1998, after ex-gay ministries used his picture for a national ad campaign that followed up on my "In Defense of Free Speech" ad. "My parents divorced when I was five," Paulk explained in an article in the *Denver Post*.

My father was hardly ever there for me, I had no male role models. I was picked on in school as a sissy, a homo. I only hung out with girls, but I had this intense longing to be accepted by boys. From the age of

14, a sexual attraction towards boys started to grow. Looking back, I know that I wanted to complement my own deficiencies by being with them.

These studies and examples of poor father-son relationships among homosexuals suggest that homosexuality may have the same root cause as juvenile delinquency, drug abuse, and many other of today's pathologies. Homosexuality may be but one more social problem that comes from the lack of a strong, loving father.

The research tends to focus on male homosexuals because most homosexuals are men. But as Dr. Socarides notes, lesbians typically also report poor relationships with their fathers.

In addition, many homosexuals were sexually abused as children. Dr. Socarides believes, based on his extensive experience, that "most homosexuals have been abused as infants, or in their early childhood." Dr. Dreikorn's study reported that 47 percent of homosexuals said they had been sexually abused during childhood. A 1992 study published in *Child Abuse and Neglect* examined 1,001 homosexuals in Chicago, Denver, and San Francisco. The study reported that 37 percent had been sexually abused as children. The researchers also concluded that because of the "methodological constraints" on the study, "our data may underestimate the amount, or inadequately describe the full range, of abusive contact that occurred."

What about the research a few years ago pointing out that homosexuals have a different brain structure from that of heterosexuals? In 1991, a gay researcher named Simon LeVay, formerly at the Salk Institute, published an article that reported that a cluster of brain cells in homosexual men was twice as large as that in heterosexual men. The media trumpeted the study. However, there were problems with his research. LeVay performed his research on men who had died from AIDS. AIDS is a disease that can affect the size of brain cells. Also, nobody could confirm that the people he said were homosexual in fact *were* homosexual. Two prominent geneticists pointed out in *Technology Review* that LeVay "could not really be certain about his subjects' sexual preferences, since they were dead."

Other research supposedly showing there's a "gay gene" suffers from major problems. Dr. Socarides has described as "invalid" and "seriously flawed" the well-publicized research of Dean Hamer of the National Institutes of Health and Drs. Michael Bailey and Richard Pillard of Northwestern and Boston Universities on the genetic basis of homosexuality. And he notes that all three researchers are homosexual—something that the media failed to report.

If all this research about homosexuality is news to you, join the club. It was news to me too. What I've learned since my speech just confirms that Paul was right about slavery to sin. Homosexuality, like all other sins, boils down to a choice. But usually, homosexuality has its roots in a tragic childhood. People don't wake up and decide to become homosexual. Failed relationships with their fathers, confusion from sexual abuse in childhood, and other factors gradually steer them toward that decision.

Still, there is a way out.

Spiritual Treatment

Those who don't believe in clinical treatment of homosexuality should remember that there's a second—and I think more effective—door to freedom: religion. At least one hundred groups across the country now minister the gospel to homosexuals. Their efforts are bringing forth a long parade of souls freed from the new slavery.

An article in the *Washington Post* told the life stories of some of the people touched by these ministries. They included a married man with five children, a sixty-two-year-old man with AIDS, a former male prostitute who said he had slept with six thousand men, a "guilt-tortured" lesbian, and an African-American man "whose sexual urges have driven him to the brink of suicide."

Bob Davies, executive director of Exodus International, tells a similar success story. As a boy and young man, Davies felt sexually attracted to men. He says he felt inferior to other men, and he dealt with his insecurities by idolizing and "sexualizing" them.

When he found Exodus, Davies began to understand the source of his confusion. He also learned to lose his sexual attraction to men. "The idea that I'm sexually unfulfilled, that I'm secretly attracted to men, is absolutely ridiculous to me," Davies told *USA Today*. "I will intellectually recognize a good-looking man on the street. What's different is that I will no longer wish to have a sexual connection to him."

Another example of God's power to conquer homosexuality is Dennis Jernigan, a popular Christian musician. As a boy, he displayed an extraordinary musical gift that allowed him to hear music only once and then play it on the piano. But in the small, rural town in Oklahoma where he grew up, his talent drove a wedge between other boys and him. By the time he was six or seven years old, Dennis says, "I thought I was different from the other boys. Because I played the piano and the other boys found out, they called me a sissy, fag, that kind of thing. My dad was one of these macho guys who worked hard to support his family, yet emotionally I didn't feel a connection. Physically, there was no affection."

Dennis now realizes that, like many other young artists, he was just "more sensitive" than the other boys. But as he grew older, he struggled with sexual confusion and attraction to men. Sexual experimentation with other boys led to homosexual relations with men in high school and college. In his senior year in college, he started to commit suicide, then pulled back.

Finally, in 1981, Dennis went to a Christian concert by the group 2nd Chapter of Acts. The music drew the guilt and sin out of his soul. He asked Jesus to help change him. He has never returned to homosexuality. Now married for sixteen years and the father of nine children, Dennis has become a prominent Christian singer and songwriter.

Dennis says that homosexuals are concentrated in the arts because "God is a creative God. If the enemy [Satan] can pervert our sexuality and our creative drive, he can permeate society. Think of the movies, TV shows, music, arts — there's really a glut of homosexuality." Dennis thinks that his sensitivity made it hard for him to relate to other boys and to men, and that this is extremely common among homosexuals. "If they answered honestly," he says, "I would venture to say that 95 percent would give you the same story."

It's one thing for homosexual activists not to want to leave their lifestyle. But it's terribly wrong for them to hold back information that can help other homosexuals who aren't as happy living that way. As Dr. Socarides and his colleagues noted, many AIDS victims would be alive today if they had only been told where to find the help they sought. The many others who've attempted or completed suicide because of homosexuality deserved to know this information too.

The intimidation must stop. Just because gay rights activists don't want to leave their lifestyle is no excuse for denying hope to people who are crying out for help.

Why Homosexuality Is Not a Civil Right

One thing I said in my speech that really seemed to upset the media was my belief that homosexuality "is a decision, not a race." Homosexual activists like to compare their cause to the civil rights movement. But they don't seem to understand, or don't care to know, that many blacks find that comparison deeply offensive.

Believe me, that's not just my opinion. I can't tell you how many of my black teammates and players on other teams told me they agreed with what I said about homosexuality. A lot of them said their parents wanted me to keep on saying it. Even guys who aren't Christian said they supported what I said. Black people I meet off the field tell me the same thing.

In fact, since the speech, I can't think of a single black person who has said he or she disagrees with what I said about homosexuality.

In the NFL, calling a fellow athlete a homosexual—or slang to that effect—is almost guaranteed to start a fight. In 1997, Michael Westbrook and Stephen Davis, two black teammates on the Washington Redskins, got into a fight that a TV crew captured on film. The media played the tape over and over again, which landed one of the players in trouble. The media didn't widely report why they'd had their brawl. Some time later, the *Washington Post* acknowledged it was because one of the players "used a derogatory term in suggesting [the other] was gay." Four months after their fight, two teammates on the Washington Wizards, a team in the National Basketball Association (NBA), had a scuffle for the very same reason.

Polls of black folk make the same point. In June 1998, as the controversy over my remarks was still brewing, *USA Today* commissioned a poll on homosexuality. Americans were asked whether they "believe homosexual behavior is morally wrong or is not morally wrong." Overall, 59 percent said it was morally wrong; 35 percent said it wasn't.

What was most striking, I think, was the racial breakdown. While 57 percent of whites said homosexuality was morally wrong, 74 percent of blacks said it was wrong. Blacks were more opposed to homosexuality than any other ethnic group. Only 19 percent of blacks thought homosexuality wasn't morally wrong.

In 1995, the *Los Angeles Times* conducted a poll about homosexuals and civil rights. The poll asked, "Do you think homosexuals should get protection under civil rights laws in the way racial minorities and women have been protected, or should homosexuals get no civil rights protection?" Forty-three percent said they should receive civil rights protection. Fifty percent said they should not.

Again, there were racial differences. While 42 percent of whites thought civil rights protection should be extended to homosexuals, only 38 percent of blacks did.

Even more remarkable is the fact that, based on at least one poll, blacks are less likely than whites to be homosexual. In 1993, *Time* magazine reported a poll showing that 2.4 percent of white men ages twenty to thirty-nine reported having had sex with men within the past ten years. Also, 1.3 percent reported having had sex exclusively with men during that time.

For blacks, the numbers were much lower. Only 1.3 percent of black men reported having had sex with men. And only 0.2 percent reported being homosexual. In other words, according to this poll, white men are almost twice as likely to be bisexual, and seven times as likely to be homosexual, as black men.

What does this mean? I'm not really sure. But I do know that these facts pose a problem for people who believe that we're all slaves to our genes. It leads them to conclude, at least regarding sexuality, that whites are inherently inferior to blacks!

That's nonsense, of course. The differences in homosexual practices come from differences in attitude. Blacks have a long tradition of opposing homosexuality. It's rooted in our religious tradition. Blacks are a very traditional and spiritual people. That's true when we're compared not only to other Americans, but also to other people of the world.

Leading the Way

Black Africans have stood firm as a brick wall against homosexuality. The Lambeth Conference in Canterbury, England, provided strong proof of this to the whole world. In August 1998, 750 bishops in the Anglican Church gathered from around the globe to discuss church doctrine. Many bishops from Great Britain and the United States wanted to change the church's laws on homosexual marriage and the ordination of homosexual ministers. African bishops made up most of the vote against these changes. They carried the day as the motions to change the laws failed.

The bishops who wanted these changes were racist in their attacks on their African brethren. The head of the Anglican Church in Scotland, the Right Reverend Richard Holloway, accused the Africans of having been bought by "chicken and sausages." That was a reference to barbecues held by conservative American bishops opposed to the changes. Bishop John Spong of Newark, New Jersey, called African Christianity "superstitious." He said it only recently "moved out from animism," and Africans had ignored "the intellectual revolution of Einstein and Copernicus."

Bishop Spong later apologized. But then he said he really didn't care how his comments were taken. "If they feel patronized that's too bad," he said. "I'm not going to cease being a twentieth-century person for fear of offending somebody in the Third World."

The African bishops who held the line against homosexuality at the Lambeth Conference are heroes. They made it clear to the whole world that blacks will have no part in watering down Christianity with homosexual rights.

Another African leader has been at the forefront of this battle. Robert Mugabe, the flamboyant leader of Zimbabwe, has spoken out against American and Western attempts to spread homosexual rights throughout the world.

America and the West have tried to force Zimbabwe to accept homosexual rights. But Mugabe hasn't bowed down, and he hasn't pulled any punches in speaking out against homosexual activists. Mugabe said of homosexual behavior, "If dogs and pigs don't do it, why must human beings?" And the media here thought *my* speech was harsh!

Mugabe received a lot of criticism from the same folks who didn't like my speech. Some members of the U.S. Congress urged him to respect homosexual rights. But he didn't back away from his comments. "Let the Americans keep their sodomy, bestiality, stupid and foolish ways to themselves, out of Zimbabwe," he said. "We don't want these practices here. Let them be gay in the United States, Europe, and elsewhere."

Bornwell Chakoadza, the government's chief spokesman, tried to explain where Mugabe was coming from. Referring to homosexuality, he said, "A lot of Africans consider it very, very revolting." The *Washington Post* reported that Mugabe's "political arrow hit a cultural bull's-eye" in his native country. "Church groups have rallied around him," the reporter noted, and "some of the educated, well-traveled elite even agree that homosexuality appears to emanate from foreigners."

Drawing the line against homosexuality was truly an Africanist position. It was also courageous. The little nation of Zimbabwe stands to lose quite a bit in this confrontation. God bless Robert Mugabe. And shame on us for bullying him and his people.

Closer to America, other mostly black nations are fighting the good fight. It's now common for homosexuals to charter cruise ships in the United States and sail to islands in the Caribbean. Once there, the ships dock, and the passengers go ashore to show off their lifestyle without regard to local beliefs.

Several predominantly black island nations in the Caribbean have begun to draw the line. In February 1998, when a ship carrying 900 homosexuals tried to dock in the Cayman Islands for the day, the ship was denied permission. The government said that it doubted the visitors could be counted on "to uphold the standards of appropriate behavior." Since then, the British foreign secretary has asked Great Britain's dependent territories in the Caribbean, including the Cayman Islands, to institute policies "more friendly" to homosexuals and to repeal sodomy laws there. So far, the Cayman Islands have held out against these strong-arm tactics.

In other island nations, people are resisting this same cultural pressure. When the Village People, a homosexual vocal group popular in America in the 1970s, announced it was going to perform in Jamaica in March 1998, local residents protested. "To promote a music festival of that nature, which is going to highlight a behavior repugnant to the majority of people in this country, is disrespectful," said the Reverend Stanley Clark, president of the Jamaica Council of Churches. The performance was canceled after one of the members of the group became ill.

In April 1998, several hundred people rallied in Nassau, Bahamas, to protest one homosexual charter ship. Protestors carried placards saying, "Keep your perversions in your bedrooms."

A group called Save the Bahamas Campaign has organized to oppose the docking of homosexual charter ships on the islands. "It is not in the best interest of Bahamians to prostitute our sun, sand and sea for the cozy and costly bedsheet of immorality," said the Reverend Mario Moxey, chairman of the campaign.

"If this madness is not stopped," Rev. Moxey warned, "it will be an integral part of our Bahamian cultural heritage. We implore anyone in government who possesses the moral fortitude to take a stand against this invasion of indecency and regain the confidence of the people in their government."

Americans should be supporting true liberty around the world, not preaching the new slavery. We shouldn't be engaged in this kind of cultural imperialism. We should show off our best side to other countries, not our worst. We definitely shouldn't be forcing these ways on other countries just so we can feel better about ourselves.

The Meaning of Civil Rights

Gay rights activists who compare their cause to the civil rights movement greatly insult the brave men and women who marched for civil rights, and risked death, out of loyalty to a race they were born into. The civil rights movement was completely different from the gay rights movement. Preachers such as the Reverend Martin Luther King Jr. led the civil rights movement. It was founded on solid Christian principles. It appealed to our better nature.

The gay rights movement is an attempt to turn a sin into a civil right. To put it bluntly, it's not a sin to be black. It's a sin to be a practicing homosexual.

I thought that Colin Powell explained these differences well a few years ago. Back in 1993, when President Clinton decided to relax the military's restrictions on homosexual conduct, General Powell pointed out that there's a big difference between race and homosexuality. "Skin color," he said, "is a benign, nonbehavioral characteristic, while sexual orientation is perhaps the most profound of human behavioral characteristics."

One young black writer, Jason Riley, took up this point in an article in the *Wall Street Journal*. He noted that the "gay rights lobby . . . constantly seeks to appropriate the prestige of the black civil rights struggle." Although other groups try the same thing, "it's especially galling to see gays doing it, since what they want is protection for their *conduct*, not their status per se." Riley added, "The victims of segregation suffered not because of their behavior but because of their race, something over which they had no control."

Homosexual activists argue that discrimination based on "sexual orientation" should be just as illegal as discrimination based on race, sex, and national origin. Lately, they've had quite a bit of success with this argument. In 1998, President Clinton signed an executive order that added sexual orientation to the laws against discrimination in the federal workplace. Congress tried, but failed, to override the order.

The Supreme Court has created special civil rights for homosexuals. In 1992, the people of Colorado passed a state initiative declaring that homosexuals should not enjoy the same special civil rights protections as blacks and other minorities. But in 1996, the Supreme Court struck down this law.

Ironically, the Court said that the Fourteenth Amendment—which was passed after the Civil War to guarantee equal protection of the law for ex-slaves—required that homosexuals receive the same extra civil rights protections given blacks and other minorities. As far as I'm concerned, the Supreme Court's decision in *Romer v. Evans* was a slap in the face of every one of the vast majority of black Americans who disapproves of homosexuality.

Why do blacks resent comparisons between the civil rights movement and the gay rights movement? It's because we know real slavery when we see it. Homosexuality is slavery by another name. It's simply not a civil right. It's the opposite of what the civil rights movement was about.

Battles on the Horizon

The masters of the new slavery have won important victories lately in their campaign to enact homosexual rights across the country. The executive order signed by President Clinton in 1998 and the Supreme Court's decision in *Romer* were major wins in the battle against God's rules on homosexuality. The fight continues at many levels. The nation's largest churches are wracked with controversy over whether to declare homosexuality no longer a sin, to uphold gay marriages, and to ordain homosexuals as ministers. Homosexual activists want homosexual couples to have the same rights to health insurance and public benefits as married heterosexual couples. In newscasts, movies, and TV shows, the media continue to promote homosexuality as normal and acceptable.

Our children have become the focus of these efforts. Homosexual activists want the right to be scoutmasters. In New Jersey, the state supreme court recently "found" this right in the state constitution. Homosexual parents want equal rights to child custody. Homosexual activists want the right to adopt children, even while heterosexual couples without children go wanting.

In school districts across the country, children are being labeled and "protected" as homosexuals. In 1993, Massachusetts became the first state to ban antihomosexual discrimination in public schools and establish a statewide "safe schools" program. In a landmark 1996 case, a Wisconsin school district paid nearly $1 million to a young man and his lawyers after a federal jury held school officials liable for failing to protect him from antihomosexual abuse. A student in Arkansas recently filed and won on a similar complaint under Title IX, the federal statute that prohibits sex discrimination in schools that receive federal funds.

In both Wisconsin and Arkansas, two young men had been beaten up by antihomosexual bullies. But instead of fighting for greater protection against school bullies—something that every school administration should be committed to—the students and their lawyers wanted something else. The lawyers, some of whom worked for gay rights groups, wanted settlements that legitimized the homosexual lifestyle in high schools. That's what they got. Homosexual support groups are increasingly common in high schools today.

I find that extremely sad. It reminds me of a conversation I had with a confused seventeen-year-old at a Christian convention in Charlotte, North Carolina, in 1998. The young man came up to me and told me he thought something was wrong with him. He was convinced he was gay.

"Why do you think you're gay?" I asked him.

"Because the kids call me a faggot. Plus, I thought maybe I was gay because I'm a virgin and I don't want to have sex yet."

I was amazed. I told him, "Don't let them tell you you're something that you're not. You're not gay. You should take pride in your virginity."

The young man walked away grateful, or so it seemed. But he walked off into a society that's telling him exactly the opposite of what God wants him to do.

The most important battleground over the new slavery is society. Public opinion polls show that homosexual activists are gaining ground here. Sixty percent of Americans think it's okay for homosexuals to be employed as high-school teachers. Fifty-five percent think it's acceptable for homosexual teachers to be hired for elementary schools. Fifty-three percent think that homosexuals are entitled to serve as members of the clergy. In 1977, only 27 percent favored homosexuals as elementary school teachers and 36 percent as clergy.

Congress recently has tried to stem the tide. The House of Representatives in 1998 passed a measure that would bar adoptions in the District of Columbia to individuals "who are not related by blood or marriage." The *New York Times* article reporting this vote carried the headline "House Votes Another Antigay Measure."

The bill's sponsor, Representative Steve Largent, a former NFL player and Hall of Famer, explained what motivated him. "It might give some gay rights activist a warm feeling to see gay couples treated as if they were married," he said. But adoptees have already had a rough start in life, and "it is simply wrong to turn them into trophies from the culture war, to exploit them in order to make some political point."

These bills can go only so far. Until enough of us return to God's rules on homosexuality, we'll continue to fall prey to those who want us to swap our freedom for the new slavery. The masters of this new slavery have shown in their treatment of me and anyone else who opposes them that they mean business. They won't give up without a tremendous fight.

We must be willing to make this fight. Too many homosexuals are suffering needlessly from a condition they can overcome. We must never give up sharing the truth with them. In the truth, they'll find freedom from the terrible pains of childhood that haunt them. They'll find freedom from the broken image of God that their masters would force on them.

We must all do our part in manning the Underground Railroad fighting the new slavery. Homosexuals who want to escape the new slavery should know that we will be there to support them, no matter what abuse and persecution we endure. If they want someone to stand with them in their fight—even someone to join hands and sing "we shall overcome" with them—I for one will be there.

Chapter Three

Going Our Separate Ways

You've probably heard the cliché that a football team is like a family. That cliché actually has a lot of truth to it. For example, have you ever noticed that black kids tend to go out for team sports like football and basketball instead of individual sports? This isn't a stereotype—it's a provable fact. Why is this so?

I've sometimes thought it's because, to a black kid these days, a team is like the family he never had. On a team, he'll find a male coach who serves as a father figure. The coach lays down rules he has to follow. The other guys, who also have to follow the rules, become like his brothers. I've seen guys on sports teams who clearly look up to certain coaches or players as father figures. I've even felt that some of the guys on the Packers looked at me that way.

As our families continue to crumble, more and more young men will have to look to things such as team sports to fill the void. Today, the American family is coming apart. Marriages are breaking up, children are growing up without fathers, and society is reaping the whirlwind. At last, after years of denial, people are acknowledging these facts. But even now, we're still reluctant to talk honestly about *why* our families are breaking up.

Until recently, the breakup of the family was considered too touchy a subject for public discussion. It's easy to understand why. It's hard to talk about the breakup of the family without causing pain. Our decisions about marriage and children are some of the most personal choices we ever make. All of us who've been married and had children like to think of ourselves as good spouses and parents. When others challenge this view of ourselves, we naturally grow angry, defensive, and even tearful.

I don't wish to cause anyone pain. Still, I feel I must add my voice to the chorus of those defending the traditional family. The family is essential for society. We can't afford to see it disappear.

Why is the family so important? Children learn how to love in the family. Children learn from watching their parents love each other and make sacrifices for their children. When children see their families breaking up due to lack of love, they take it hard. They also take this lesson to heart. I believe this lack of love and family support is one of the main reasons why so many children are declaring war on our society.

Most likely, you've already heard the statistics I'm about to list, or at least some of them. But I think it's important for us to know just how bad things have gotten.

Right now, one out of three babies born in America is born to a single mother. The out-of-wedlock birth rate is 68 percent for blacks and almost 20 percent for whites. For Mexican-Americans and Puerto Ricans, the rates are 36 and 57 percent, respectively.

The rise in illegitimacy rates among whites is especially alarming. Between 1980 and 1992, out-of-wedlock births to white women rose 94 percent. Among blacks, the increase was only 7 percent. The increase was even greater among white professional women. Their out-of-wedlock birth rate more than doubled during that time.

Divorce statistics are just as disturbing. Almost half of new marriages end in divorce. Children who grow up in a divorced home aren't much better off than children born to single mothers. They know their fathers only for a little while. Sixty percent of all children will spend some portion of their childhood living with only one parent.

These trends have been in the making for some time. I can remember back in the seventies, when I was in high school, one of my classmates had already fathered five children. But until the last few years, our leaders haven't had much to say about the matter.

In 1992, Vice President Dan Quayle finally ended the silence. He criticized the TV show *Murphy Brown* for glamorizing single parenthood. Afterward, the media gave him what I'm tempted to call the "Reggie White treatment." Then again, maybe he'd call the media's treatment of me after my speech the "Dan Quayle treatment."

Suffice it to say that Dan Quayle took a lot of heat over that speech. But a year after his speech, he was vindicated. A scholar named Barbara Dafoe Whitehead published an article called "Dan Quayle Was Right." In the article, she went over the data surrounding single parenthood. She found that children of single parents are far more likely to become delinquents, to have children out of wedlock, and to suffer from alcoholism, drug abuse, depression, and other problems. In 1998, Candice Bergen, the actress who played Murphy Brown, admitted that she thought Dan Quayle's remarks were on target.

There aren't many people left who think single parenthood and divorce are no cause for worry. A child needs both parents. Two parents are better able to serve a child if only because there are two sets of hands instead of just one.

Of course, when we're talking about family breakdown, we're really talking about the absence of fathers. A father is critical to a child's upbringing. I know from my own experience. I was raised by a single mother, and I know what it's like to grow up without a father. I also know, from raising my own children, how important a father is for raising good children.

The Bible talks quite a bit about fatherless children. The ancient Jews and early Christians realized that growing up without a father was more than an inconvenience. It was definitely not just a lifestyle choice. They looked upon it as a calamity.

God set down rules in the Bible to preserve the family. He wrote these rules very clearly. He told us that it's wrong to have sex outside marriage. It's wrong to commit adultery. It's wrong to divorce our spouses, except in rare circumstances.

These standards are challenging. They're tough for people to live up to. But God gave them to us for our own good. They're designed to keep families together.

These rules make sure that children grow up with two parents. They also make sure that when a man and a woman marry each other, they know that their love will be for eternity. In this day and age, when the word *love* is used cheaply to describe sex, isn't eternal, unconditional love a beautiful vision? This vision can be a reality for America's couples and families if we remember the true meaning and source of love.

A Crisis of Selfishness

There are various explanations for why the family is breaking up. Some say the family is falling apart because of money. They say that welfare has encouraged men not to marry the mothers of their children because the government will support them with welfare checks. Some people also point to the "marriage penalty" in the federal tax code. That law makes it a little more expensive to be married. The marriage penalty, they say, creates an incentive for people, including parents, to stay single.

I think that this economic theory falls short of the truth. Welfare or taxes don't determine whether people decide to have sex outside marriage or to divorce their spouses. People don't pull out and examine their checkbooks before doing these things. Economics may play some role in these choices. Mostly, though, these are decisions of the heart. Our sex lives reflect our souls.

Other people offer a different explanation. They say racism has made black families, in particular, vulnerable to family breakup. Slavery and segregation, they argue, have robbed black men of their manhood and discouraged them from taking responsibility for their families.

I agree that the problems in the black community are partly the legacy of slavery. I marvel that the black family has done as well as it has, given all the obstacles black folk have had to overcome. It's important to remember, though, that until only a few decades ago, the illegitimacy rate among blacks was as low as that of whites. So there must be something more recent at work here.

My explanation for the decline of the family is more simple than these theories. I think all of us know what's really going on. We don't need any grand sociological or political theory to break it down for us. Our families are falling apart for one basic reason: selfishness.

Selfishness is a tough word. Let me explain what I mean.

God's rules are designed to make us serve Him and our fellow human beings. Throughout the Bible, we're told to love others as we love ourselves, to be the servant of all, and to believe that it's more blessed to give than to receive. All of these rules have one thing in common. They teach us to deny ourselves.

God knows that lurking inside our hearts is selfishness. Whether or not you believe in original sin, there's no denying the selfish side of human nature. God's rules help us to fight this inclination.

When we break God's rules, we do it out of selfishness. We do it because we don't want to serve others. We want to be supreme. We want to call the shots. We want to have it all.

The breakup of the family is a prime example of this kind of runaway selfishness. We split up from our spouses because we'd rather have things our own way. We have sex and babies out of wedlock because we follow our pleasures and appetites wherever they lead us. We ask paid strangers to raise our children in day-care centers so that we can work and have higher incomes.

When we do these things, we send a powerful message to our children. Whether we intend to or not, we're telling them that they should do the same thing. We're teaching them that they, too, should worship selfishness.

Families tie us, as individuals, to the rest of society. If we can't hold together our families, how can we hope to hold together our country? That's what's at stake in the debate over family values. The fundamental question is: Are we willing to deny ourselves for the good of our families and our country?

Now, people who oppose family values often use some sophisticated language to try to justify their views. They talk about *rights* and *choices*.

They say they're entitled to do as they please because it's part of their *freedom*.

This is bogus freedom. If we all practiced this irresponsibility, our society would fall apart. And that's exactly what's happening. When you hear words such as *rights* and *choices* being used in debates over family values, you should keep in mind what these words really mean. In this context, these terms are simply code words for selfishness.

We don't have the right to abandon or neglect our loved ones. To say that the life or death of an unborn child is a choice left up to the mother, just so that we can have sex without consequences, is horrible. What a perversion of rights!

The founders of our country didn't create these so-called rights. They're nowhere in the Constitution. They're nowhere in God's rules, either. God knows that the "freedom" to sin is no freedom at all. It means slavery to sin and selfishness. And selfishness means misery for everyone it touches.

God told us that adultery, sexual immorality, and divorce are against His rules. For those of us who believe in these rules, the choice is simple. For those who don't believe in God's rules, the choice becomes more complicated. Their minds can become clouded with selfishness. Too often, they give in to their worse nature.

The State of Our Unions

The selfishness that's ruining our families takes many forms. I think it's important for us to look at these different kinds of selfishness. That's the best way for us to judge our own lives and decide if we're contributing to these problems.

But first, let me emphasize that I'm not holding myself up as a model of perfection. Nobody's perfect. All of us break God's rules from time to time. So when I discuss these matters, I hope you'll remember where I'm coming from.

Although I believe in defending God's rules, I'm not judging others.

We can all stand to be better spouses, parents, or children of God. My goal is to clarify God's rules in an age when a lot of people would just as soon see these rules ignored or broken.

Sexual Immorality

Today, most Americans believe that sex outside marriage is morally acceptable. In a 1997 poll, only 39 percent of Americans said that "having sexual relations before marriage" is wrong. Among Americans between the ages of eighteen and twenty-nine, 75 percent said that premarital sex was not wrong.

These values are apparent in the way we live our lives. Only one in five young people today doesn't have sex while a teenager. Our teenage pregnancy rates are twice as high as those of England and Canada and nine times those of Japan.

All around us, we can see how destructive fornication is. Sex outside marriage leads to babies outside marriage, which leads to children without fathers. Only marriage can ensure that both parents will be there to raise the child. Each year, three million teenagers—one in four who are sexually active—contract a sexually transmitted disease. One out of three babies conceived by a teenage mother is aborted.

I don't hold myself up as the best person to preach on premarital sex. We've all done things in life that we regret, especially when we were young. Because I'm not without sin in this area, maybe I can at least speak with the authority that comes from personal knowledge of sin. I know the temptations that pull at young people. But the fact that these temptations are so strong is all the more reason why we should hold fast to God's rules. These rules are our only shield against sin and unhappiness.

When I talk to kids about abstaining from sex, I try to level with them. I'll say, "Don't get me wrong. I did it when I was young. I can't change that. But I want to keep you from repeating my mistakes."

Some argue that birth control and "safe sex" make fornication acceptable. But these inventions can't erase sin. Sex outside marriage violates God's rules. Sex is an activity that God reserved for people who are married.

Protecting our bodily health with contraceptives doesn't safeguard our spiritual health. For that matter, contraceptives sometimes don't work.

Fornication is especially harmful for women and girls. Let's face it: men enjoy casual sex much more than women do. Women desire relationships, not casual sex. Sex for women is more an expression of love than a pursuit of physical pleasure. In my ministry, I've found that many young women have been confused and hurt by casual sexual relationships.

In the inner city these days, the popular culture encourages promiscuity. There's extreme pressure to have sex. Young men often brag about how many women they've had sex with. The young men who've had many sexual partners are called "players," "pimps," and "mack daddies." It's considered manly to be sexually active. These days, young women who are sexually active also pressure their friends to do the same thing.

This same peer pressure is common in the suburbs—a lot more common than you might think. In 1998, three former high-school seniors in Grosse Pointe, Michigan, a wealthy suburb of Detroit, were convicted of having sex with three fourteen-year-old freshman girls. One of the seniors was Dan Granger, the senior class president at Grosse Point North High. After a high-school yearbook was published with a photo of Granger exposing his genitals, an investigation led to the discovery that Granger and the other seniors had used alcohol to seduce the girls. The three girls cried in court as Granger was sentenced for conspiracy to contribute to the delinquency of a minor.

Unfortunately, there are many other examples of this predatory behavior in the suburbs. In 1993, in Lakewood, California, members of a high-school clique called the Spur Posse had a secret contest to see how many girls they could have sex with. A few years before that, in Glen Ridge, New Jersey, a well-off suburb, several high-school football stars lured a mentally impaired girl into a basement and persuaded her to perform sex acts with a baseball bat and broomstick. They also lured unsuspecting girls into bedrooms and had sex with them as their teammates watched from nearby closets. Three of these young men were convicted of sexual assault.

I've overheard enough conversations in locker rooms and elsewhere to know that predatory sex is rampant in just about every city and town in America. It's not only athletes or black kids who are involved. The polls on teenage sex show how rampant such premarital sex is. Forty-seven percent of teenagers between the ages of thirteen and eighteen said that they've done something sexual or felt pressure to do so before they were ready. One out of four teenage girls said that her first sexual experience was unwanted.

Premarital sex is so common because we tell our boys that there's nothing wrong with it. The parents in Lakewood were an example of this attitude. "Nothing my boy did was anything any red-blooded American boy wouldn't do at his age," said the father of one boy. Another boy recalled his father bragging about his exploits to his friends. One mother dismissed all the controversy as a "testosterone thing."

It's wrong for young men to take advantage of young women this way. The macho, "love 'em and leave 'em" attitude that America has toward sex takes a terrible emotional toll on women.

Why are so many women and girls being treated this way? Obviously, the men doing this are disgusting. I also think that this is happening because women have lowered their standards. They're not demanding that men treat them like ladies anymore.

Women, as a whole, used to hold men to higher standards. Women used to demand that men marry them before they would agree to have sex. Why? For one thing, people used to follow God's rules more faithfully. People were more religious and cared more about God's teachings on sexuality.

Also, women seemed to understand better why marriage is so important. Marriage was proof positive that sex was about more than the man's pleasure. Sex was a reflection of the couple's *permanent relationship* to each other. Marriage showed that the woman was more than the man's passing fancy for the evening.

Today, men are free to have it all without making any commitment. These standards have changed, I think, because our culture is telling women and girls to act more like men. How else do we explain why the rates for crime, drug and alcohol abuse, and other social problems have risen so much among women and girls? Why else is the rate for sex outside marriage so high for girls today? Girls today aren't made any different from girls of years past. I think these trends are happening because we're telling our girls that they should act more like boys.

Mother Nature gives men every reason to seek fornication where they can get it. But women, thank God, aren't put together that way. They prefer to have a permanent relationship first. This desire helps to make sure that a father is around after the baby arrives.

When society tells women that they're crazy for demanding marriage before sex, society is fighting Mother Nature. When we do this, we shouldn't be surprised when Mother Nature fights back. The result is millions of women and children deserted by men enjoying their "freedom."

It's time to remind ourselves that there's nothing wrong with women holding men to higher standards. There's nothing wrong and everything right with women being feminine. Women should be proud of their important contributions as wives and mothers. They're the most important contributions that anyone makes to our society.

We've all heard the old saying, "Why buy the cow when you can have the milk for free?" Fornication will be less common only after women insist that the men in their lives live by these higher standards—God's rules. I'm not saying men aren't responsible for the current state of affairs. In fact, I'd say they're mostly to blame. I'm just pointing out that men have more of a natural incentive to fornicate than women do. Our rates of sex outside marriage will fall significantly only when women start to demand a wedding ring before letting men do what comes naturally.

Cohabitation is another trend that's harmful to women. It's become almost as common for unmarried couples to live together as it is for them to have sex. Almost one out of three currently married couples admit that they lived together before they got married. For married couples ages eighteen to twenty-nine, almost half say they lived together. In 1989, 19 percent of married couples said they cohabited. In December 1997, the number had risen to 31 percent. This is a 61 percent increase in only eight years.

There's no getting around it. Living together without being married is a sin. It's just one more way of trying to have the benefits of marriage without entering into this sacred covenant.

From the male point of view, cohabitation is mostly about having sex without having to get married. The woman he is living with often ends up cleaning, buying groceries, and doing chores for the man as if they were married. In many cases, the woman puts up with this because she thinks it's the best arrangement she can hope for from the man in her life. But by agreeing to cohabit, she runs the risk of never getting married, or of getting divorced soon thereafter. A 1995 survey of 1,300 U.S. couples found that those who had lived together before tying the knot had a divorce rate 50 percent higher than those who'd lived apart before marriage.

The men in these arrangements should grow up and accept their responsibilities. They should either fish or cut bait. And the women who settle for living together instead of getting married should hold out for something better. If the men won't give them a wedding ring, they're not worth cleaning for.

The flood of pornography in our society is further evidence of how we've come to accept a loveless, macho view of sex. By pornography, I mean the entertainment and magazines that appeal to our sexual and more perverted appetites. Today, we're overwhelmed with pornography at every turn.

People who say pornography is a private matter that doesn't affect society or our souls are kidding themselves. First, pornography encourages men to lust for women other than their wives. Jesus told us that any man who lusts for a woman who isn't his wife has committed adultery. Pornography encourages adultery, both in the mind and in the flesh. It entices men into looking outside their marriages for sexual gratification.

Second, pornography inevitably becomes available to children. The idea that we can keep pornography out of the hands of children by keeping it behind drugstore counters is naive. Once pornography is available in society, it's only a matter of time before it falls into the hands of children. The Internet is now full of X-rated material as well.

Pornography is especially degrading to the women who are attracted to the industry by the big money it promises. Many of these women were victims of sexual exploitation or abuse while growing up. The further sexual abuse they go through by posing or dancing naked for men's sexual gratification only adds to their pain and guarantees it will continue.

Women whose husbands turn to pornography suffer a deep and hurtful insult. No wife with any self-respect can say that kind of behavior doesn't bother her. If the shoe were on the other foot, no man with any self-respect would tolerate it, either.

Even if pornography could be kept away from children, it still wouldn't be good for society. Pornography corrupts men, degrades women, and ruins families. It's hard enough for people to do the right thing with temptation beckoning all around. Letting pornography loose on society makes it that much harder for us to hold our families together.

Divorce

Because of Dan Quayle and Barbara Dafoe Whitehead, the pain and problems that divorce causes for children are well known. My discussions with kids have taught me that children of divorce often lose trust in their fathers. I believe a child judges how much his father loves him by how much his father loves his mother.

People leave their spouses usually for selfish or frivolous reasons. One 1992 poll showed that the main reason is communication problems. Second is infidelity. The other top reasons are constant fighting, emotional abuse, falling out of love, and unsatisfactory sex. Physical abuse is far down the list.

Divorce "touches a nerve in middle-class audiences," according to William Galston, a University of Maryland professor and former adviser to President Clinton. As the *Wall Street Journal* noted, "Unlike social issues that set off finger-pointing at the poor—welfare reform, teen pregnancy, out-of-wedlock births—divorce is more an issue of 'us' than 'them.'"

When Michigan tried in 1996 to repeal its no-fault divorce law, people who'd been left by their spouses came forward to speak out against the law. One man, David Michael, said, "I almost blame the state as much as I do my wife" for their divorce. He admitted that he had been domineering and financially irresponsible. But he said he didn't drink, didn't abuse his wife or children, and had never been unfaithful. Now, Michael reports, his daughter has put on too much weight, and his son drinks and has become violent.

Christine Kurth, a forty-seven-year-old divorced woman who lives in a suburb of Detroit, said that when her husband left her, she was financially devastated:

> Instead of starting a career for myself, I helped my husband get his business started. I had four children. I made the beds. I cooked the meals. I cleaned the house. I kept my marriage vows. Now I find myself divorced in midlife with no career. My husband makes $100,000 a year, and we're struggling to get by on a quarter of that.

Marriage is a lifelong challenge. It requires us to consult another person in making our biggest decisions in life: where to live, what career to pursue, how to raise our children, what to buy. One of the most beautiful aspects of marriage is that it makes a man and a woman deny themselves for each other. It forces them to work out their problems and live well with others, both inside and outside the home. The driving force behind this cooperation and sacrifice is love.

Like any other married couple, Sara and I can tell you that marriage can be tough going at times. God gives us wills of our own. Marriage forces us to turn these two wills into one.

In my case, I had a tough time accepting Sara as an equal. I came into the marriage thinking that if I asked her to cook or clean, she should hop to it. I thought that's what a preacher's wife should do. I even prayed to God to change her into that mold.

From these prayers, however, I got a different answer. I was the one at fault. Sara, I realized, was only responding to my leadership, which was poor and misguided. Sara deserved to be treated as an equal. More than that, she deserved to be treated like a queen—because in our household, we reigned as equal partners.

Over the years, we've grown to understand each other better. There are certain things that Sara does better than I do, such as managing money, so I just let her handle them. In return, on certain things, she defers to me for the same reason (for instance, she'd have a tough time busting through an offensive line). Because we know we're a partnership, we sort through these issues as they come up, guided by God's love. In the process, we've grown much closer. And I've come to learn that the saying, "Behind every successful man is a good woman," really should read, "*Beside* every successful man is a good woman."

Sometimes, it seems simpler just to walk out and do your own thing. However, just because it's easier doesn't mean it's better, for ourselves or our children. Sara and I have found that the peaks and valleys of a marriage make the journey together that much more worthwhile. We live better when we live together.

I know many people feel trapped in hopeless, loveless marriages. I wish I could offer a guaranteed solution for shoring up these marriages. It's no simple thing for two persons—full of their own individual tastes and interests—to live together happily. I hope it's some consolation for them to know that they're not alone, that we all go through rough spells in our marriages.

There's one thing I do know. Our odds of holding together a marriage go way up when we entrust our marriages to God. He's our best hope for forging a permanent union out of two souls. He's also our best source for comfort and love when our marriages are troubled and seem headed toward divorce.

One of my former teammates with the Packers, Sean Jones, told me that his grandfather used to say to him, "Your marriage is successful only if you die married." That's a great motto for any marriage.

Cloning

Ever since a Scottish research team announced in 1997 that it had successfully cloned a sheep named Dolly, we've been scrambling to figure out the proper moral response. I thought that President Clinton did the right thing by banning the use of federal money for research into human cloning. But so far, Congress hasn't passed any laws that would go beyond that.

I think we need a law that bans human cloning and related experiments. Cloning would greatly undermine parenthood and the family. Without new laws, scientists will continue their research until human cloning is a reality, which would be truly an evil development.

Cloning is dangerous for several reasons. It's worse than having a child out of wedlock because it denies children *any* parents at all. The person whose DNA is used for cloning is not a parent. The DNA could be taken from a child who's not even old enough to have children. Besides, parenthood requires *sharing* one's DNA with another person of the opposite sex in creating a child. Anything else isn't true parenthood.

Cloning would destroy individuality. When a child is formed, the child takes from the genes of both parents. That makes the child unique. The child is his own person, with an individuality that no one else can ever share. Cloning would change that. It would make children the identical copy of another person.

Without regulation of human cloning, scientists could conduct experiments on unborn children without any legal consequences. If they botched these experiments, creating children with terrible disabilities or suffering great pain, they would face no legal penalty. In vitro fertilization has left behind thousands of unclaimed embryos. It's bad enough that abortionists can cause similar suffering in their business. Cloning would make matters worse by tinkering with the very *creation* of human life.

Cloning raises another issue: would cloned humans belong to people like slaves? If a scientist creates a human being, could he demand that the work of his brow be treated as his property? Nothing in the law today says otherwise.

And what about so-called designer children? What if wealthy parents someday want a genetically engineered "perfect" child? Are we willing to do away with the diversity of life so that this whim can be satisfied? Will poor people be entitled to the same thing? If so, would the taxpayers pay for it?

Cloning raises a lot of disturbing questions, but one thing about cloning is clear. Cloning is an act of great selfishness. The cloned child is valued not for himself, but for how much he reminds his "parents" of another person. Talk about a recipe for low self-esteem.

Some might argue that parents who lose a child should be able to replace the child through cloning. But why can't they have another child or adopt one? I believe the dangers of cloning far outweigh its advantages.

Human beings are meant to reflect God's image. Creating human beings in our own image is an insult to our Creator and a grave danger to parenthood and the family.

Strengthening Our Families

Strengthening our families requires admitting the reason for their weakness today. Our families are dissolving because too many of us aren't willing to put our families first.

To strengthen our families, we have to rediscover the value of marriage. We need to remind ourselves that marriage can add much happiness to life. Also, marriages become stronger when we view them as sacred. I'm convinced Sara and I have stayed together all these years because we put God above all things—even above each other.

Sara and I also recognize that each of us has certain responsibilities in the marriage. Take, for example, our family's finances. My responsibilities include earning an income to support us. Sara's include making sure that the income is spent wisely. For another couple, these responsibilities might be reversed. Each couple has to work through these issues. In our case, the decision was simple. When I married Sara, my finances were so messed up that she had to straighten them out for me. I learned to leave well enough alone.

Recently, politicians have considered passing laws that would strengthen marriages. Some have proposed repealing the no-fault divorce laws that swept the country in the 1970s. Polls show the public is divided on this issue. Although 50 percent of Americans think it "should be harder" to get a divorce, 46 percent do not. When the question is phrased, "Should the government make it harder for people to get a divorce?" 37 percent say yes, and 59 percent say no.

A new, innovative approach to our high divorce rates is called covenant marriage, and two states have adopted it. Covenant marriage allows couples to choose a kind of marriage that makes it harder to get divorced. Couples can divorce only after proving fault—that one of the spouses committed adultery, abuse, or something similar. But it's not clear that covenant marriage will really change things much. In 1998, a year after Louisiana passed the first covenant marriage law, only about 1 percent of newlyweds there were opting for it.

I think covenant marriage is a good idea. But covenant marriage isn't likely to gain many takers until we change the hearts and souls of people. We must once again look upon marriage as something permanent and ordained by God. It can't be seen as a mere contract that we can get out of at any time.

There is some good news. The rates for teenage births, teenage abortions, and teenage sexual activity have leveled off or declined in recent years. Teenage birth rates have declined 12 percent since 1991. The percentage of American high-school students who've had sexual intercourse has fallen 11 percent during the 1990s. The adult divorce rate has leveled off too.

Still, the level of teenage sexual activity remains way too high. Each year, nearly one million teenage girls become pregnant. Two-thirds of Hispanic and white teenage mothers are unmarried, as well as 95 percent of black teenage mothers.

Critics of family values say these trends can't be reversed. They say we can't return to the days of *Leave It to Beaver*. Yet most of the people who say this are trying to justify their own values and lifestyles.

In my ministry I've seen God's power to transform young predators into family men. One young man I came to know in Milwaukee sticks out in my mind. He was a leader of a Hispanic street gang. After he committed his life to Jesus, he not only gave up his life of crime, he also gave up sex until he married his girlfriend several months later. And this young woman had already had two children by him.

I know these are old-fashioned values I'm preaching. But they've been around for a long time for good reason. They're the best values for America's families. Children raised under these values are better off. The society they're raised in is better off too.

All of us benefit from these values. Things such as romance and courtship have more meaning when we're not so obsessed with sex. The word *love* becomes more than a come-on line. True love has nothing to do with sex. It doesn't fade away because of new passions. It burns more deeply and grows more perfect with time.

That's the kind of love we need to strengthen and sustain our families. The source of such love isn't hard to find. It's found in every heart that truly seeks to follow that holy command: "If anyone would come after me, he must deny himself and take up his cross daily and follow me."

Chapter Four

The Complete Image of God

One of my favorite movies is *Glory*. It tells the story of the Fifty-fourth Massachusetts Regiment, an all-black unit that fought for the Union in the Civil War. In my mind, one character really stands out: an ex-slave named Trip. He's portrayed by Denzel Washington, who won an Academy Award for his performance.

Trip is an idealistic but angry young soldier. He ran away from home when he was twelve, escaping to freedom in the North. When the war broke out, he signed up to crush the slavery he had fled as a boy. But his experiences as a slave, and then as a soldier who suffers discrimination in the Union army, make him extremely bitter toward America.

After a battle in which Trip fights with great valor, his commander, who is white, takes him aside. He tells Trip that he's going to honor him for his bravery by letting him carry the regimental colors—the American flag. But Trip refuses. He explains that he wants no part of honoring America. While he's committed to the fight against slavery, he says, "I still don't want to carry your flag."

Later, Trip's true loyalties are revealed. In a fierce battle, Trip's commander falls and drops the flag. For a moment, the troops are frozen, not knowing what to do.

Trip shows them the way. He picks up the flag. Then he yells at his comrades to follow him onward.

Glory teaches several powerful lessons. It recalls the heroism and sacrifice that blacks have shown in defense of our country. It shows us how important religious faith was to the black soldiers who fought for the

Union. And the character Trip forces us to think about what it means to be an American.

Like Trip, every American must decide whether to put aside his personal prejudices for the common good. Too many of us aren't willing to do that. We'd rather blame our country for its flaws than stand up for it. Too often, we blame America for the hard times or injustices that we or our loved ones have suffered. We blame our society for supposedly favoring or coddling other races. In the process, we come to cherish hatred instead of love.

We do this to avoid accepting responsibility for our own shortcomings and sins. And we do this, all too often, because of racism and prejudice.

All races in America have members who are guilty of bias and racial hatred. Too many whites remain hostile to blacks and other minorities. They blame their anger on affirmative action, black crime rates, or inner-city welfare dependency. These are only excuses. Too many blacks, for their part, still hold hard feelings toward whites over slavery and segregation. Other minorities also are bitter over the mistreatment they've suffered.

This mistrust among the races is a tragic national legacy. Racial injustice is a red stain that runs through our history. Even our greatest presidents seemed unsure of how to deal with it. Jefferson and Lincoln, for example, both proposed resettling blacks in colonies in Africa or Central America. Obviously, we've made a lot of progress since then. Black Americans and other minorities are here to stay. The civil rights movement has helped to make America much more of a level playing field for minorities. A large black middle class has taken root. Black celebrities in various careers—movies, sports, TV, music—have become some of the wealthiest people in the world.

Yet racial tensions lie barely below the surface of American life. The L.A. riots in 1992 and the O. J. Simpson trial in 1995 were harsh examples of just how far apart we remain. Too many of us still look at society and at one another through the distorted lens of race. We're still very much a nation divided.

Opening Our Hearts and Minds

How do we put an end to this cycle of revenge, distrust, division, and wrath? How do we become, at last, one nation under God?

I think there are two solutions to the race problem. The two go hand in hand. Both are spiritual solutions. One demands that we open our hearts. The other demands that we open our minds.

The first solution was given to us two thousand years ago. It's captured in one of the simplest but most important commands ever given: "Love your neighbor as yourself."

God commands us to love everyone, even our enemies. No matter how much we've suffered at the hands of others, we must let go. We must forgive so that we may be forgiven. We must love so that we will not hate.

Forgiving a great injustice is not an easy thing to do. But that's what we're commanded to do. It's a righteous command and the only thing that can save us from constantly being at one another's throats.

It may sound trite, but it's absolutely true: more love can solve almost any problem. Racism and racial division are no exception. In fact, love would go a lot farther in solving these problems than any law or political program.

I believe there's a second solution to our racial troubles. It has to do with how we think about one another. Along with greater love for one another must come greater understanding and appreciation of our differences.

Obviously, the races are different from one another in at least some ways. For one thing, we look different. On that, at least, we can all agree. Too many people, however, want to leave it at that. They say that although we look different, there are no other meaningful differences among us.

The people with this belief were some of my loudest critics following my speech. Most of these critics were white journalists. It's still not totally clear to me why they were so outraged. I suspect that some of these critics hated what I said about homosexuality and wanted to discredit me by portraying me as ridiculing my own people, blacks. "Divide and conquer" is an old strategy.

I can understand why minorities are sensitive about discussing racial issues. For centuries, racial stereotypes have been used to put us down. In the past, generalizations about race almost always have been negative toward minorities. They've been used to make fun of us and keep us "in our place."

I'm talking about something else. What about differences that exalt us? What about those that help us to serve God's purpose? What about differences that are not negative, but positive—blessings, even?

As the saying goes, God doesn't make junk. If He made us different, it's for good reason. It makes no sense to deny or cover up our differences if they exist. For if they exist, whether because of genetics or culture or some other reason, they are blessed by God's will.

I believe that we should admit and delight in the differences that God has created in the races. I'm not saying that one race is the smartest or best looking or anything like that. I'm also not speculating whether these gifts are a result of genes or culture or another factor. I have no idea, to tell you the truth.

What I am saying is that God has given each race a *special gift* that it contributes to the world. These are special gifts *in addition to our own individual talents and blessings.*

We all have certain strengths, certain great qualities, that we lend to the human race. I believe this is as true of the races as it is of individuals. We don't serve God well when we deny the gifts He has given us because denying these gifts means not making the most of them. To use the example that Jesus gave us, it's like burying your five talents in a field instead of investing them for the betterment of others.

Let me give you another example. There's a basic fact about teamwork in the NFL that a lot of fans don't know. When a team wins the Super Bowl, it's not just the players who receive championship rings. Everyone associated with the team gets one. The team's equipment managers, ticket vendors, secretaries, the players' wives—everyone gets a ring.

This rule serves a purpose. It shows that a team is more than just the players on the field. There are a lot of people behind the scenes who make victory possible. By the same token, the team wins because everyone recognizes his contribution to the team. On a good team, a ticket salesman doesn't say, "I'm tired of selling tickets. Why don't you let me play defensive end for this game?" He knows that his contribution to the team comes in other areas. Unless he's interested only in his own gridiron glory, it shouldn't matter to him who's on the field as long as his team wins.

This isn't to say that the ticket vendor doesn't have a right to try out for the team or that he won't make it. And again, I'm not suggesting that the races can contribute only in certain ways. Blacks, for example, have offered to American society a diverse array of great men and women. They've excelled in careers as varied as the military, business, politics, ministry, athletics, science, and so forth. All races raise up talented individuals who blaze paths of distinction through society.

The point I'm making isn't about the talents of individual people. It's about God's special gifts to the races, in addition to the talents of individuals. If each of the races has a special gift from God on top of the blessings bestowed on its individual members, why shouldn't we be proud of these gifts? I say that we should. I believe it's time for us to start praising and thanking God for these gifts of the races.

These gifts provide a wondrous diversity. God tells us that He created us in His own image. When we're all viewed together as members of the human family, we form a brilliant mosaic. That mosaic is the complete image of God.

The Gifts of the Races

The Bible teaches us that God marks out certain peoples for His purposes. He made the Jews a special people for all time. The Egyptians, the Babylonians, and the Romans also served God's purposes. The Egyptians even held God's chosen people in bondage for a specific reason. As God, speaking through Moses, explained to Pharaoh, "I raised you up for this very purpose, that I might display my power in you and that my name might be proclaimed in all the earth."

If God could allow us to develop different languages, customs, and so on along racial lines, then maybe, through genetics or culture or whatever, He also saw fit to give each of us a special gift and purpose. And maybe the best way for all of us to live together happily is to acknowledge these special gifts of the races while striving to do even more, as individuals, races, and nations, to serve others.

Before we discuss whether these gifts do in fact exist, I'd like to clear up an issue. The main objection to my speech on this point was that I was offering stereotypes. Well, I ask you: If these gifts exist, how can they be stereotypes? Stereotypes are negative and false images of a race. The gifts that I mentioned aren't negative at all. If these gifts do exist, as I believe they do, they can't possibly be stereotypes. That is, unless one thinks that God believes in racial discrimination.

Consider what Thomas Sowell, a senior fellow at the Hoover Institution at Stanford University, has argued in his acclaimed studies of race and culture. He points out that the word *stereotype* is used too often to block legitimate discussion of race issues. Sowell states,

> One of the obstacles to understanding what behavioral characteristics follow each group around the world is the widespread use of the term "stereotypes" to dismiss whatever observations or evidence may be cited as to distinguishing features of particular group behavior patterns. But behavior has consequences, and when these consequences are the same for the same groups in disparate settings, that is an empirical fact not to be waved aside.

Sowell, a black man, has devoted three lengthy books to documenting these differences. Some of the greatest figures in the history of the black community have said much the same thing. To be honest, I didn't know that so many others had talked about these gifts of the races when I gave my speech. I'd based my remarks only on my own experiences.

Since then, I've learned that I'm not alone. Throughout history, other people, including some famous and impressive figures, have come to the same conclusions. Let me quote some of them in my defense as we discuss the gifts of the races. Maybe the journalists who poked fun at my speech will take notice that these authorities say the same thing I said. And maybe from this discussion, these critics will understand it is the message, not the messenger, that counts: we must learn how to live together as brothers and sisters.

Blacks and the Gift of Worship and Spirituality

In my speech, I stated that blacks are gifted at worship and spirituality. Blacks, I argued, have a way of worshiping God that's truly extraordinary. This may not be true of every black church in America, but it's true of every black church I've ever been to. And as a traveling minister, I've been to plenty of them.

The main thing you'll notice in a black church service is tremendous joy. The faithful sing loudly, clap, dance, and shout praise to God, all with no embarrassment. The preacher fills the church with a booming, dynamic voice. Marcus Garvey once said that Anglican preachers too often fail in their mission "because their congregations do not hear them." That's not a problem for black preachers, he observed, "because they talk loud enough to be heard and have more emotion in their expressions than other preachers." For example, the most famous black preacher of all time, Dr. Martin Luther King Jr., developed his powerful style of speaking by giving countless sermons in black churches across the country.

In black churches, a dialogue occurs between preacher and congregation. Cries of "hallelujah" and "amen" from the congregation punctuate the preacher's sermon. And then there's the music. My biased opinion is that black gospel music is the finest music ever offered up to almighty God.

That's been my experience in every black church I've visited since my grandmother took me to her church in Chattanooga, Tennessee. When black ministers belt out their sermons with passion and energy, often to the point that they're sweating, you can see they're "in the Spirit." By speaking with such authority, they command your attention.

I've always especially loved the choir. I've never been much of a dancer, but something about black gospel music sung by a church choir inspires and energizes me. The music sends a spiritual surge through the whole congregation. I've noticed that almost every time I've attended a black church, the joy and emotion evoked by the music move someone to tears.

I'm certainly not the first person to comment on the unique beauty of black church services. Warren H. Stewart, pastor of the First Institutional Baptist Church in Phoenix, makes the same point in his book *Interpreting God's Word in Black Preaching*. Pastor Stewart notes that when it comes to making church services more powerful and vibrant, "The black preaching tradition has made a significant contribution to the Christian community in this area. . . . There is probably no other context in the United States of America in which preaching as dialogue has been so evident, vital, and authentic as in the black church."

Pastor Stewart adds, "Things happen when the written Word is proclaimed from a black pulpit! The participation by the preacher *and* the pew causes a dynamism and creative atmosphere that are not apparent in many other Christian communities." Maybe that's why many white churches—which, quite honestly, I find to be too laid-back—seem to be moving toward the dynamic model of worship found in black churches.

Most popular music today has its roots in black gospel music. Black churches and spirituals kept alive the African music that today is integral to popular music. Black music has become so popular that, as Jonetta Rose Barras has observed, "African-American culture is becoming American culture."

It's my belief that blacks are gifted at spirituality as well as worship. The evidence suggests that blacks around the world are especially spiritual. Here again, I'm not saying that blacks are better servants of God than members of other races. I do think, however, that it's valuable for us to analyze the deep spirituality of blacks in Africa and around the world.

The greatest black thinkers in history were keenly interested in the spiritual dimension of life. The writings of Booker T. Washington, W. E. B. Du Bois, Marcus Garvey, Martin Luther King Jr., Malcolm X, and the other leaders of the black community are full of religious references. It's impossible to separate their overall message for society from the spiritual message that, in most cases, drives it.

One of the best authorities on the black religious experience is Edward Wilmot Blyden. Born in St. Thomas, Virgin Islands, in 1832, Blyden immigrated to Liberia, Africa. There, he eventually became the editor of the leading newspaper, the *Liberia Herald*, secretary of state of Liberia, president of Liberia College, and one of the most brilliant thinkers of the nineteenth century. His writings inspired Marcus Garvey, among others.

Blyden argued that Africa was the spiritual center of the world. He also contended that the greatness of his fellow blacks—the "African" or "Ethiopian" people, as he called them—lay in their being a uniquely spiritual people.

In his book *Christianity, Islam, and the Negro Race*, Blyden observed: "Every race is endowed with peculiar [unique] talents, and watchful to the last degree is the great Creator over the individuality, the freedom and independence of each. In the music of the universe each shall give a different sound, but necessary to the grand symphony."

Blyden believed that God's gift to the black race is spirituality, and that He gave blacks a special place in history: "When the African shall come forward with his peculiar gifts, he will fill a place never before occupied." He reminded us that Homer and Herodotus, the great Greek historians, are some of the "ancients [who] recognized these qualities. . . . They seemed to regard the fear and love of God as the peculiar gift of the darker races."

Blyden related, "There is not a tribe on the continent of Africa, . . . which does not stretch out its hands to the Great Creator." What's more, "there is not one who does not recognise the Supreme Being. . . . There are no atheists or agnostics among them."

Blyden also noted Africa's importance in the Bible. Africa offered a home for Abraham, Jacob, Joseph, Moses, and baby Jesus. Black Africans have played a central role in the Bible, from Moses' marriage to a Cushite woman in Numbers to Philip's conversion of the Ethiopian eunuch in Acts. And Blyden said,

> In the final hours of the Man of Sorrows, when His disciples had forsaken Him and fled, and only the tears of sympathising women, following in the distance, showed that His sorrows touched any human heart . . . what was the part that Africa took then? She furnished the man to share the burden of the cross with the suffering Redeemer. Simon, the Cyrenian, bore the cross after Jesus.

Blyden saw that God has bestowed on blacks a spiritual, instead of a materialistic, gift. He didn't believe that in doing so, God had shortchanged blacks. On the contrary, Blyden regarded the gift of spirituality as a far more powerful gift. It's as great a gift as our Maker can bestow on any race.

Scientists like George Washington Carver, political leaders like Dr. King, selfless heroes like Harriet Tubman, soldiers like Colin Powell, entertainers like Bill Cosby, and entrepreneurs like Oprah Winfrey are only a few of the diverse leaders to rise up from the black community. I think we should celebrate our special gift as a people. If it comes from God, it isn't junk. It's a gift. And what a gift it is!

Whites and the Gift of Organization

After my speech, nobody really complained about what I said about whites. I complimented whites as being talented at setting up businesses and making good use of money. I guess all those white reporters liked what I said because they picked on me only for what I said about the other races!

The compliment was deserved. I believe that like blacks, whites have a special, God-given gift. It's what I call the gift of organization.

Let's be honest: who runs the world today? By and large, it's whites. It's been that way for centuries. The world's dominant language is English. American computers run the world's businesses. American jet fighters and aircraft carriers keep the peace around the globe. The U.S. dollar is the most important currency. The American economy is the largest and most powerful in history. American movies are shown everywhere there's a TV or a movie theater.

Whites' dominance of the globe is a remarkable thing. It didn't just happen, of course. For centuries, European nations have competed against one another to be masters of the earth. And while the names of the victors have changed over the centuries—the Italians, Portuguese, Spaniards, French, and British each have had their turn—whites have shown a remarkable ability to come out on top.

Europeans founded America and created its main political and economic institutions. And now America has become the latest in this line of great nations to dominate the material world.

Why have whites been so successful at global politics and business? I believe God has blessed them with a mighty gift. Whites are gifted at creating organizations, administering them, and investing money in worthwhile projects.

Look at the list of the one hundred wealthiest people in the world. There's no denying it: whites are very gifted at creating wealth. If money is all that matters to you, then you'll consider this fact a tragedy for non-whites. But those of us who worship a Higher Power know that money isn't everything. It can be a curse if not used wisely.

Heaven knows this gift of organization hasn't always been used for God's glory. The European colonialism that covered the globe when this century began was slavery by another name. America hasn't always used its power in the right ways, either. Lately, we've been telling the rest of the world, through our movies and entertainment, that easy sex, violence, and materialism are the way to go.

Examples of how this gift of organization has been abused over the centuries could fill a whole book. The point I'm making is simply this: all gifts can become warped for Satan's purposes when they're devoted to the wrong cause.

Whites, as I see it, have a great talent for organizing people, things, and ideas. This talent is reflected especially in politics, business, war, and the sciences. Maybe there's a better way of describing this gift than calling it the gift of organization. That seems to me as good a term as any.

Regardless, I really don't see the harm in acknowledging that the whites' gift of organization has brought about great progress for mankind in many areas. That is, as long as this gift of organization is seen for what it really is. It's all part of a larger scheme, a fuller portrait of man: the complete image of God.

Hispanics and the Gift of Family

Some whites seem to think that minorities are the only people who can be the butt of a racial joke. The joke I'm about to repeat should clear up that misimpression. It's a joke from Mexico that was printed on a pro-life newsletter a few years ago.

The people who didn't like my speech probably won't like this joke, either. I have to admit it's really not all that funny. It's definitely politically incorrect. But it does help to make a point—one of the points I was criticized for making in my remarks about Hispanics.

One night, four dogs are sitting around and talking: a Mexican dog, an African dog, an Asian dog, and an American dog. The Mexican dog starts to brag to the other dogs. "When I want some food," it says, "I just have to bark and my family gives me some."

The African dog asks, "What's food?"

The Asian dog asks, "What's barking?"

The American dog asks, "What's a family?"

Say what you will about the "stereotypes" used in this south-of-the-border joke. The moral to the story is clear—and painful. The world knows what we know. The American family is going through some terrible times.

In rebuilding our families, we could really use some good examples of strong families. We need to learn all over again the happiness and honor that come from a good family life. I think these examples are all around us. They're the strong, joyful Hispanic families that are now the fastest-growing part of our population.

In my speech, I talked about how God has blessed Hispanics with the gift of family. God has exalted Hispanics with stable marriages and many beautiful children. To illustrate my point about Hispanics' gift of family, I pointed out how many Hispanic families live together under one roof. I said that twenty or thirty Hispanic relatives might live together in the same house.

Examples are easy to come by. My coauthor, Andrew Peyton Thomas, is married to a Mexican-American woman who grew up in southern California. She comes from a family of ten children. At one point during her childhood, she had a grandparent, an aunt and an uncle, and three cousins living with her. At various other times in her childhood, between twenty and thirty other relatives and friends of the family lived or stayed with her family.

She admits that sometimes she felt cramped. But she always felt blessed too. She grew up with a strong sense of family that's carried over into the family she's raising today.

My main point about Hispanics is that they have a strong family structure. And Hispanics are more likely to have members of their extended family living with them than are whites or blacks.

Recent statistics from the U.S. Census Bureau shed some light on this tendency. The Census Bureau keeps track of how many family members over the age of eighteen live in a household in addition to parents and children. That would include people such as grandparents, aunts, uncles, cousins, and so on.

In 1997, 10 percent of white households and 14 percent of black households had members of the extended family living with them. For Hispanics, the number was 20 percent. In other words, Hispanics are twice as likely as whites to have members of the extended family living with them.

Hispanics' gift of family is also evident in their values. Women born in Mexico have a birth rate more than double that of U.S.-born women. The divorce rate in Mexico is one-tenth that of the United States. More Hispanics say that abortion is "an act of murder" (63 percent) than members of any other ethnic group. Elida Vargas, who directs the adolescent program at Mary's Center, a nonprofit clinic in Washington, D.C., says, "Once a Latino girl gets pregnant, I would say 98 percent do not see abortion as an option."

The same holds true on other questions of family values. Eighty-four percent of Hispanics believe that homosexual relations are wrong. Hispanics have the highest percentage of members who say that getting married is "very important" to them (74 percent), and that "having close relationships with relatives" is "one of the most important things" in their lives (43 percent).

Hispanics' gift of family is a glorious gift in any age. It's become even more important today, with so many families falling apart from sin and selfishness. Strong family values boil down to great self-denial by the parents. Hispanics have been willing to make these sacrifices. Increasingly, the rest of us haven't.

Our Hispanic brothers and sisters should be proud of this gift of family. I only wish the rest of us were more willing to learn from their example.

Asians and the Gift of Inventiveness

Some of the largest economies in the world are in Asia. Many of these countries enjoy few natural resources. Yet they produce some of the finest cars, appliances, electronics, ships, and other goods in the world.

Think about Japan. It's smaller than California. A little more than fifty years ago, Japan was bombed with nuclear weapons and devastated by war. Japan imports all of its oil, iron ore, copper, and lead. It has little land suitable for agriculture. Yet today, even after years of recession, Japan is the second-largest economy in the world. Japan will enter the twenty-first century as one of the world's most powerful nations.

Throughout Asia, the same success story has been repeated. Over the last twenty years, up until recently, China's economy has been the fastest-growing economy in the world. Taiwan, South Korea, Singapore, Hong Kong, and other Asian nations large and small have become unlikely economic powerhouses. The recent economic troubles there can't erase these tremendous gains.

Why have these countries enjoyed such success? I argued in my speech that Asians are blessed with the gift of creativity. Not only can they make ends meet despite living on islands or mountainous land with few natural resources. They can take Western inventions, improve on them, and sell them to the world at great profit—and against great odds.

Now, the term *Asian* is a broad one, I know. It covers a lot of different people. I use *Asian* to refer to the people from East Asia. The people of East Asia, the Orient, are very gifted at what you might call "making something out of nothing."

Thomas Sowell has noted the special qualities of Asians along these lines. The Japanese, he observes, "seized upon Western technology . . . and, after decades of being technological copiers and producers of shoddy imitations of Western merchandise and machinery, eventually forged to the forefront of technology and became the world's standard for quality in such fields as optics and automobiles." Sowell is aware that Japanese emigrants around the world also have shown this gift: "The behavior and performance of Japanese emigrants have certainly produced remarkable economic advancement in the most varied countries on three continents."

Several factors are at work here. For one thing, Asians benefit from strong personal values. They believe in hard work, family, and public order. Some leaders of Asian countries have called these "Asian values" because Americans and Europeans don't seem to believe in these institutions anymore.

Obviously, that's going too far. Asians don't have a monopoly on good values. We've turned away from God's rules lately, and our society is paying the price. But God will reward us if we return to His ways.

I also believe He'll reward us for being grateful for the gifts that He has given us. That means not only our individual talents. It means thanking Him for the gifts of the races—even if, for some strange reason, some people find these gifts offensive instead of glorious.

True Teamwork

Our forefathers were not perfect. They left it to their descendants to stamp out slavery, segregation, and racism. But even though they weren't equal to these tasks themselves, they left us a valuable list of instructions for dealing with them.

The founders of this country, for all their faults, were God-fearing people. They gave us a spiritual inheritance to guide us: our Judeo-Christian faith. This faith tells us that with God, all things are possible. If it be His will, even racism shall be exterminated from the earth.

We must do our best to seek this vision. I believe that through greater love and understanding of the races, we can take giant strides toward this goal. Tackling the scourge of racism requires courage as well as kindness. We shouldn't be afraid to acknowledge obvious facts. We shouldn't deny the blessings that God, in His wisdom, has seen fit to give us.

Of course, to repeat, God's gifts to the races don't diminish God's gifts to individuals. All of us, as individuals, are blessed with multiple gifts. For example, when I was a professional football player, I was also a minister and a leader off the field. There are NFL players who have run for Congress and even president, opened successful businesses, practiced law, set up large charities, and done many other things. But I'll bet that all of them never forgot what helped to get them where they were in life. It was the gift of football talent. They invested this talent wisely, and it paid off in a big way.

As a nation, we are a brilliant mosaic of different peoples and races. We should be proud of who we are. We should delight in the differences that God has created among us.

These differences are not defects of God's creation. The opposite is true. We're a stronger nation because of these differences. They come together in a powerful synergy. It's no coincidence that America is the most multicultural nation on earth and also the greatest power on earth.

I know how sensitive my own people are when it comes to matters of race. Who can blame us? In America at least, blacks have suffered more than any other race. But that doesn't mean we should deny the special gifts

God has handed us. God, I believe, wants us to make the most of these gifts. Just because blacks' special gift is worship and spirituality doesn't mean that we can't also serve mankind in other ways, as individuals and as a race. I know that we can because we already have.

Edward Wilmot Blyden summed it up best, I think. Almost a century ago, he compared blacks' contributions to the world to those of whites. They were very different contributions then, just as they are today:

> The Negro is, at this moment, the opposite of the Anglo-Saxon. Those everywhere serve the world; these everywhere govern the world. The empire of the one is more wide-spread than that of any other nation; the service of the other is more wide-spread than that of any other people. . . . The one wears the crown and wields the sceptre; the other bears the stripes and carries the cross.

Blyden went on to describe the plight of blacks as "not unlike that of God's ancient people, the Hebrews." He noted that their lot "resembles also His who made Himself of no reputation, but took upon Himself the form of a servant, and, having been made perfect through suffering, became the 'Captain of our salvation.'"

Blyden asked his people:

> Tell me, now, ye descendants of Africa, tell me whether there is anything in the ancient history of your African ancestors, in their relation to other races, of which you need to be ashamed. . . . Is there anything, when you compare yourselves with others, to disturb your equanimity, except the universal oppression of which you have been the victims? . . . We may say, then, in the language of the poet—
>
> > In all the ills we bore,
> > We grieved, we sighed, we wept—
> > We never blushed.
>
> We could not blush physically, and we had no need to blush mentally or morally.

In the end, our Creator will judge us as individuals. Each soul must answer for the life he has led. Still, while we're on this earth, let's not shy away from recognizing and praising God for *all* the gifts He has given us, even those that aren't individual gifts. Gifts from God are meant to be invested in His service. When our diverse talents are blended together in united service of a higher cause, no power on earth can stop us.

Chapter Five

A Covetous People

A sermon against greed may sound strange coming from a professional athlete like Reggie White. Many people think that because pro athletes make a lot of money, they must be greedy. Now *that* is a stereotype.

Pro athletes do earn very high salaries. But that doesn't mean all athletes are greedy, any more than it means all doctors or other highly paid professionals are greedy. It means we live in a rich society that likes ball games. Pro athletes are paid only as much as people are willing to pay them for their services.

I believe there's nothing wrong with earning a large salary as long as we earn it honorably. I happen to agree with what John Wesley, the founder of the Methodist Church, said on the subject of money: "Gain what you can, save what you can, give what you can." As long as we make our money the right way and do the right things with it, we shouldn't feel guilty about the blessings that come to us through hard work and God's grace.

I've tried to be generous with the large salaries I've earned in the NFL. After half of my salary goes to the government in taxes (call it forced charity), I give another 10 percent to my church. I give large donations to charity, including Urban Hope. And I try to help out relatives and friends in need.

In addition, I've passed up large sums of money when I thought God wanted me to. When I spoke up for God's rules in my speech, I lost several multi-million-dollar contracts. Praise God! I'm just glad He gave me the strength to do the right thing.

Even for a well-off athlete — or maybe especially for a well-off athlete —

it's easy to become caught up in money. These temptations tug at all of us. Even a rich man can feel he doesn't have enough money in the bank.

What concerns me is that our nation seems to be surrendering to these temptations without a fight. Money is becoming our god. Not only are our souls suffering from this surrender, but our children are paying a high price as well.

Today, America is blessed with incredible wealth and prosperity. We are, by far, the richest country in the world. We're almost twice as wealthy as the next wealthiest country, Japan. Our economy accounts for one-fourth of the entire global economy. We're also among the richest people in the world *per capita.*

So why don't we act that way? Too many of us act as if we can never have enough. In America, life at the end of the twentieth century has become a money chase. Our lives increasingly revolve around careers and income. As a people, we've come to focus our lives on making as much money and buying as many luxuries as possible.

Look at the lives we lead. We spend almost all our income, and even go into debt, to buy luxuries and keep up with our neighbors. I'm convinced that this is one of the main reasons America is experiencing a record number of bankruptcies. Both parents of small children work so that there will be two incomes, even when the second income isn't really needed. We vote for politicians based on whether we think they can put more money in our pockets.

The love of money is as old as money itself. Money means economic freedom and security. But money buys us more than our daily bread. Money also means power. It means that other people have to serve us instead of vice versa.

Beyond that, money allows us to buy extra goods and services from others that aren't essential. We call these things luxuries. Some luxuries are fairly inexpensive, such as VCRs and answering machines. Some are very expensive, such as large houses, prestigious cars, designer clothing, and boats.

People have always been tempted to seek more wealth and possessions than they really need. We may do some of this treasure hunting because we want extra security or an inheritance to leave to our children. But these days, a lot of these purchases, I think, are made for a different reason. They're made because we're just being greedy.

Greed is a sin you'll find in every human community. For that matter, it's inside every person, waiting for a chance to show itself. The tenth commandment deals with greed. It states: "You shall not covet your neighbor's house. You shall not covet your neighbor's wife, or his manservant or maidservant, his ox or donkey, or anything that belongs to your neighbor."

The commandment against coveting is interesting not only for what it says, but also for what it doesn't say. God didn't command us, "Thou shalt not be greedy." The tenth commandment makes clear that greed flows not so much from the love of possessions or money for their own sake. Greed usually comes from coveting what other people have.

Coveting drives our greed. And what is coveting? It means "keeping up with the Joneses." Coveting means trying to have the luxuries that other people have so we can impress them and feel better about ourselves. These days, "keeping up with the Joneses" seems to be America's new motto. It has certainly become more popular than "in God we trust."

Our whole society is built around buying and possessing. You see it in the ads on TV, the stores all around us, the huge malls that are the cathedrals of today. TV shows glamorize the rich and famous and urge us to covet what they have. Greed has always motivated people. Still, I wonder if any other nation, on the whole, has been as covetous as we are.

The late Dr. Sandy F. Ray, pastor of the Cornerstone Baptist Church in Brooklyn and one of the great black preachers of our time, noticed these trends twenty years ago. In his sermon "The Perils of Plenty," Dr. Ray remarked, "Poverty is not the greatest threat of our nation. The management of plenty is our greatest threat." The tenth commandment has fallen by the wayside. It has become about as relevant to people's lives as the second commandment, which forbids idol worship. Maybe that's because money has become our idol.

Our attitudes about money have changed a lot just in the last twenty years. In 1975, Americans were asked to define *the good life*. A majority listed only a few things, such as a car, a lawn, and a home; a happy marriage; an interesting job; and being able to afford college for their kids. Today, people say that the good life means a job that pays "much more than average," "a lot of money," and other things we used to consider luxuries. Four out of ten Americans say that living the good life means having "really nice clothes," a second car, a vacation home, and travel outside the United States. Thirty-seven percent mentioned a swimming pool.

These are wants, not needs. When we satisfy one, another takes its place.

It's fair to say that over the last couple of decades, money has become an obsession for Americans. In the process, we've forgotten some old truths. We've forgotten how the love of money corrupts the soul. "For where your treasure is," Jesus told us, "there your heart will be also."

Again, my point isn't that money is bad or that we shouldn't buy any luxuries. I'm not calling for us to live like monks. I just think we need to guard against the temptation to obsess over money and possessions. We need to resurrect the tenth commandment.

We can't let the love of money consume us to the point that we do things to earn money that are wrong in God's eyes. That means we don't steal. We don't sacrifice the welfare of our families to earn more money. We don't make decisions as citizens based on which politicians will put more money in our pockets.

What happens when we live for money? I think we're seeing the answers to these questions in a lot of our social problems today. We see it in children killing one another in the inner city for a pair of high-priced athletic shoes. We see it in the suburbs in a different form: the grueling rat race. Neither is good for body or soul.

"He Who Dies with the Most Toys Wins"

To see how materialistic our society has become, take a look around. From the way we behave, you'd think we're struggling just to put bread on the table. We race from home to job back to home, and sometimes from job to job, to make as much money as we can. Polls show that many of us feel constantly frazzled and tired because of the demands on our time. But these demands are mostly, I think, demands we place on ourselves by trying to keep up with the Joneses.

Shop Till You Drop

Look at the spending spree we've been on lately. In 1998, consumer spending in the United States hit an all-time high. We spent more money than ever before for cars, electronics, appliances, and other goods and services. New home sales also set a record in 1998.

The economy has been booming, and a spending spree seems only natural. After all, most of us have more money to spend, so why not spend it? Also, interest rates have been low, and economists say that leads to more sales of new homes, and new homes lead to still more purchases. As one analyst told a reporter for the *Washington Post*, people who buy new homes "tend to buy things to fill them up."

As I said, I don't think there's anything wrong with buying new homes and appliances as long as we earn our money the right way. But that assumes we have the money to pay for these things. Lately, that hasn't been the case. We're not just spending our extra income from the good economy. We're going into debt, spending our savings, and filing for bankruptcy in record numbers.

In 1998, Americans set a record for consumer debt. Total consumer debts reached $1.3 trillion. At the same time, our savings rate hit an all-time low. The Commerce Department reported in June 1998 that personal saving as a share of disposable personal income fell to 0.2 percent. We're not saving for our children's future the way we used to.

Even worse, we're not honoring our debts. We've set an all-time record for personal bankruptcies. In 1997, despite a robust economy, 1.3 million personal bankruptcies were declared. That was the third straight year in which Americans had set a record.

Things have reached the point that, as Congressman James P. Moran pointed out, "We have more bankruptcies than college graduates each year." In 1998, Congress responded by trying to change the bankruptcy laws to make people accept more responsibility for their debts. Imagine Congress having to tell adults to pay their bills.

Credit card companies exploit our covetousness. They're tempting people as they've never been tempted before. In 1997, two billion credit card solicitations went out to consumers through the mail. That's roughly eight solicitations a year for every American. Corporations can be greedy too.

The fact that corporations sometimes exploit us can't excuse our irresponsible or greedy decisions. It's wrong to borrow money and not pay it back. When people don't pay their debts, other people must pay them. That means the rest of us—because the companies that lost money then raise their prices to make up the difference. In 1997 alone, bankruptcies unfairly cost American businesses $40 billion. The rest of us eventually pick up the tab.

Americans are blessed with generous bankruptcy laws. Our laws allow poor people to get back on their feet. But we shouldn't take advantage of these laws. We have to hold ourselves accountable for our financial decisions. We have to pay our bills.

Don't get me wrong: I'm not on a high horse here. Through the grace of God, I'm financially well off today. There was a time, however, when I was almost broke. It happened when I started playing pro football with the Memphis Showboats of the United States Football League (which itself filed for bankruptcy soon after that).

When I started playing, I received a signing bonus of $240,000. Although that's a relatively small amount by today's NFL standards, back then it was a huge amount for me. At twenty-one years old, I really didn't know how to handle it.

I ended up wasting much of it. People took advantage of me because I knew so little about personal finances. I sank money into a condominium—a lot more than it was worth. I also gave quite a bit of money away. By the end of my first year with the 'Boats, I was $50,000 in debt.

Ironically, the people who have preyed on me most successfully over the years were so-called Christians. Throughout my career, wicked businessmen have picked my pockets far less often than dishonest Christians. At least non-Christian con men don't mask their greed and covetousness in religion.

How did I pull out of my bad financial situation? I married wisely. Sara straightened out my finances, and she's handled them ever since.

No matter how much money you're making, it's possible to overspend. Sometimes, we do this by making dumb decisions. But too often, we overspend because we're being covetous. We see what other people have, and we think we're entitled to the same thing. Sometimes it reaches the point that we can't control how much we're spending. Our appetite for money runs our lives.

By Hook or By Crook

We're not only surrendering to covetousness by borrowing our way into bankruptcy; we're also increasingly resorting to breaking another one of God's rules: thou shalt not steal.

Since 1960, the property crime rate has gone up 258 percent. Property crimes are thefts. During this same period, the robbery rate has risen 337 percent. The larceny rate has almost tripled. The motor vehicle theft rate has risen 287 percent.

The materialism of the inner city accounts for some of these statistics. People believe they have to steal their way into prosperity. They think that in material possessions, they'll find happiness. In *The Gospel for the Ghetto: Sermons from a Black Pulpit,* Rev. Manuel L. Scott saw in 1973 what we see today—too many "ghetto-dwellers are so absorbed in acquiring physical and material needs that they face a powerful seduction to sidestep moral and spiritual values." He added, "While the rich and well-to-do can be alienated from God by their abundance, the poverty stricken can be separated from God by their scantiness."

The amount of theft by employees throughout our society also has risen sharply. The Association of Certified Fraud Examiners reports that every year, workers steal about $435 billion from their own employers. This is about 6 percent of the revenues for the average firm. There's three times as much employee theft today as there was in the 1960s.

Cheating on taxes is rampant. In his book *The Complete Book of Greed*, M. Hirsh Goldberg notes that about 25 percent of Americans *admit* to cheating on their taxes. Their cheating costs society $100 billion a year. Securities and banking fraud costs the country another $15 to $30 billion a year.

Stealing is a grave sin. So is coveting. When you put the two together, you've violated two of God's most sacred rules. These are sins for which we (literally) all pay a price.

Who's Raising the Children?

Today, many young parents are paying strangers to raise their children for them. The usual reason is that both parents work outside the home.

For some parents, day care is hard to avoid. Single mothers have an especially tough situation. Basically, they either have to live near parents or relatives who are willing to help them or resort to day care. But these parents are in the minority. Most people who use day care are married. And I believe that most people who use day care do so because they're being covetous.

Let me explain where I'm coming from. I'm fortunate to have been a professional athlete. Sara has been able to stay home and raise our two children. My income has helped to make that easier.

But look at my situation another way. What if we decided we needed to live in a mansion instead of a modest house? What if we chose to live in Beverly Hills instead of Green Bay? What if we decided that every little bit counts, and Sara had to pull her share of the load by working outside the home?

That's not so far-fetched. I'll bet that's the kind of thinking that led most parents who use day care into that situation. They bought expensive houses, cars, clothes, and other possessions that they really couldn't afford.

They realized the only way to make ends meet was to have a second income.

Money can be tight for families on one income. But let's be honest. Very few families in America can't afford to put food on the table and a roof over their heads on one income.

Every day, more of us put our children in day care. We're doing it because of the love of money. We're doing it because we covet what our neighbors have, and we want others to covet what we have.

We find it hard to level with ourselves about the way the next generation of kids is being raised. About six in ten parents today believe they spend more time with their kids than their parents spent with them. Only two in ten say they spend less time. Fifty percent of mothers, in particular, say they spend more time with their children than their mothers spent with them. Twenty-five percent say less time; 25 percent say about the same time.

That can't be true. Far more mothers are working outside the home today than ever before. It's impossible for mothers to spend time with their children when they work somewhere away from them.

What's even more disturbing is the age of many children in day care. Fifty-five percent of new mothers return to the workforce within *one year* of giving birth. In 1976, by contrast, only 31 percent did. From 1965 to 1997, the percentage of mothers with children under six who work outside the home rose from 25 percent to 65 percent.

We know that these trends aren't good for kids. In 1997, 74 percent of Americans agreed that "too many children are being raised in day-care centers these days." But we aren't willing to change our behavior.

I'm no social scientist, and I'm not going to pretend to be an expert on the effects of day care. However, as a minister, I must speak out against placing money or careers above the welfare of our children. Many experts are convinced that day care—a symptom of our covetousness—is damaging the next generation of children.

Research beginning in the early 1970s has found that children raised by day-care centers are more likely to be violent or disruptive, or to suffer learning disabilities, when they grow older. A 1974 study in *Developmental Psychology* concluded that children who entered day care before their first birthday were "significantly more aggressive" than other children. They also were more "physically and verbally abusive" of adults. A 1985 study reported in *Child Development* compared two groups of day-care children. It found that those who had spent more time in day care suffered from more harmful effects, regardless of the quality of care. Teachers were more likely to describe these early care kids as "having aggressiveness as a serious deficit of social behavior."

Jeree Pawl, director of the infant-parent program at the University of California-San Francisco, says that in day care, the loudest, least disciplined children receive most of the attention. They're rewarded for bad behavior. Pawl observes that "in most day cares, it's a pecking order; it's like a bunch of wild chickens in a hen yard."

In 1998, the National Institute of Child Health and Human Development released a long-term study of more than 1,300 children in ten states. The study looked at kids from diverse ethnic and socioeconomic backgrounds. It found that a child's placement in day care provided a "significant prediction" of poor interaction between mothers and children, and of learning difficulties in the children.

Karl Zinsmeister of the American Enterprise Institute has noted that children in day care are more likely to become ill. The American Pediatric Association estimates that infants under the age of one in group care have eight times as many colds and other infections as babies cared for by their families. Children in day care are four times as likely to require hospitalization.

A moving personal account of life in a day-care center comes from William and Wendy Dreskin. For five years, the Dreskins ran their own nonprofit nursery school and then day-care center near San Francisco. Their teachers had to have a college degree. The Dreskins tried in other ways to make their day-care center special and geared toward teaching children new skills.

After a while, though, the Dreskins began to lose heart. They said,

·We typically saw scenes like this: Carl's mother arrives at 6:00 p.m., tired and frazzled. Carl tries to show her a picture he has painted. "Show me later. Get your lunch box. Come on." She is already halfway out the door. Carl trails after her, crying at the rebuff and at the effort of trying to balance his painting, his lunch box, his fire engine, and the cup of fruit salad he made in a cooking project that afternoon. We can tell from his mother's mood what sort of evening Carl will have. So much for the precious two hours he will get to spend with his mother between leaving day care and going to bed.

After watching such scenes over the years, the Dreskins said they were "so distressed by our observations" that they closed their center.

Why have we ignored these facts? Harvard psychiatrist Armand M. Nicholi Jr. believes it's for "the same reason society ignored for scores of years sound data on the adverse effects of cigarette smoke. The facts demand a change in our lifestyle that we simply do not want to change — or have difficulty changing."

I think that we don't deal with these facts because our covetousness won't let us. We've convinced ourselves that we need the money from a second income. We can't imagine life without the luxuries we've grown attached to.

The most common reason that people give for putting children in day care is the need for more money. But the median income for two-earner families is $56,000, compared with only $32,000 for one-earner families. The truth is that families can get by at either salary. Where's the money going? A lot of it is going for things such as bigger homes. New homes are 38 percent larger now than in 1970. We're not even spending the extra money on our children.

This is a tough message. I suspect that's why not many ministers have been talking about day care. But we can't afford to ignore this problem any longer. Nobody really believes that a stranger can raise a child as well as a parent can.

I can't say what it's like to give up a career for a family. But my wife,

Sara, can. Through four years of college, she trained to be an officer in the U.S. Army. Halfway through her senior year, I proposed to her. We knew we'd be starting a family soon, so we were relieved when she received a commission for reserve, instead of active, duty. Sara took this as a sign that God meant for us to be married and to raise a family together.

Sara loved the army and was successful while she served. She was promoted to first lieutenant, and was on the verge of making captain, when she left the army. Sara never pursued active duty because she knew our two babies would suffer from her working full-time.

While I was playing for the Philadelphia Eagles, Sara worked twenty hours a week as a counselor at a mental hospital in New Jersey. It was something she felt called to do. Sara worked at night so that I could be home to watch the children. Her bosses offered her more pay and responsibilities, but only if she agreed to work forty hours a week. She turned them down, because that would've forced us to put the kids in day care.

She did this of her own free will because she thought it was best for our kids. I'll never know all the frustrations, big and small, she has gone through by staying home with our children. But I do know that when I leave my house to do my job, I never worry about who's minding my children and how well they're doing it. As long as Sara is there, I know my kids will get the best upbringing they possibly can.

They'll get the best upbringing not because Sara is the best mother in the world (although I happen to think she is). They'll get it because, except for me, Sara loves them more than anyone else in the world. Love is the best child-care program around.

Voting for Dollars

How do most people decide on which politicians to vote for? Political experts say they vote based on pocketbook issues. Most people vote for politicians based on who they think will put more money in their pockets.

The same experts say that interest groups support candidates based on who they think is buttering their bread. Unions support Democrats because they think they'll get a better deal from them; big business supports Republicans for the same reason. When you add up all the interest groups, maybe we all belong to one.

Let's hope not. Because it's wrong to worship money to the point that our votes, and even our souls, are for sale.

I'm a minister, not a political pundit. I don't follow politics the way some people do. I'm not even a Democrat or a Republican. Still, when I see what I've seen lately, I feel I have to speak out. The love of money is corrupting our political system.

Here, I'm not talking about political contributions and corruption of the political system. I'm talking about corruption of *the people*. This is far more serious, in my opinion. Americans have come to believe it's all right to vote for people based on who will help us out financially. I think that's a bad sign for our democracy. It's another sign of our covetousness.

It's one thing to vote based on money issues when we're in a depression. But in these times, supporting politicians based on money issues means trading our votes for mammon.

Look at the relationship between the state of the economy and political support for the president. Most Americans base their decisions on which presidential candidate to vote for and whether they like a president once in office on how well the economy is doing. That was true before President Clinton was elected. One political commentator, David Broder, has pointed out that President Reagan's job-approval ratings also rose and fell with the state of the economy. In March 1983, when the country was deep in a recession, President Reagan's job-approval rating was only 35 percent. Later, "the climb back up to the level preceding his 1984 reelection landslide tracked the steady recovery of the economy."

Polls show that voters care most about the state of the economy. When the economy is doing well, they tend to vote for the guy who's in office because they give him credit. When the economy is in the tank, they're more likely to vote for change.

President Clinton's troubles have given us even stronger evidence of our materialism. The president has been criticized by just about everyone for what he's done in the Oval Office. He's admitted that he sinned. There's no need to beat up on him anymore.

Also, let me say that I can understand why so many black folk have stuck up for President Clinton. It's clear from his past and from the company he keeps that he truly cares about black folk and is very comfortable around them. Quite frankly, that's something we don't see very often in a president.

I'm frustrated about the reaction of the American people to his sins. When news of the Monica Lewinsky scandal broke in January 1998, a lot of political experts thought his public support would drop like a rock. But it didn't. Instead, President Clinton's ratings shot up. They ended up hitting the highest levels of his presidency.

Maybe the good ratings happened because people thought the media were giving him a hard time. It's difficult for me to criticize anyone for being tough on the media. But the polls since then have made things clearer. The people think President Clinton's sins are no big deal. His poll numbers never really went down. And almost all the political pros agree that that's because the public likes the way he's handled the economy.

A few weeks after the scandal broke, a *New York Times* poll showed President Clinton's job approval ratings at 68 percent. Other polls showed his support at more than 70 percent. Another poll showed that 60 percent didn't think it was important whether he had committed adultery with a White House intern. Sixty-five percent said they would want him to stay in office even if the allegations were true.

This number has stayed about the same ever since. The numbers didn't change even after one woman, Kathleen Willey, said on *60 Minutes* that the president had sexually groped her; after the president admitted lying about what he did with Monica Lewinsky; and after the details of the Starr Report were released.

Why did nobody care? People loved their money more than their government. The economy was roaring, and nobody wanted to rock the boat.

President Clinton was elected based on the slogan, "It's the economy, stupid." He stuck to that theme once he got into office. As one political commentator, Paul Gigot, put it, many people now view him as "the icon of our economic boom." A *Wall Street Journal* reporter found after interviewing people in a Chicago suburb that people have stood by President Clinton because they think he's been an effective "CEO" for the country.

One woman in New York seemed to sum it up when she explained why she still supported the president. When asked by the *New York Times* for her reaction to the evidence in the Starr Report, she said, "The stock market is doing well. There are more jobs for people. Basically, I think the American people are happier than they've been in many years."

Political experts agree that the strong economy is the main reason why President Clinton has remained popular in his approval ratings. "It's not Paula Jones, it's Dow Jones," the saying goes. Or as another expert, Charles Krauthammer, put it in the *Washington Post*, "Americans continue to resist trading in their new Ford Explorer for clean government."

Some have pointed out that this is poor economic reasoning. The president, they say, has little to do with the state of the economy. But I think that's really beside the point. We give credit to politicians when economic times are good, and we turn on them when times are bad. The problem is that we care too much about the economy and money.

Look at the example we've set before the soldiers who defend our country. Military leaders say they're worried about the double standard that's been established. If soldiers see that the commander in chief can commit adultery and lie under oath—two offenses that would mean a court-martial for a serviceman—then why shouldn't they do the same thing? These military leaders fear that this example "may cause a devastating and irrecoverable erosion" in their respect for the president and "further damage sagging morale in the ranks."

Worst of all, look at the example we're setting for our children. At least our children know what the president has done is deeply wrong. In this respect, they seem to know more than their parents.

Notice what some of the kids in New York City had to say when a *New York Times* reporter asked them for their thoughts after the president admitted his adultery. Keith Lynch, an eleven-year-old from the Bronx, said, "He's lying to people who love him and trust him." He added, "That's no President to me. He should be ashamed of himself for teaching kids bad things."

Almost all of the kids said the same thing. Tyrone Strother, age fifteen, called the president a "player." That's street slang for a man who cheats on women. Tyrone continued, "He went to lie school, not law school."

We've come up with all kinds of excuses for the president's adultery. We tell ourselves that the president's sex life doesn't affect how he does his job. But part of his job is serving as a hero—or "role model," as some people say—to kids. When even kids realize that he's set a bad example, we should ask ourselves why our kids have better morals than we do. These children are reminding us of what Jesus said so beautifully: "I praise you, Father, Lord of heaven and earth, because you have hidden these things from the wise and learned, and revealed them to little children. Yes, Father, for this was your good pleasure."

Many other examples illustrate how covetousness has corrupted the political system. For one thing, we've rung up $5 trillion in national debt, most of it in peacetime, because everyone has his hand out to the government. This is money borrowed from our children and grandchildren, which they'll be paying interest on for years to come.

If you're angry with the way our government has been corrupted, don't join a militia. Don't blame the politicians. They're doing what we want them to do. This is a democracy.

If you don't like what's happened to our government, the best advice I can give is to look in the mirror. It's our fault. We're the reason why it's embarrassing for our kids to watch the evening news and hear what our leaders have been up to.

Rest for Our Souls

How do we become less covetous? Ministers, for starters, must speak out more on this issue. I also think that ministers who preach a "gospel of prosperity" do us a disservice. Jesus said repeatedly that we are to seek His kingdom, not the treasures of this earth. There's enough covetousness these days without ministers of the gospel contributing to the problem.

Let's remember that true happiness won't be found in money, luxuries, or careers. It comes from centering our lives on God and the blessings of family and love. Paul told us that "godliness with contentment is great gain." Careers can't provide the happiness that we can gain from serving God and our families.

Neglecting a family for a career can lead to deep regrets. An article by Jeffrey K. Salkin, entitled "Smash the False Gods of Careerism," talks about this. Salkin quotes a turn-of-the-century Yiddish song, "Mayn Yingele" ("My Little One"), which is sung by a father to his sleeping child:

I have a son, a little son,
A boy completely fine.
When I see him it seems to me
That all the world is mine.
But seldom, seldom do I see
My child awake and bright;
I only see him when he sleeps;
I'm only home at night.
It's early when I leave for work;
When I return it's late.
Unknown to me is my own flesh,
Unknown is my child's face.
When I come home so wearily
In the darkness after day,
My pale wife exclaims to me:
"You should have seen our child play."
I stand beside his little bed,
I look and try to hear.
In his dream he moves his life:
"Why isn't Papa here?"

To escape covetousness, all we have to do is to seek the source of true peace and riches. God is the one true solution to the modern rat race. Jesus pointed the way when He said, "Come to me, all you who are weary and burdened, and I will give you rest. Take my yoke upon you and learn from me, for I am gentle and humble in heart, and you will find rest for your souls. For my yoke is easy and my burden is light."

Chapter Six

Crime, Drugs, and Salvation

In 1994, a ten-year-old boy in Janesville, Wisconsin, became one of the youngest murderers in the history of the state. As his father was lying on a couch and watching TV, the boy walked up to him carrying a 12-gauge shotgun. He aimed the shotgun at his father's head and pulled the trigger. Then the boy walked to the police station, holding his pet beagle. He told a detective there that he'd just killed his father.

In 1998, the boy was let out of a juvenile treatment center—just as the nation was coming to grips with a series of school shootings by other disturbed young men. Like those young men, the boy in Janesville had no good explanation for what he did. He told authorities that he was mad at his father for drinking alcohol and for making fun of him in front of his friends.

Things definitely have changed a lot since I was a youngster. When I was growing up in Chattanooga, Tennessee, if two kids got into a fight, a bloody nose was about the worst thing you could expect. Of course, you might be mad at the guy for a while. I can remember not talking to a friend for a week after we duked it out. But soon, things would blow over, and you'd find yourself playing basketball or hanging out with him again.

I carried this lesson over into life. When I'd get into fights with my teammates, either on the field or in the locker room, I wouldn't let things fester. Afterward, we'd apologize to each other for the good of the team. Usually, I'd end up feeling closer to the teammate. The fight actually drew us together.

Troubled teenagers aren't learning these lessons today. For that matter, they don't settle things with their fists. They open fire on their classmates. And they seem to do it for no reason at all.

The recent rash of school shootings has shown us just how rampant these problems are. Between February 1997 and May 1998, nineteen people were killed and fifty injured in school shootings from Alaska to Mississippi to Pennsylvania. Try to make sense of these shootings:

- Evan Ramsey, sixteen, of Bethel, Alaska, had threatened to kill his principal and a popular student who always teased him. On February 19, 1997, he followed through on his threats. He walked into the lobby of his high school carrying a shotgun. First, Ramsey shot sixteen-year-old Josh Palacios in the stomach. With his gun in one hand and a bag of shotgun shells in another, he roamed through the hallways. When his principal, an ex-marine, confronted him, he shot and killed him. A school secretary said that Ramsey's expression that morning was "gleefully evil."

- Luke Woodham, sixteen, of Pearl, Mississippi, said his mother blamed him for her divorce. He also was angry at his former girl-friend. Woodham fell into a satanic cult called the Kroth. On the morning of October 1, 1997, Woodham said demons told him that he was "nothing and that I would never be anything if I didn't get to that school and kill those people." Woodham first stabbed his mother to death in her bed. Then he went to school armed with a deer rifle. He shot and killed the girl who'd spurned him, then his prom date from the previous year. He wounded seven others.

- Michael Carneal, fourteen, went to Heath High School in West Paducah, Kentucky, on December 1, 1997, with a handgun in his backpack. He fired into a crowd of classmates who'd gathered for a prayer session. He killed three and injured five others. Carneal said that a scene from a 1995 movie, *Basketball Diaries*, had inspired him to commit the shootings.

- Mitchell Johnson, thirteen, felt slighted after a three-day romance with Candace Porter ended. He warned his classmates, "Something big is gonna happen." Mitchell and an eleven-year-old friend, Andrew Golden, went to Westside Middle School in Jonesboro, Arkansas, on April 24, 1998. With a 30.06 hunting rifle and other guns, they slaughtered a teacher and four classmates in the school yard. Ten others were wounded.

- Kip Kinkel, fifteen, grew up in a comfortable middle-class home in Springfield, Oregon. But he had shown violent tendencies for a long time. His parents tried to appease him by buying him guns, including a Ruger semiautomatic rifle. On May 21, 1998, he helped his mother carry some shopping bags into the house. Then he shot her in the chest. Two hours later, he shot his father in the back of the head. After hiding in the woods all night, Kinkel went the next day to Thurston High School, carrying his Ruger. He walked into a crowded cafeteria and fired fifty rounds, killing one student and injuring twenty-three others.

These kids had some things in common: they felt rejected by a girl or their peers, they were depressed and angry, and they were able to get guns easily. Kinkel actually talked his parents into buying him guns.

Many of these youngsters came from divorced or broken homes. In his testimony at trial, Luke Woodham said his mother didn't love him, and she blamed him for her divorce. During his trial, he lashed out at the prosecutor. At other times, he couldn't stop crying. "I didn't want to kill my mother," Woodham said at one point. "I do love my mother. I just wanted her to understand."

Mitchell Johnson of Jonesboro also came from a divorced family. His grandmother raised him because, according to neighbors, "his parents were always working." Another young killer, Barry Loukaitis of Moses Lake, Washington, walked into his school in February 1996 and shot his teacher and two students. He did that shortly after his mother told him she was getting a divorce. "I didn't think about Barry at all," she testified in her son's case.

Also, all of these young men were white. I think that's one of the main reasons the media paid so much attention to these shootings. Black folk have known for a long time just how bad a problem school violence has become. The worst school year for school-related violence was 1992–93, when nearly fifty people were killed. Because most of the killings were in inner-city schools, the media didn't pay much attention. Now that these problems have made it to the suburbs and the heartland, the media are starting to take notice.

These trends are frightening. At least school killings in the inner city usually are related to gangs or fights over money or girlfriends. Obviously, these aren't excuses for murder. But at least they're explanations. They make some sense. The recent school shootings are so scary because they were so random and senseless.

The government and the media have been telling us lately that crime rates are down and the streets are safer. But as these school shootings prove, there's more to the story. As I travel around the country for games and speaking engagements, I see the same thing in every hometown newspaper I pick up. Crime is down, but it's not out.

First of all, crime rates haven't fallen by that much. We've seen a minor drop in the crime rate. From 1991 to 1996, the overall crime rate fell 14 percent. The violent crime rate went down 16 percent, the property crime rate 14 percent. The homicide rate dropped 25 percent—but according to the Department of Justice, it's still near an all-time high. Even if the violent crime rate keeps going down at the current rate, it'll take us twenty-five years to get back to where we were in 1960.

The crime problem is becoming worse among whites. Between 1965 and 1991, the violent crime rate among white Americans rose nearly 250 percent. The FBI has reported that the juvenile crime problem is not confined to "minority youth in urban areas," but has become a major problem among "all races, all social classes and lifestyles." Between 1985 and 1994, the number of whites incarcerated increased by more than 50 percent. The percentage of white high-school students admitting they've stolen something worth more than fifty dollars on at least five occasions has more than doubled since 1984.

The recent, small drop in crime rates may be overstated. Police departments feel great pressure to show progress in fighting crime. Some police departments have tried to keep up with public expectations by lying. Charges of falsely reporting crime statistics have hit police departments in New York, Philadelphia, Atlanta, and Boca Raton, Florida. As a result, high-ranking police commanders have resigned or been demoted.

Philadelphia, where I ministered to inner-city youth while playing for the Eagles, has a terrible crime problem. The police there have been underreporting crime for years. The FBI no longer even counts Philadelphia's numbers in its crime statistics. The new police commissioner of Philadelphia, John F. Timoney, admits that because of his new emphasis on accuracy, "I can guarantee you my crime [rate] is going to be way up this year."

Even if the good news about crime is true, we don't have cause for great joy. Think about what we've become. America now has the highest incarceration rates of any nation in the industrialized world. More than one million Americans are in prison. Another half million are in jail. Almost four million more are on probation or parole. The incarceration rate has risen 209 percent from 1980 to 1996.

Now, don't misunderstand me. A lot of criminals deserve to be behind bars. Fifty-two percent of the new male prisoners in 1997 were convicted of violent offenses. Obviously, these offenders need to be kept off the streets.

But we should admit that our crime problem has made us a more dangerous and hard-hearted society. One thing that really bothers me is what's happened to young black men during this time of high crime rates. One out of four black men in their twenties is incarcerated or on probation or parole. Today, 1.4 million black men—13 percent of the total black male population—aren't eligible to vote because of past felony convictions. In ten states, more than 20 percent of black men are barred from the voting booth.

These numbers are unacceptable. We have to find a way to keep so many of our young black men from throwing their lives away. Jesse Jackson said recently in *Emerge* magazine, "You simply would not have this level of massive incarceration of white youth. . . . These [black] youth are dispensable and disposable."

Then there's capital punishment. Since 1960, the murder rate has gone up 85 percent. During that time, the number of people on death row has risen 1,445 percent. Regardless of how you feel about the death penalty, it's obvious that the crime problem is hardening our hearts.

Crime control has become big business for private prisons, security-guard companies, home and car alarm manufacturers, and other corporations. Many Americans now have a financial stake in our high crime rates. Like it or not, that makes us more likely to be complacent about our crime problem.

The drug problem has been even harder to tame. Unlike crime rates, the rates for drug use are still going up. Since 1981, arrests for drug abuse violations by adults have almost tripled. The situation is even worse for our youngsters. From just 1991 to 1996, juvenile drug arrests increased 271 percent. If Americans had to take random drug tests like NFL players, I believe many of us would have a lot of explaining to do.

How do we deal with these awful plagues? Criminals who refuse to obey God's rules and society's laws must be held accountable. We need enough police, prosecutors, and prisons to deal with these offenders.

On the other hand, throwing people in prison and forgetting about them is not a Christian solution to the crime problem. In the last six years, forty states have made it easier to prosecute juvenile offenders as adults. Is this really the best we can do—writing off a generation of kids because we haven't raised them right?

Juvenile shock incarceration programs, or boot camps, sound tough, but don't really work in practice. All fifty states have such programs. But kids graduating from them don't do much better than juvenile offenders who don't. Roughly half of boot camp graduates are convicted of new crimes and returned to prison.

I think we expect too much of these camps. They're supposed to transform a kid into a model citizen in a few months. Then we return him to his old neighborhood and expect him to behave himself. That's unrealistic. Anyone who has grown up or ministered in those neighborhoods knows that these kids need something that will stick. Self-discipline is a good start, but it's only that—a start.

I also think that sometimes we're too hard on offenders who are sincerely trying to turn their lives around. A few years ago, I came to know a barber in Knoxville, Tennessee, who had recently left prison. After some convictions for petty theft and drug offenses, he had received a fifteen-year prison sentence. Upon his release, he took up a trade, married a good woman, and started a family. When I met him, he was working his heart out to support his loved ones.

Eventually, though, he went into debt. All his hard work wasn't enough to make ends meet. Feeling overwhelmed by the pressures, the man reverted to using drugs. When his parole officer found out, the prosecutor threw the book at him. His parole was revoked, and he was sentenced to two more years in prison.

Our church, which the barber had been attending, offered to help him overcome his drug problem. Faith-based ministries have a proven track record of liberating drug users from their addictions. But the state authorities would have none of it. They seemed more interested in shipping him back to prison and breaking up his family.

I'm not saying that this barber was in the right when he used drugs and violated his parole. But surely under the circumstances, the state should've shown him some leniency. Drug dealers deserve to go to prison, but drug users should be given a chance to kick their habit—especially when a faith-based program can help them do just that.

Other crime authorities have argued for even tougher, and more disturbing, policies. One well-respected criminologist, John J. DiIulio of Princeton, has proposed that the state remove children from "criminogenic communities," or high-crime inner-city neighborhoods, to prevent them from growing up to be criminals. In response, Professor Glenn

103

Loury of Boston University pointed out, "It is certainly fair to ask whether the failure of parents to adequately care for their children is limited to high-crime-generating communities or extends more broadly through the society." If crime rates start to go up again, we can expect similar proposals to crop up.

We shouldn't rely too much on tough-on-crime strategies. At some point such strategies are just a way of shifting the blame away from ourselves and our society's failures. America didn't always raise so many young people to commit so many crimes.

Jesus warned us in Matthew 24:12 of how heartless people will become in the end times. "Because of the increase of wickedness, the love of most will grow cold," Jesus said. I don't know if these are the end times. But I do think that the public reaction to the crime and drug problem reflects a lack of love. We see so much crime and wickedness around us that our hearts have grown cold. We shouldn't forget that the people who commit these crimes—even the most terrible of crimes—have souls too. We shouldn't just lock up these people and go about our business.

As the problems of the inner city become problems for the rest of our society, I suspect there will be less finger-pointing at the inner cities and more searching for lasting solutions. That searching should lead to our souls.

A Moral Problem

Only recently have we come to see the crime and drug epidemic as, above all, a moral problem. It all starts with families breaking up. Seventy percent of juvenile offenders come from single-parent homes. And it's not just inner-city kids who are at risk. Boys from divorced families also are at a disadvantage.

Boys from divorced families are more likely to be hostile and withdrawn than boys from intact families. In one study, one out of three boys from divorced families became a delinquent who committed serious crimes. One out of ten girls did the same. The study also found a "surprisingly high incidence of alcoholism" in these kids.

A 1998 study by Sara McLanahan and Cynthia Harper showed that young men who grow up in homes without fathers are twice as likely to end up in jail as those who come from traditional two-parent families. This was true regardless of race, income, and other factors. Even when their mothers remarry, the boys suffer. In their fourteen-year study, McLanahan and Harper found that boys who grow up with a stepfather in the home run an even higher risk of being incarcerated than boys without a stepfather. Boys with stepfathers are roughly three times as likely to be incarcerated as boys raised by their natural parents. White youths whose families split up are at a higher risk of incarceration than their black peers.

It's not hard to understand why fatherless children get into trouble. I remember one Hispanic kid in Milwaukee who offered a good explanation. He told me why he ran with gangs and sold drugs. He said that the drug dealer he worked for was like a father to him. The drug dealer was there for him. He looked out for him. And he cared for him—even if it was for selfish reasons. That's why drug dealers are so successful at recruiting young boys and turning them into "little G's," or gangsters. They fill the void for kids who don't have fathers.

I believe that the problems in our families and our streets are related in other ways too. They spring from the same seed. The crime and drug problem comes from the same sin that's breaking up so many of our families. It's selfishness.

People who commit crimes do so because they don't care about other people. They rob, rape, or brutalize others because they want their way. Maybe they're after money or sex or a power trip. Whatever the reason, they're willing to do anything—including breaking God's most sacred rules—to get what they want.

The same is true of drugs. People use drugs because they want to enjoy the pleasure of getting high. They don't care about how it affects others, including their loved ones.

People sometimes talk about drugs as if they're no big deal. People think that drug users are hurting only themselves. But that's not true. Look at all the newborn babies on crack, or the infants and children neglected by drug-addicted parents. In Iowa, a state where the population is almost entirely white, 10 percent of newborn babies are affected by drugs. For 90 percent of these babies, the drug is methamphetamine, known on the street as meth, speed, crank, or ice.

These babies are damaged for life. One child psychologist in Des Moines said she counsels a three-year-old who screams for up to forty-five minutes every time she's wiped after using the toilet. Another pediatrician treats a five-year-old whose hands shake so much that he can't hold a crayon. A seventeen-month-old named Harley screams whenever somebody reaches for him. One doctor believes that the child thinks the person's hands will go right through him.

The root of this horrible selfishness is the rejection of God. People are seeking things and pleasures instead of obeying God's rules. Remember, in one way or another, every crime is a violation of at least one of the Ten Commandments.

Some have argued that our crime rates are so high because so many poor people live lives of despair. I agree that we as a people should do more financially to help the poor. I've tried to put my money where my mouth is by founding and funding Urban Hope. It provides economic as well as spiritual assistance to people of the inner city. I've supported this charity with large donations—including a portion of the royalties from this book.

We can't just let the poor fend for themselves. But we also can't be misled about why we have such a bad crime and drug problem. What really ails America isn't a lack of money. Rev. Manuel L. Scott once reminded the members of his inner-city congregation, "Morals are free." Scholars have pointed out that crime rates actually went down during the depression. For that matter, crime rates went up dramatically during the 1960s, a period of great prosperity.

A good economy alone can't solve the crime and drug problem. This problem comes from sin and selfishness. Until people learn to follow God's rules, there will be no justice and no peace.

The Solution: Spirituality

The solution to our crime and drug problem is right before our eyes. It's spirituality. God is the only power that can break down the forces of selfishness and sin and show us how to love and serve one another.

Crime experts and social scientists finally have come to realize that religion is the key to tackling crime and drugs. One social scientist, Thorlief Pettersson, reported in 1991 in the *Journal for the Scientific Study of Religion* that while "religion has not been totally neglected in criminological research," he found only sixty studies of the relationship between religion and criminality. This is out of literally tens of thousands of criminological studies that are on the library shelves of almost any major university. Pettersson said, "Most of these studies have reported a negative association between individual religiosity and criminal behavior." He added that "there seems to be substantial empirical support for the conclusion that among those 'attending church services frequently, there is manifestly a strong tendency . . . to commit fewer crimes.'"

A study in 1983 by Charles Tittle and Michael Welch, published in *Social Forces*, drew similar conclusions. They found sixty-five studies of the relationship between personal religiosity and criminality, drug abuse, or related behavior. Fifty-five of those, or 85 percent, reported an inverse relationship. In plain English, the greater a person's commitment to religion, the less likely he will be to commit a crime.

The same is true of drugs. A group of researchers noted in *Youth & Society* in 1993, "Individuals affiliated with a religion have lower rates of drug use than do those not affiliated with a religion. Regardless of denomination, people who attend church regularly have lower rates of drug use than do those who do not attend regularly."

A 1991 study of eight-hundred white male adolescents in the Seattle area reached the same conclusion. According to the study in *Deviant Behavior*, adolescents who never attended religious services were almost four times as likely to use drugs as kids who attended church services weekly.

Even among prisoners, the most hardened of criminals, spirituality provides great hope. A 1992 study by researchers at Rutgers University concluded that, spiritual help aside, prisoners benefited from religion in some very practical ways. They found that inmates who were involved in religion were less likely to break prison rules and to be disciplinary problems. The study also found "two major ways that religion might help to improve adjustment to prison: dealing with the emotional strains of incarceration and dealing with the deprivations of the prison environment."

The researchers reported, "Many religious inmates did not excuse their guilt. Instead, they seemed to accept a profound personal responsibility for their crimes and for the wrongfulness of their conduct." Several inmates talked about how religion had turned their lives around:

- "Being a Christian, I can go and ask Jesus Christ to forgive me for my sins and to give me the strength to deal with my problems."

- "If you talk to everyone here, they'll tell you they're in prison because of a mistake. Most of them, it was a bad attorney, a judge, a stupid mistake in the way they did the crime. The religious inmate, he realizes the mistake was doing the crime in the first place."

- "I am able to live a normal life and uphold my character with dignity. The first objective of prisons is to strip you of your dignity. It takes your self-esteem, your dignity, and everything about you. Religion has helped me to regain this."

- "I've seen some guys who don't really realize that they are in prison because it is not the prison that they see, it is the walk with God. Prison doesn't bother them anymore."

One inmate said it best: "My faith has made me excited about when I go home. *This* person has never been on the streets before."

The Rutgers researchers concluded, "Involvement in religion can reinforce attitudes and behaviors that circumvent the traditional hustles of prison life." These inmates are likely to "associate with other, like-minded religious inmates, and generally surround themselves with a protective social cocoon of religion."

Let's remember that when Jesus began His ministry to the people of Israel, He went to the synagogue in Nazareth and read the following scroll from Isaiah:

> The Spirit of the Lord is on me,
> because he has anointed me
> to preach good news to the poor.
> He has sent me to proclaim freedom for the prisoners
> and recovery of sight for the blind,
> to release the oppressed,
> to proclaim the year of the Lord's favor.

Groups such as Charles Colson's Prison Fellowship are helping to "proclaim freedom" and "release the oppressed," as Jesus commanded us, by liberating inmates from their sin and hopelessness. Now, finally, criminologists and scholars are seeing the power of these ministries and the God they serve.

Despite all this evidence of the effectiveness of religion, the powers that be in our country have only recently taken notice. This change in elite opinion was clear by 1998 when *Newsweek* ran a cover article entitled "God vs. Gangs." The cover declared that religion now has become the "hottest idea in crime fighting."

The article focused on the ministry of Rev. Eugene Rivers of Dorchester, Massachusetts. When Rev. Rivers left his studies at Harvard and moved into a rough neighborhood in Dorchester, he sought out a local drug dealer and gangbanger named Selvin Brown. Brown took him around the neighborhood and introduced him to the people who lived and worked in the crack houses there. When Brown explained why he was so successful recruiting kids to help him sell drugs, he used almost the same words that the kid in Milwaukee told me a few years ago: "I'm there when Johnny goes out for a loaf of bread for Mama. I'm there, you're not. I win, you lose. It's all about being there."

The people these ministries have saved are some of the hardest cases around. The changes in their lives are truly miraculous. Robert L. Woodson Sr. points out in *The Triumphs of Joseph*, "The testimonies of hundreds of men and women who have experienced dramatic turn-arounds in their lives reveal that many of the people who were ultimately freed of their addictions through faith-based programs had previously been hostile to religion and spirituality."

Woodson also notes,

Many faith-based substance-abuse initiatives, for example, have success rates as high as 70 and 80 percent, while the success rates of most secular therapeutic programs hover in the single digits. A comparison of recidivism rates of the two types of approach would reveal even greater evidence of the long-term impact of faith-based programs.

Stories from the Street

In the fight against crime and drugs, the best evidence of God's power isn't in scholarly works. It's in the testimonials of the countless criminals and drug addicts God has touched.

One of the most famous of these is Nicky Cruz. Nicky was born in Puerto Rico to parents who practiced witchcraft. The villagers called his home "the Witch's House." One day, when Nicky was eight years old, his mother was talking to several other mediums. She told them that the boy was "Satan's child." Then she went into a trance. "Leave me, devil!" she screamed at him.

After that, Nicky became filled with hate. He was sent to live with his brother in New York when he was fifteen. He soon joined a street gang called the Mau Maus, one of the toughest in New York. He shot, stabbed, and beat up his rivals with no remorse. Not long after that, Nicky was voted president of the gang.

Nicky recalls in his autobiography *Run, Baby, Run*, "A life motivated by hate and fear has no room for anyone but self." A court-appointed psychologist told Nicky that he was "on a one-way street to jail, the electric chair, and hell." Nicky's life changed only after David Wilkerson, a preacher from rural Pennsylvania, kept after him and eventually persuaded him to repent and accept Jesus as his Lord. At a neighborhood revival put on by Wilkerson, Nicky found himself crying for the first time since he was eight years old.

Nicky has gone on to become one of the world's greatest evangelists. He and Wilkerson established the first Teen Challenge center in Brooklyn. Nicky says the first center was a "kind of Holy Ghost hospital, where the Lord put people back together." Teen Challenge centers now are open in every major city in America. The drug-cure rate for men and women who complete the entire program at Teen Challenge has remained consistently about 70 percent.

Nicky's revival meetings have drawn thousands of lost souls to God. His latest campaign, T.R.U.C.E. (To Reach Urban Children Everywhere), gained 3,500 converts in San Antonio alone in 1993. In 1997, his revival in the Bronx attracted what one New York police officer called "the biggest crowd for any event in the Bronx, except for a Yankees' game, that I have ever seen." Vaso Bjegovich, a former street minister for Urban Hope, is now Nicky's T.R.U.C.E. coordinator. He tells me Nicky has been taking his message to Paducah, Kentucky, and other places where white youths are starting to show the same problems that have affected the kids of the inner city.

One person Nicky helped bring to the Lord is Sonny Arguinzoni. A former heroin addict in New York City, Arguinzoni came into Nicky's Teen Challenge center in Brooklyn in 1962. For three days, Nicky prayed with him and tended to his needs. Arguinzoni committed himself to Jesus and turned his back on substance abuse. He then left New York to attend a Bible college in La Puente, California, and become a minister. Soon, Arguinzoni and his new wife, Julie, were receiving drug addicts into their home to minister to them.

In 1967, Arguinzoni founded the first Victory Outreach Church. Its mission was to reach out to drug addicts, gang members, and their families, and to provide a residence where they could live as they grew in the faith. Victory Outreach Special Services Homes offer biblical counseling, prayer, worship services, Bible studies, and "an atmosphere of God's love." Residents receive twenty-four-hour supervision and are asked to live there nine to twelve months while their faith takes hold. Victory Outreach now calls itself the largest "Christian Home organization in the world." It boasts more than ten thousand men and women in residence in more than two-hundred locations worldwide.

Other street ministers are just as creative in trying to bring kids to God. They try to interest young people with projects that will get them off the streets. In different ministries, these have included computer training and job placement, college tours, building homes for the needy, and tae kwon do.

Why are kids these days causing so much havoc? Nicky Cruz believes it's because of loneliness. He says loneliness is "eating our youths alive." Cruz, like many other street ministers, believes these youths need a second family to make up for the one that let them down. He tries to fill their lives' with love and hope, knowing that's the best way to get them to respond in kind.

My experiences with Urban Hope have taught me the same lesson. Above all, troubled kids need someone who'll love them like a father.

Some of the young people we've reached through Urban Hope have ended up changing *my* life. One was a young man named Rafeal. He grew up in a tough, dangerous part of Philadelphia. When he was six years old, he tried to burn down a store. As a boy, he also sold crack. Between the ages of twelve and nineteen, Rafeal grew up in foster and group homes. When he became a teenager, he was arrested numerous times for aggravated assaults and other crimes. Finally, after Rafeal got into a fight and broke a kid's ribs, he was kicked out of high school.

I met Rafeal through Vaso, who was then with Urban Hope. Vaso came across Rafeal after Rafeal had moved to Milwaukee with only five dollars in his pocket. One day, Vaso brought him up to Green Bay to hear me preach. Before we went to church, they came by our house. I took an instant liking to Rafeal.

Later that day, at the service, I called for anyone who wanted to accept Jesus as his Savior to walk up to the altar. When I saw Rafeal come forward, I was filled with joy. After the service, Vaso and Rafeal came back to our house. I talked to Rafeal for a couple of hours about what was in store for him. I warned him that the devil was going to go after him, and that he needed to stay grounded in his new faith.

Afterward, I kept in touch with Rafeal. I spoke to him two or three times a week. And I also did something unusual to reach out to him. He'd told me he'd always wanted to be a pro athlete. Of course, a lot of kids have this dream. But I thought it would be good for Rafeal to have this chance. If he failed, at least he would know that pro sports wasn't what God had in mind for him.

I set up a private tryout for Rafeal with the Packers. I rented him a motel room and made sure he was treated like any other recruit. In the end, the Packers thought he had talent as an athlete, but not enough to make it in pro football. They didn't offer him a position.

After he heard the bad news, Rafeal got really mad. When Vaso saw him, Rafeal had the same angry glare in his eye that he had had before he accepted Jesus.

Vaso confronted him about his attitude. "So this whole thing's been a big act?" he said to Rafeal. "You just wanted a chance with the Packers, and that's all this was about?" Rafeal was furious. He and Vaso had a terrible fight. It was obvious that Rafeal was really hurting. I wasn't sure where things would go from there.

But the next day, something remarkable happened. Rafeal went to Concordia College in Mequon, Wisconsin, outside Milwaukee. He approached the coach of the football team and vowed, "I will go to college here. I will play football here. And I'm gonna play in the NFL."

Rafeal is now in his third year in college. He's started his own company working with young people. He speaks at schools in Milwaukee about overcoming adversity. He's engaged to be married. Soon, he'll receive his college degree. All of this has happened to a kid who, in high school, was in special education.

The story gets even better because Rafeal went on to do for another kid what we had done for him. After Rafeal was saved, he came to know a troubled white kid. I'll call him John. John had had a rough childhood. When he was four years old, his sister's friends would give him marijuana and show him pornographic movies. They'd also shoot guns outside for kicks. John grew up with violent urges he couldn't really understand. "I developed a lust for guns and violence," he would later say.

When John was in the eighth grade, he took a gun to school. He intended to shoot up the cafeteria. He might have joined the list of angry, lonely youths I mentioned at the beginning of this chapter — except that he brought the wrong bullets. When someone found him carrying the gun, he was arrested. John committed eleven felonies as a juvenile, all armed robberies or crimes with a gun. He was in juvenile detention from the ages of twelve to eighteen.

Finally, John got a break in life — he met Rafeal. John was sent to live in a juvenile group home in Milwaukee where Rafeal was working. Rafeal made John a part of his life. He'd take John fishing, working out, and driving around town with him.

Rafeal also introduced John to Vaso and me. As I did with Rafeal, I helped John out by buying him some new clothes, giving him some pocket money — that kind of thing. I'd also invite John to Packers games in Green Bay.

Today, both Rafeal and John are living lives dedicated to Jesus. Instead of becoming hardened criminals rejected by society, they've opened up their hearts to God. I know that if God could touch their hearts, nobody is beyond His power. What worked for Rafeal and John will work for any-one — guaranteed.

Supporting Our Street Fighters

I've also learned from Urban Hope that you have to treat these kids as a father would. Just as our Father in heaven pours out His love to us, we have to show fatherly love to the kids whose fathers on earth aren't there for them. The problem is that so many kids are hurting.

All of us need to pitch in and help these kids. We can help by funding full-time street ministers who can fill this role of a second father. Nicky Cruz operates an international ministry on a remarkably small budget. Other ministers in the inner city who are sharing this gospel of hope get by on a fraction of what's collected in suburban churches.

Now, God surely enjoys the sight of the beautiful churches that have been built in our suburbs. But He's a God of love, not of buildings. If churches in the inner cities and the suburbs could join forces—financial and spiritual—to reach these kids, the synergy would be powerful.

In fact, I've seen this synergy in action. It happened a few years ago in Charlotte, North Carolina. It all started with a black woman named Barbara Brewton, whom I talked about in my autobiography *In the Trenches*. Some years ago, her husband was shot to death in a crime-ridden Charlotte neighborhood known as Double Oaks. The *New York Times* once described the neighborhood as one of the five most violent urban zones in America. She moved away from the neighborhood after the shooting. But over the next few years, as she grew closer to God, she felt that God was calling her to return to Double Oaks.

When she moved back, Barbara Brewton started a Friday night ministry for neighborhood children. She taught the kids about Jesus. She also taught some of them reading and writing. When she'd hear gunfire, she'd race outside to pull kids off the playgrounds. Before long, Barbara was ministering not only to the kids, but to their parents too. Eventually, a church grew from her efforts. The Community Outreach Mission Church sprang up with Barbara Brewton as its pastor.

Then Barbara Brewton met another female minister, Mary Lance Sisk. Mary was from the southern, well-off part of Charlotte. Mary runs an international ministry. She's also involved in the wealthy and mostly white Forest Hill Evangelical Presbyterian Church. Mary felt God calling her to help the children of Charlotte's inner city. She contacted Barbara Brewton-Cameron (who had remarried) and approached her with an idea. Together, she thought, the two women could make a great team.

Barbara and Mary started a project to clean up and improve Double Oaks. They started a partnership with the church, the city of Charlotte, and civic groups. It bought run-down houses from the slumlords in the area. Then it renovated them and sold them to carefully screened low-income applicants using low-interest loans. The revitalized part of the neighborhood was renamed Genesis Park.

As part of this effort, Forest Hill started a fund-raising drive for their black sister church. The goal was to raise $150,000. I came to speak at a men's rally at Forest Hill in March 1996. I can't tell you how thrilling it was to see all those white and black faces together in celebration of the Lord. The emotional support they gave me during my sermon was phenomenal. They had come together to bring hope and peace to the poor, fatherless, and oppressed people of Charlotte's inner city—and I felt the power of their love.

Instead of raising $150,000, the two churches raised more than double that amount. A banquet in May 1996 that was supposed to be a kick-off banquet turned into a celebration banquet because they'd already met their goal. After Barbara Brewton-Cameron spoke to the people at the banquet, they ended up raising more than $300,000—from the donations made that very night.

Private ventures such as the Double Oaks partnership are critical to winning souls back from the devil. But I also think that the government should be willing to fund some of these programs. I know that some people will have a problem with that. They think that the government has to stay away from anything spiritual. They call this separation of church and state.

But the phrase "separation of church and state" isn't even in the Constitution. The fact that these court rulings are so recent tells you that they have a lot more to do with our modern hostility toward God than with the Constitution. The founders of our country were deeply religious and never would have supported such "separation." One historian opposed to government support of religion, Leonard W. Levy, nevertheless admits that six of the original thirteen states, and seven of the states that voted on the Bill of Rights, aided churches directly with tax dollars.

Let me give you an example of how silly this "separation" has become. A black preacher in Milwaukee put on a religious play after school, on Fridays and Saturdays, in an inner-city public school. It was a motivational play designed to steer kids away from crime, drugs, and sin. The play was a big hit with the kids.

But then the preacher found out that he couldn't pass the hat and ask for donations from the audience. He ended up owing the school several thousand dollars for use of the facilities—with no way of asking for support from the audience. Eventually, I found out about the minister's situation and paid the bill. But the court rulings that have caused such silliness have got to go.

The government should fund faith-based ministries that have a proven track record of turning around the lives of offenders and drug addicts. The evidence is in. Their programs are working better than secular ones. We shouldn't discriminate against them just because they use spirituality as their message. If we want to be a nation under the rule of law, we must first accept the rule of God.

These faith-based programs can't possibly be a worse investment than some of the things the federal government has funded in fighting juvenile violence and drug abuse. In 1998, the *Los Angeles Times* looked at the almost $6 billion that the U.S. Department of Education has spent as part of the Safe and Drug-Free Schools and Communities Act. The reporters "found that taxpayer dollars paid for motivational speakers, puppet shows, tickets to Disneyland, resort weekends and a $6,500 toy police car."

The reporters continued, "Federal funds also are routinely spent on dunking booths, lifeguards and entertainers, including magicians, clowns and a Southern beauty queen, who serenades students with pop hits." In Richmond, Virginia, where a ninth grader shot and wounded a basketball coach and a teacher's aide before school recessed in June 1998, state education officials spent $16,000 to publish a drug-free party guide that recommends staging activities such as Jell-O wrestling and pageants "where guys dress up in women's wear." You can bet that a teenage Reggie White wouldn't have gone along with that!

More important than money, however, are true love and caring. It's not enough to add up how many kids we've saved and put notches on our belts. We have to stay with these kids for the long haul. When they need a second parent, a friend, or a counselor in God's service, we have to be there for them. Otherwise, our faith is a hollow faith, and these kids will know it. What's more, God will know it.

In the fight for the souls of America's outcasts—criminals and drug addicts—we must be creative, dedicated, and tough. In that respect, cheating the devil out of their souls isn't that different from sacking a quarterback. The difference is that when we sack the devil, we help a soul to gain eternity. Our crime and drug problem won't truly be in decline until we blitz the devil in every neighborhood and town, wearing what Paul called "the full armor of God." That armor never fails to protect and to serve.

Chapter Seven

Deaths in the Family

There aren't many open minds left when it comes to abortion. But no matter where you stand on the subject, I hope you'll read on. I doubt you've heard much of what I'm going to say in this chapter. It's what I consider the black perspective on abortion.

When Sara and I speak out on abortion, we're mindful that many women who've had abortions were terribly abused. The fathers of their babies walked out on them or pressured them into getting an abortion. The abortion industry talks about abortions as if they're nothing more than minor surgery. The federal government has declared abortion nothing less than a constitutional right. Most media executives and reporters are strongly for abortion rights. These days, the pressure to have an abortion is ever-present and intense.

The pain that these women feel, even years after an abortion, can be overwhelming. I found that out a few years ago after I preached a sermon in my church in Knoxville. During my sermon, I said that abortion is a terrible sin. I added, though, that if we're truly sorry and seek His forgiveness, God will forgive even the taking of a human life. The blood of Jesus washes us clean.

I also said that if we accept Jesus and repent of our sins, God has something else in store for us. One day, we'll see our children again in heaven — including our aborted children.

After my sermon, a black woman came up to me. She had tears running down her face. She told me that she had had five abortions. She realized now that what she'd done was terribly wrong. I could see she was filled with pain.

But then I could see a glimmering of joy through her sadness. She told me that until she'd heard my sermon, she'd never thought about the fact that one day, she'd see her five children again. It hadn't occurred to her that God would reunite her with her lost children in paradise. That knowledge seemed to lift a heavy burden from her.

My experience is that that kind of suffering is typical for women who've undergone abortions. We just don't hear much about it because the media prefer to ignore it.

Too many powerful forces in our society are pulling women into abortion clinics. I think it's time to push back against these forces. It's time to tell the other side of the story.

There's one side of the story, in particular, that you probably haven't heard before. Abortion is the most divisive issue since slavery. Maybe that's because, like slavery, abortion is a racial issue. Throughout this century, abortion has been used as a tool for population control. The population that's been targeted? Blacks and other minorities.

Let me state my accusations up front and clearly. I accuse the abortion industry of pursuing genocide against the African-American community. I accuse the government of permitting and even funding this genocide. And I accuse the media of covering it up.

There's no way to sugarcoat the points I'm about to make. Quite simply, the history of the abortion rights movement is a history of genocide against black Americans.

Abortion on Demand

Abortion has become a major institution in this country. But it wasn't always this way. In 1973, the U.S. Supreme Court ruled in *Roe v. Wade* that abortion was a constitutional right. The court said this right exists through all nine months of pregnancy. Before *Roe*, this "right" didn't exist.

Roe was a ridiculous ruling. The Constitution doesn't even mention abortion. The Constitution doesn't mention a right of privacy, either, which the right to an abortion supposedly grew out of. The court just dreamed this up "right" and imposed it on the country. The justices acted like referees who wanted one team to win. In doing that, they violated their sacred trust to interpret the laws honestly and to protect the innocent.

The winners in this fixed competition were those who want sex without consequences. Many people who strongly support abortion rights also back homosexual rights and believe there should be little to no limits on pornography, sex on TV, divorce, and so on. It's all part of the same package: sex without consequences.

The losers in *Roe v. Wade* were the 31 million American babies who've been killed in the womb since the court handed down its ruling. Today, one out of four babies in the United States dies at the hands of an abortionist.

In the vast majority of cases, abortion means either sucking the baby's body out of the womb with a vacuum (suction aspiration) or chopping up the body with a knife (dilation and curettage). In the case of partial-birth abortion, the abortionist grabs the baby's legs with forceps, jams scissors into the base of the baby's skull, sucks out the brains until the skull collapses, and then removes the baby's body. Since babies have a nervous system by the ninth week of development and can feel pain, these procedures are truly unspeakable torture to the most innocent and defenseless among us.

It's legal and common for doctors and scientists to conduct experiments on aborted babies. In 1998, scientists were talking up the fact that they'd found a way to make brain cells multiply. They said their findings might someday help people with head or spinal cord injuries. But their experiments were like something out of a horror movie. It turned out that they had used brain tissue from aborted fetuses to conduct these experiments. No matter how much was learned from them, the deliberate, violent taking of tiny human lives was too high a price. Personally, I can't see much difference between these experiments and those of Nazi Germany or the Tuskegee Syphilis Experiment.

Today, the right to an abortion is very popular. Sixty-one percent of Americans support the right to an abortion during the first three months of pregnancy. But not many Americans support *Roe's* right to an abortion through nine months of pregnancy. By a margin of 66 percent to 15 percent, Americans believe abortion should be forbidden during the second three months of pregnancy. And only 7 percent of Americans believe in a right to abortion in the final three months, versus 79 percent opposed.

When asked whether "abortion is the same thing as murdering a child, or is abortion not murder because the fetus really isn't a child?" 50 percent of Americans agree that abortion is murder. Thirty-eight percent say the fetus isn't a child. Americans basically view abortion as justifiable homicide under certain circumstances.

But other than after rape or incest or when the mother's life is in danger, under what circumstances can such homicide be justified? The reasons given for abortion almost always are self-centered. Three-fourths of those who choose an abortion say that having a baby would interfere with work, school, or other pursuits. About two-thirds say they can't financially support a child. Half say they don't want to be a single parent or they're having problems with their husband or companion. Forty-seven percent of those seeking an abortion have had at least one already.

Babies definitely make demands on our time and money. They turn our daily schedules upside down. But babies don't create themselves. We create them. To destroy babies because they interfere with our lives or cost us a little money is terribly wrong.

Look at all the harmful side effects of abortion. In the years since *Roe v. Wade*, violence has become much more common and accepted in our culture. Our children see that we don't care about the unborn. So, they figure, why should they care about other kids or people who they think have done them wrong? As Pastor Warren H. Stewart says in his book, *How to Handle Giants: Sermons to African American Youth and Their Mentors,* "How can we tell a gangbanger to respect life when they are a part of a generation that the law allows to 'dis' life in the womb through abortion as birth control?"

Almost every day, we hear stories about babies being abandoned in garbage bags, flushed down toilets at proms, and grossly abused and neglected. Before *Roe*, we rarely heard such things. As this book was being written in late 1998, the *Milwaukee Journal-Sentinel* ran a story about a mother of two who lives in Milwaukee. She became pregnant by a married man, who then wouldn't have anything to do with her. She decided she "couldn't take care of another child" so she gave birth in an alley, put the newborn boy in a plastic bag, and dumped him in a trash bin. The baby suffocated.

The woman said afterward she realized she did a "horrendous and selfish act." At least she owned up to more than the abortion industry ever will.

Isn't it obvious that our devaluation of human life in the womb has affected the value we place on babies outside the womb? For that matter, why was it any worse morally—and a crime that earned her fifteen years in prison—for that teenager in Delaware to flush her baby down the toilet seconds after giving birth? Her only crime was not leaving the prom early enough to get to an abortionist before delivering.

Whatever else can be said about abortion, let's at least admit that there can be no doubt about where God stands on abortion. The Bible repeatedly says that human life begins in the womb. Consider these passages from Scripture:

> For you created my inmost being,
> you knit me together in my mother's womb.
> (Ps. 139:13)

> As you do not know the path of the wind,
> or how the body is formed in a mother's womb,
> so you cannot understand the work of God,
> the Maker of all things. (Eccl. 11:5)

This is what the LORD says—
he who made you, who formed you in the womb,
and who will help you:
Do not be afraid, O Jacob, my servant,
Jeshurun, whom I have chosen. (Isa. 44:2)

The word of the LORD came to me, saying,
"Before I formed you in the womb I knew you,
before you were born I set you apart;
I appointed you as a prophet to the nations."
(Jer. 1:4–5)

A touching passage appears in Luke 1:41. It's about John the Baptist when he was an unborn baby: "When Elizabeth heard Mary's greeting, the baby leaped in her womb, and Elizabeth was filled with the Holy Spirit."

Pastor Stewart, who led the fight for a state holiday in Arizona in honor of Dr. King, is also a great champion of civil rights for the unborn. In making his case for the "most fundamental human right—the right to life," he notes, "There is no Scripture in the Bible that justifies, rationalizes, condones, and/or commends abortion. No word of God places more value on a woman's body than her unborn baby."

He adds this chilling thought: "Do you remember that Mary, the mother of Jesus, was an unwed teenager who became pregnant by someone other than her fiancé? What if abortion as a cover-up had been as available to Mary and Joseph as it is today?"

We may call our sins *rights*, yet no fancy words can change the nature of what happens during an abortion. Babies are having their heads crushed, their arms and legs ripped off, their bodies smashed and sucked out of the womb—often at a stage when they can feel pain. Our God is a just God. He can't possibly look at this as anything but a slaughter very similar to what King Herod ordered.

Even if you're not a Christian or Jew, think about what abortion means.

It means some people (adults) have greater rights than others (the unborn). Abortion means survival of the fittest. And as we'll see, that's what abortion has always meant.

Genocide

I'm especially concerned about how abortion is ravaging the black community. I believe that predominantly white abortionists and proabortion organizations have, either deliberately or effectively, targeted the black community for genocide.

Let me emphasize that I'm not saying whites are trying to destroy blacks. I love my white brothers and sisters. I believe the great majority of whites would not support these genocidal efforts if they knew about them. But it's a fact that many wealthy and powerful whites in the abortion industry have aggressively pursued a proabortion agenda at the deliberate expense of blacks. And these people have very influential, and mostly white, allies in government and the media.

From the very beginning of the abortion–rights movement, this predominantly white elite has targeted blacks and other minorities. Planned Parenthood and its founder, Margaret Sanger, promoted birth control and abortion among black folk in an attempt to limit the growth of the black population. I believe this motive still drives Planned Parenthood and the abortion industry. Ample evidence supports this conclusion.

Does this campaign of population control qualify as genocide? The United Nations Convention for the Prevention and Punishment of Genocide has held that attempts to wipe out part of a group constitute genocide. I say that by these measures, the black community was and remains the target of genocide.

Illegitimate Birth

Today's abortion rights movement is the legacy of Margaret Sanger. Sanger founded the Planned Parenthood Federation of America in 1942 as the capstone of her years of activism on behalf of birth control and abortion rights. Sanger was born in Corning, New York, in 1883. Her father was an Irish Catholic immigrant who was very skeptical of religion. On one occasion when she was a little girl, Margaret's father teased her when she was saying her prayers.

As a young adult, Margaret met William Sanger, an up-and-coming New York architect. They were married a few months later. Through her husband, she came to know many of the activists of the day who wanted to loosen sexual morals. Eventually, she started her own publications, including *The Birth Control Review*. Her writings advocated sex without consequences by celebrating the virtues of birth control, abortion, and a promiscuous lifestyle.

In her writings, Sanger called marriage a "degenerate institution" and sexual modesty "obscene prudery." One article stated that "rebel women" have "the right to be lazy, the right to be an unmarried mother, the right to destroy . . . and the right to love." She was indicted for publishing obscene materials in violation of the federal Comstock Laws. She fled the country for a while, then returned and used her connections to get the authorities to drop the charges.

Margaret Sanger had a broad following among rich whites who favored eugenics. Eugenics was the theory that social progress depends on reducing the birth rate of "inferior" races or ethnic groups. Followers of eugenics thought that people in these groups should be discouraged from having children.

This view was all the rage in the early twentieth century. The rich and famous of the day supported eugenics. People such as Alexander Graham Bell, H. G. Wells, George Bernard Shaw, and Justice Oliver Wendell Holmes of the Supreme Court believed in eugenics.

In 1919, Sanger proclaimed in *The Birth Control Review*, "More children from the fit, less from the unfit—that is the chief issue of birth control." Across the top of the November 1921 issue of the magazine, Sanger declared, "Birth control: To create a race of thoroughbreds." Some groups, she thought, were "inferior races" and "human weeds" that needed to be curbed. Sanger said she believed there was "an ever-increasing, unceasingly spawning class of human beings who never should have been born at all."

Sanger argued in a 1932 article, "A Plan for Peace," that society should "apply a stern and rigid policy of sterilization and segregation to that grade of population whose progeny is already tainted, or whose inheritance is such that objectionable traits may be transmitted to offspring." Ironically, she said that these measures would mean "defending the unborn against their own disabilities."

Sanger sought to put her theory of "race betterment" into practice. She opened her first birth control clinic in 1916 in Brooklyn. It was in one of the "coarser neighborhoods and tenements" where she hoped to attract "immigrant Southern Europeans, Slavs, Latins, and Jews."

Sanger and other eugenicists were also very concerned about the black population. Many worried about racial intermarriage. In 1921, over half of the papers presented at the Second International Congress of Eugenics discussed the harmful effects of intermarriage. The titles of these papers included "Some Notes on the Negro Problem," "The Problem of Negro-White Intermixture," and "Intermarriage with the Slave Race."

The Ku Klux Klan was a big advocate of eugenics. Dr. Hiram Wesley Evans, Imperial Wizard of the Ku Klux Klan, cited the work of eugenicists. In 1936, Earnest Sevier Cox, a Klansman, published an article in *Eugenical News* arguing that all blacks of "breeding age" should be deported to Africa.

Eventually, Sanger and her allies tried to put their theory about blacks into practice. One of Sanger's biggest undertakings was Planned Parenthood's so-called Negro Project. In 1939, the American Birth Control League and the Clinical Research Bureau combined to become the Birth Control Federation of America (BCFA). Sanger was tapped to be honorary chairman of the board. That same year, the BCFA established a Division of Negro Service. The Negro Project was one of Sanger's pet programs.

In 1938, Sanger laid out her reasons for pursuing the Negro Project. She claimed in the project proposal, "The mass of Negroes, particularly in the South, still breed carelessly and disastrously, with the result that the increase among Negroes, even more than among whites, is from that portion of the population least intelligent and fit, and least able to rear children properly." That year, Sanger obtained a $20,000 grant from Albert Lasker to begin the project.

In 1939, Sanger wrote a letter outlining her plans for the Negro Project to Dr. Clarence J. Gamble. Gamble was a member of the board of directors of BFCA and heir to the Proctor and Gamble fortune. "It seems to me," Sanger said,

> From my experience where I have been in North Carolina, Georgia, Tennessee and Texas, that while the colored Negroes have great respect for white doctors, they can get closer to their own members and more or less lay their cards on the table which means their ignorance, superstitions and doubts.

> They do not do this with the white people, and if we can train the Negro doctor at the Clinic, he can go among them with enthusiasm and with knowledge, which I believe, will have far-reaching results among the colored people.

Sanger knew it was important to persuade black ministers to back her project:

> The ministers [*sic*] work is also important and also he should be trained, perhaps by the Federation as to our ideals and the goal that we hope to reach. We do not want word to go out that we want to exterminate the Negro population and the minister is the man who can straighten out that idea if it ever occurs to any of their more rebellious members.

In a memorandum written that year, Gamble echoed her views: "There is a great danger that we will fail because the Negroes think it a plan for extermination. Hence let's appear to let the colored run it." The Negro Project worked hand in hand with "southern state public health officials." As George Grant pointed out in his excellent book, *Grand Illusions: The Legacy of Planned Parenthood*, these officials were "men not generally known for their racial equanimity."

The problem was that there were many more "rebellious members" among the black community than Sanger and her backers would have liked. Dorothy Roberts, a supporter of abortion rights, acknowledges in her 1997 book, *Killing the Black Body: Race, Reproduction, and the Meaning of Liberty*, what Sanger's writings make clear: "Black people were suspicious of white-controlled birth control programs from the very beginning, and white-controlled programs had no intention of allowing Black people to take the reins." Roberts notes that many residents of Harlem were wary of the birth control clinic that Sanger and her associates founded there in 1930. "Many potential patients," Roberts says, "suspected that the clinic was really intended to promote race suicide rather than racial betterment."

I believe this mistrust still exists. Two surveys in 1972 and 1973 found widespread concerns among blacks that family planning programs were "a potential means of racial genocide, especially if the programs provided sterilization and abortion and were run by whites." One of the surveys stated that nearly 40 percent of blacks questioned believed that the programs were designed to exterminate blacks.

Leaders of Planned Parenthood since Margaret Sanger's time in office have expressed pride in her work. Dr. Alan Guttmacher, who succeeded Sanger as president of Planned Parenthood, once said, "We are merely walking down the path that Mrs. Sanger carved out for us." Another Planned Parenthood president, Faye Wattleton, said she was "proud" to be "walking in the footsteps" of Margaret Sanger. And Wattleton is a black woman.

A Community Under Siege

The genocidal legacy of Margaret Sanger and Planned Parenthood is clear and shameful. White women today obtain 61 percent of all abortions in America. But they are 81 percent of the female population. Black women, who make up 14 percent of the female population, account for

31 percent of all abortions. Black women are nearly three times as likely as white women to have an abortion. Hispanic women are roughly two times as likely as their white counterparts.

Today, for every three black babies born, two are aborted. Every month more than 41,000 black babies are killed in the womb. Since *Roe v. Wade*, more than 10 million black babies have died in this American holocaust.

Not only are black abortion rates three times those of whites, but Planned Parenthood targets the black community with its abortion clinics and propaganda. Today, according to the Life Education and Resource Network (LEARN), a black antiabortion group, 78 percent of abortion clinics are located in or near predominantly minority neighborhoods. Grant also notes that in the 1980s, more than one-hundred school-based Planned Parenthood clinics opened in the United States. None was opened in a suburban, middle-class school. All were in black, minority, or ethnic schools.

Of course, pregnant black women are more likely than their white counterparts to be single and poor. But just because a woman is single and poor doesn't mean that her pregnancy has to end in an abortion. For one thing, she could put the baby up for adoption. A lot of us believe that the high crime and poverty rates among blacks are a legacy, to some extent, of slavery, segregation, and discrimination. I believe the high abortion rates among blacks are also a legacy of racial injustice and genocide.

Besides, it's not enough to look only at a woman's economic circumstances. You also have to look at the temptations surrounding her. The temptation to want sex without consequences is strong in all of us. When society backs up this temptation with a "right" to abortion, and Planned Parenthood conveniently locates a clinic in your neighborhood, outside factors influence a woman's "choice."

Consider this fact: while the black abortion rate is almost three times higher than that of whites, blacks are more likely than whites to believe that abortion is wrong. When asked whether abortion is an act of murder, 48 percent of whites say yes. But 56 percent of blacks answer yes. Blacks are less likely than whites to support the right to have an abortion for any reason whatsoever. Like whites, the vast majority of blacks think that abortion should be legal only under certain circumstances.

Akua Furlow of LEARN has pulled together data showing the devastating effects of abortion on black women. A study of black women by the Howard University Cancer Center from 1989 to 1993 concluded that among those who had received an abortion, there was a significant increase in the risk of breast cancer. In 1994, a survey of 126 black women who had had an abortion found that 81 percent suffered from one or more psychological complaints. Sixty percent had feelings of guilt. Fifty-five percent reported crying and depression. Thirty-five percent said they were unable to forgive themselves.

One black psychiatrist, Dr. Karen Stevenson, shared her experiences in treating patients who had undergone abortions:

> I have encountered tortured women who were struggling with depression, suicidal thoughts, anxiety, and drug and alcohol abuse who have had encounters with this thing called "the women's right to choose." I've seen women touched by the horror of abortion, yet during my training, this issue was never discussed by my professor as a possible contributor to the person's present state of emotional turmoil.

Given that blacks don't think highly of abortion and are suffering from it, why is the black abortion rate so high? People who might blame this fact on black ignorance or selfishness should first consider a few critical facts. Today, the white leaders of the abortion industry are spending millions of dollars in advertising and propaganda to encourage this behavior. And they've been doing it for decades. Targeting blacks has been an integral part of the abortion rights movement from the very beginning.

Planned Parenthood has become widely respectable, and it has many allies. Influential people still promote abortion of black babies as the solution to our social problems. One example came in 1992 with the publication of Jared Taylor's harsh book on race relations, *Paved with Good Intentions: The Failure of Race Relations in Contemporary America.*

Several conservative leaders spoke highly of the book. Taylor argues that one of the best ways to reduce teenage pregnancy rates among blacks is to provide them "sex education, free contraceptives, and free abortions."

This history is probably news to you. You can check out the history yourself by reading the sources I've cited in the back of the book. Obviously, Planned Parenthood is aware of this history. That's why the organization's supporters have worked so hard to keep it from coming to light.

Why haven't you heard this information before? Because the media are suppressing the truth. Media executives and leading journalists are overwhelmingly in favor of abortion rights. You can bet that many of the same people in the media who attacked me for what I said about homosexuality feel just as passionately about abortion rights. As I said, it's all part of the same package—sex without consequences.

A definite slant is evident in the news in favor of abortion rights. When was the last time you heard an antiabortion story or statement from a leading journalist? Every time some nut shoots an abortionist, it's national news. But 1.4 million aborted babies a year are just a number hidden on the back pages of newspapers.

The major news networks and newspapers are biased in favor of abortion rights. George Grant discusses how ABC, CBS, and NBC, as well as newspapers such as the *New York Times*, have been slanting their coverage in favor of abortion rights for many years. Stephen Hess, a senior fellow at the Brookings Institution who specializes in the media, has said that "with those issues like abortion, there is a very distinct tilt that reflects class more than political views." That "tilt" favors abortion rights and favorable publicity for Planned Parenthood. And that means support for the continuing genocide against the black community.

The Fight for Life

Most Americans think a fetus is a baby, but our government doesn't. It's time for the government to stop siding with the abortionists. The

Supreme Court should overturn *Roe v. Wade*. The federal government should stop funding Planned Parenthood, which is a racist organization. Our black elected officials in Washington should be especially vigilant in opposing this funding.

Nineteen federal statutes, and hundreds of state and local laws, allow public funds to go to "family planning" programs and policies. These programs are a multi-million-dollar cash cow for Planned Parenthood, which also receives millions of dollars in funding from the United Nations Fund for Population Activities, the World Bank, and the Agency for International Development. President Clinton opposed Congress's attempt in 1998 to stop U.S. tax dollars from going to Planned Parenthood and other groups that lobby foreign countries to loosen abortion laws. We shouldn't be spending our tax dollars on that kind of cultural imperialism.

Charities such as the United Way and March of Dimes give large amounts of money to Planned Parenthood. They shouldn't be supporting a racist organization this way.

Let's also not forget adoption. Many childless couples are desperate to adopt babies. The number of children adopted has risen from 118,000 in 1987 to 127,441 in 1992 (the most recent year available). And that was during a time of high abortion rates, when most unwanted children were being aborted instead of put up for adoption. Americans have had to look to other countries to find babies available for adoption. It's no surprise that since 1990, the number of children adopted from other countries has doubled.

We need to make it easier for black families to adopt. The extended family is a strong institution in the black community. Black families informally adopt ten times more children than are placed through adoptive agencies. These family members are grandparents, aunts, uncles, and other relatives. One private organization in Detroit, Homes for Black Children, focuses on black extended families and doesn't charge a fee. In its first year of operation, Homes for Black Children placed more children in stable, loving homes than Detroit's twelve other public and private adoption agencies combined.

State adoption agencies sometimes discriminate against blacks. Robert Woodson tells the story of a black military couple who wrote to him after his appearance on *Oprah*. They had tried unsuccessfully for years to adopt a child. They had an impressive home and background. However, the local social service agency put them through an outrageous ordeal. The agency's representatives asked the couple questions such as "if we get along with our families, how much we weigh, and what our fantasies are." The screen-out rate for blacks seeking to adopt ranges between 90 and 99 percent, according to an Urban League study.

Of course, we also shouldn't discriminate against white couples trying to adopt black or minority babies. Instead, we should thank God that the mothers of those babies made the right choice by choosing life. Then we should do our best to find them good, loving homes.

We need to be more caring toward unmarried mothers. Unmarried mothers who choose life for their babies deserve our support—financially, emotionally, and spiritually. Pro-lifers shouldn't just focus on overturning *Roe v. Wade* or protesting at abortion clinics. We need to reach out to women in need.

A few years ago, when Sara and I were living in Tennessee, we opened a crisis pregnancy facility on the grounds of our home in Knoxville. We called it Hope Palace. It was a home for unwed mothers who needed support. Unfortunately, Hope Palace didn't receive as much backing as we had hoped from pro-life organizations and Christian churches. After a couple of years of keeping it afloat, we ended up having to close it.

Still, I remember one success story that made all our efforts worthwhile. One fourteen-year-old girl from Cleveland, Tennessee, came to stay with us. She was pregnant and scared. She really missed home and cried many times asking to go back.

Finally, her homesickness was too much for her. She decided to go back home and try to cope with her pregnancy in Cleveland. After that, Sara and I prayed for her and her baby. We wondered if we'd ever know how things had turned out.

Two years later, we found out when the young lady, who was then sixteen, drove up to our home—holding a beautiful baby. Sara and I were overjoyed. That was one black baby who made it safely into her mother's arms.

For more than a million babies every year, the story doesn't have such a happy ending. We've moved far away from God's rules on life. The good news is that abortion rates have leveled off. The percentage of women of childbearing age who obtained abortions dropped 5 percent from 1994 to 1995, and has dropped 20 percent since 1980.

The bad news is that big obstacles remain in front of us. At current rates, an estimated 43 percent of women will have at least one abortion by the time they turn forty-five years old. Guilt, shame, and denial make it hard for these women to admit that what they did was wrong.

We must not give up on these women. They are suffering. I remember one young white woman who came into our lives through Urban Hope. When she became pregnant, Sara counseled her strongly against abortion. The young woman ended up not following Sara's advice. But Sara stayed in touch with her, trying to deepen her faith and conscience.

Sometime later, the young woman became pregnant again. Sara again lobbied her to keep the baby. This time, Sara's love and compassion for the young woman paid off. She kept her baby, and she's now a mother.

Now, was it the best thing in the world for this baby to be born without a father? Obviously not. But was it better for the baby to be born than to be killed? Of course it was. His mother chose life, and we're all better off because of it.

We live in a time when abortionists, politicians, and celebrities tell women that abortions are no big deal and even a constitutional right. These lies have seduced many of us, especially in the black community. We can't let our guilt over these sins consume us.

God sent us His only begotten Son, and shed His precious blood, so that we wouldn't feel tormented by our sins. I believe that one day, we'll see a lot of beautiful little faces in heaven who'll know us not by our sins, but by God's grace.

Chapter Eight

Personal Fouls

I'll never be able to thank God enough for the chance to play professional football. It had been my dream since I was a boy. When I was twelve years old, I informed my mother that one day, I would be both a pro football player and a minister. A lot of parents might've had their doubts about their child growing up to play in the NFL. But that wasn't my mother's response.

"A minister?" she said in disbelief.

My careers have supported each other. Through football, I've been blessed with friendships and opportunities that otherwise never would've come my way. Football has given me a high platform from which to talk about God and my ministry. And, of course, there's the game itself. I'm extremely grateful that God and the fans make it possible to play a child's game for a man's salary.

These days, sports have tremendous influence on our society. At a time when Americans are deeply divided over values and related issues, sports bring people together. Cities unite behind their ball clubs. People across the country come together to cheer for the same team. When I travel around the country and see Packers fans in every city, I see the unifying power of sports.

Because I love football and sports so much, it's hard for me to say anything critical about either of them. But that same love for the game compels me to speak out. I've seen trends in football and other sports recently that I think are negative for the players, the fans, and society.

Too many players in the league, especially younger players, put themselves ahead of the team. Their main concerns are landing a big contract, being selected for the Pro Bowl, and gaining personal glory on the field. To these players, the team comes in a distant second. There are also too many athletes who are getting in trouble with the law and having babies out of wedlock. The money chase in sports is another negative development.

Yet hopeful news is also coming from pro sports today. The NFL, for example, is experiencing a great increase in expressions of faith. A growing number of players aren't ashamed to show their obedience to God. Many contribute anonymously and generously to charities and churches.

So after we look at what's wrong with sports today, I'll urge you to remember what's right as well. God is exalting many poor kids in this country by raising them up to be remarkable athletes. Many of them are honoring God in return. To me, that sight all by itself is reason enough to be a sports fan.

Self Ahead of Others

Pro athletes are just as human as the rest of us. In fact, I'd argue that because they're celebrities, they face more opportunities to sin. Unfortunately, these sins are on display in front of everyone because these athletes work in a high-profile profession.

Publicity comes with the territory when you play in pro sports. Still, I think it's a shame that the media dwell on the negative. Every time an athlete does something wrong, it's all over the front pages and TV news. But when an athlete spends Christmas serving food to homeless people or spends time in a hospital with kids who are ill, often the media are nowhere to be found.

That's not to say pro athletes shouldn't be held responsible for their conduct on and off the field. They should be. The best way for athletes to stay out of trouble in both settings is to remember not to put themselves above others. These days, too many athletes are falling into sin because they put their interests and appetites ahead of everyone else. That's the number one problem I see with athletes today.

That's especially true of the young players coming into the league. I see too many who just don't have the will to win. They want to be an All-Pro, but they're not willing to do what it takes to win a championship. They're more interested in signing a big contract, buying a mansion, or gaining personal recognition.

To me—and to the vast majority of athletes, I might add—nothing is more precious in sports than a championship ring. It means you're the best. For one year, at least, you topped everybody. Players who aren't totally committed to the team lessen the team's chances of reaching this goal. If players are looking out only for number one, they're not committed to true excellence.

A few years ago, after I became a free agent and decided to leave Philadelphia, I had to decide where I wanted to play. I looked at several teams around the league. Before I ended up signing with the Packers, I considered one team in California that said they were very interested in me.

I liked the tradition of the team. I thought they had many talented players. But I ended up not going with them. Why? I told one of their coaches that I didn't think the players were committed enough to the team. I told him I thought he had too many players who seemed more interested in being in the movies than in playing football.

While I was a player, football wasn't just a side business. It was my job. Despite all my interests off the field, I tried hard never to lose my focus. The only way to do a job right is to give it 100 percent. In football, as in all other sports, that means going all out with one goal in mind—a team championship.

Off the field, players can be just as distracted. They may get into trouble because they've gone along with the wrong crowd or don't want to "dis" the friends they had before they made it to the pros. Serious problems can happen when these old friends expect you to share your new wealth with them. One star player in the NBA, Gary Payton, recently talked about the problem. He was asked about another NBA star who has had widely publicized problems off the court. Payton said that like this other, troubled star, Payton "employs" five of his old friends. "Most guys in this league employ their friends," he said, "and a lot of times some of them are knuckleheads. But if you love them, you love them."

Obviously, players who stand by their friends this way are extremely loyal and generous. But by the same token, players who "employ" their friends can afford to be choosy. They should be. If a player's friends get into trouble, they can ruin his reputation in a hurry. If they do drugs, carry guns, or abuse women, and that player is identified as their buddy, that player will be judged by the company he keeps.

Too many players in pro sports have had scrapes with the law. A book that came out in 1998, called *Pros and Cons*, estimated that 21 percent of the players in the NFL have some kind of criminal record. However, that number should be taken with a dose of skepticism. The authors included everything from juvenile records up to the present. I thought that was a cheap shot. That number doesn't say anything about what those players are like today.

We've all done things in our past we're ashamed of. That's part of growing up. Is it fair to still hold juvenile offenses over players' heads when they're responsible citizens now? I don't think so.

Another area where a lot of pro athletes run into trouble is in their relationships with women. In 1998, *Sports Illustrated* ran a cover story about pro athletes who father children out of wedlock. The cover asked, "Where's Daddy?" The cover ran a photo of an infant boy whose father plays in the NBA.

The article was pretty hard-hitting. It talked about one NBA superstar who has had seven children by six women. When another NBA star (who was married) found out a former girlfriend was pregnant, he called her four times a day pleading with her to have an abortion. When she refused, she alleges that the player had one of his former college teammates—who now plays for another NBA team—call and say that if she kept the baby, "I will get you."

Players who act this way deserve our contempt. Those players can't be good fathers to so many children by different women. And you know how I feel about abortion.

Still, some of the women involved weren't exactly blameless. Many of the athletes were married, and the women obviously knew it. The article talked about how some of the women in question would threaten the athletes, saying that unless they married them, they'd make their lives miserable or wouldn't let them see their children.

Think about the boy whose face was on the cover of *Sports Illustrated*, and who was identified on newsstands everywhere as an illegitimate child. Would a good mother do such a thing? As far as I'm concerned, *she* should be put on public display.

A certain percentage of the women attracted to pro athletes are looking to get either a husband or a paycheck. At the NFL rookie orientation in 1998, two HIV-positive former NFL groupies talked about how they used to seduce players. The chaplain for the San Francisco 49ers, Pat Richie, told *Sports Illustrated* he's seen the same thing. He said, "I don't condone players who have had affairs, but the fact is, there are women who hunt pro athletes in the hope of becoming pregnant and filing paternity suits to make an income."

Athletes should be more realistic in their dealings with members of the opposite sex. I tried to drum that lesson into some of my younger teammates when I was with the Packers. One time I asked several of the guys, "How many of you think that women are after you because of how you look?"

One guy insisted that women were after him because he's good-looking.

"You think it's because you look good, huh?" I said.

"I know I do," he replied.

"Man," I told him, "it's because you play for the Packers. You think all those women would be after you if you were pumping gas down the street?"

I'll say this—my teammate wasn't suffering from too little self-esteem!

He stuck to his guns. But he or any other athlete is crazy if he thinks that his playing in the NFL has no effect on his relations with women.

The NFL certainly has some bad apples. But let's not judge all athletes by the antics of a few knuckleheads. Look at all the players who've led good lives on and off the field, who've been solid family men. Mike Singletary, the former great middle linebacker for the Chicago Bears, has a happy marriage and a wonderful family life. His wife has given him seven beautiful kids. Christian athletes in the NFL such as Cris Carter, Hardy Nickerson, Merton Hanks, and others don't attract nearly as much attention as the guys who get into trouble. There are no *Sports Illustrated* cover stories about them.

But they're for real. And we shouldn't focus so much on the problem citizens in pro sports that we forget about the players who are heroes for our time.

"Show Me the Money"

When there are labor disputes in pro sports, the fans tend to be angrier with the players than with the owners. Maybe that's because the fans relate more to the players. The players come from the same walk of life as the fans, and the owners are rich men up in luxury boxes. Or maybe it's because all rich people seem alike to many fans. In their minds, a billionaire owner is the same as a millionaire player.

Obviously, I'm biased in favor of the players. I know that players, on average, have only a few years to play in the league. The typical NFL player has only three or four years on the field. Football is a rough sport, and a serious injury can end a career instantly. For the sake of their families, pro athletes have to try to earn as much money as they can in the short span of time they play. Just like a plumber or carpenter or auto worker, an athlete is entitled to the fair market value of his services.

The owners preside over teams that are worth hundreds of millions of dollars. Expansion teams in the NFL now are worth half a billion dollars.

Of course, some teams are more profitable than others. Yet when it comes to money, the owners are in a totally different league from the players.

Shakedown in Knoxville

Like pro sports, college athletics generate mountains of cash for the nation's universities. Top college coaches are often paid seven-figure salaries. A recent survey of twenty-five major-college athletic programs found that since 1996, they've spent or committed $1.2 billion to build or renovate sports facilities.

A few years ago, I found out firsthand how grasping some college athletic programs have become. The incidents I'm about to discuss caused some controversy when the Associated Press reported them in 1998. I'm still really disappointed over what happened.

Before my family and I moved to Green Bay, we lived in Knoxville. During the off-season, I would go to my alma mater, the University of Tennessee, to use their training and weight-lifting facilities. Several other alumni would go there too. We'd get together and work out to stay in shape.

After a while, I began to notice something. Every time I went to the Athletic Department to work out, people from the university would ask me for a donation. Now, I can understand promoting your school. But every time? It got to the point that it was annoying.

There was also the matter of my college jersey. By 1991 or 1992, I'd been in the NFL seven or eight seasons. I'd been to the Pro Bowl quite a few times, and I'd earned a reputation for my play. Many, if not most, athletes in that situation would have seen their alma mater retire their college jerseys. It's very common for colleges to retire the jerseys of alumni who go on to do well in pro sports. Even pro players who didn't graduate from college have had their college jerseys retired.

Having my jersey retired wasn't a huge deal to me. However, I'd grown up in Tennessee, and the jersey carried some sentimental value. After a while, I became curious whether officials at the university had even considered the possibility of retiring it. Finally, I thought I'd break the ice and ask.

In 1991 or 1992 (I can't remember which year), I went to the Athletic Department to work out. In the training room, I ran into Doug Dickey, who was then the athletic director. I asked him if he thought the university might retire my jersey someday.

Doug Dickey smiled. He told me, "We can negotiate." Then he walked off.

I wasn't sure what that meant. A few days later, I found out. Doug Dickey and Mitch Barnhart, then his senior associate athletic director, met with my agent, Jimmy Sexton, and me at the athletic cafeteria. I told Doug Dickey right off that I wasn't going to give money to the university to persuade them to do what I thought was the right thing. Dickey, in return, told me that except for a few war heroes, the university had never retired a player's jersey. He also complained that too many alumni players didn't give any donations to the university.

I would've been happy to donate to the university if they'd previously agreed—with no strings attached—to do the right thing with my jersey. I've given generously to charities and other good causes during my entire career in pro football. But they were asking for loyalty when I thought they hadn't shown much to me. So that was where we left things.

After the meeting, I put the whole matter out of my mind. I didn't want anything to do with any ceremony of theirs. But I didn't tell many people what had happened, mostly because I didn't think anyone would believe me.

In 1998, however, the subject came up in the press. Peyton Manning, then the star quarterback for Tennessee—and now an up-and-coming quarterback for the Indianapolis Colts—was months away from graduating. The year before, I'd heard talk about the school possibly having a ceremony for alumni who had won Super Bowls. I knew it was just a way to finesse the problem of their wanting to honor Peyton after they hadn't honored other alumni. In April 1998, the university retired Peyton's number.

I was very happy for Peyton. I've known Peyton's father, former NFL quarterback Archie Manning, for a long time. He's an outstanding Christian gentleman. Peyton is also a Christian and a fine young man.

A few months later, however, the Associated Press found out from someone in Green Bay what had happened between Doug Dickey and me. I was disappointed because I didn't want to detract from Peyton's accomplishments. But when a reporter asked me about the conversations with Dickey, I confirmed what had occurred.

Dickey denied everything. He told reporters, "I don't believe I ever had a conversation with Reggie White regarding retiring his jersey" or about "making contributions." But my agent, Jimmy Sexton, backed up my story. That took some guts, by the way, since he still has to recruit players out of Tennessee.

My guess is that episodes like the one I've just related go on all the time. There's immense pressure on college athletic programs to generate income for their schools. But the bottom line for me is that if the university ever does retire my jersey, I won't be at the ceremony.

Other Pet Peeves

I've got two more pet peeves related to money in sports that I need to get off my chest.

In football, they've changed the rules so that the offense can score more points. They've allowed offensive linemen to line up farther off the line of scrimmage. This gives them more time to block and to hold off the defense. Defensive backs can't touch receivers after they've gone five yards past the line of scrimmage. Quarterbacks can throw the ball away when they scramble outside the pocket and not be called for intentional grounding.

Worst of all from a defensive lineman's point of view, offensive linemen can hold on almost every play and get away with it. These days, I'd say that on 95 percent of the plays from the line of scrimmage, at least one member of the offensive line is holding. It's arbitrary when the referees choose to throw a flag.

I wouldn't deserve my nickname "the Minister of Defense" if I didn't speak out against what's been done to tie the defense's hands behind their backs.

The defense is half of the game. We're just as important as the offense. I feel I've worked at least as hard as the guys on offense I'm lining up against. The rules of the game shouldn't be changed just to increase profits.

Why do I say these changes were made to increase profits? Because it's widely assumed that fans won't watch games — and TV revenues will go down — if there isn't a lot of scoring. Today, if a game has a final score of 3–0 or 7–3, the press says it was an "ugly game." I disagree. To a defensive player, a game like that is a thing of beauty.

I once approached a high-level NFL official about these changes to the rules. He was up front about why he thought the rules were changed. He said, "Reggie, if the score is 3-0, people will turn their TVs off."

That's not right. To all those who would tilt the rules of the game against the defense, I say, "Let my people go!"

Another pet peeve is the dishonesty of many sports agents. If you've seen the movie *Jerry Maguire*, then you have a pretty good idea of what a lot of sports agents are like. The movie gave a very realistic picture of how dishonest and cutthroat many sports agents have become.

Let me stress that plenty of honest agents are working in the NFL. The problem is that there are so many dishonest agents competing against them, the honest ones have trouble recruiting athletes and making a living. Many of the dishonest ones are new agents who have no knowledge of the business.

My experience is that most sports agents are dishonest. They'll say anything to talk you into signing and letting them represent you. My advice to young athletes is to be very careful in choosing an agent. In particular, if an agent tells you that he can get you drafted in the first round, kick him out of the house. He's lying to you.

No agent can get you drafted. It's up to you and your ability. The pros will look at how well you did in college, at the combine, and so forth. No agent can make that kind of guarantee.

And by the way, he definitely can't be counted on to "show you the money."

Women in the Locker Rooms

Why do we allow female reporters in the locker rooms? I can't see any legitimate reason for forcing male athletes to walk around naked in front of women who aren't their wives.

Let me tell you what really goes on in locker rooms after games. Reporters come in and do interviews while players are showering and dressing. If they choose to, female reporters and camerawomen can film guys showering or walking to their lockers stark naked. They can keep the film for themselves, make copies, and give it to friends — who knows? The truth is, nobody knows. That's what's really scary about the policy.

Let me assure you I'm not alone on this. The policy of letting female reporters walk around locker rooms is extremely unpopular among NFL players.

And why shouldn't it be? I have no idea if someone has film of me standing naked in a shower. For all I know, someone does. The person could've shown it to other people or put it on the Internet. With all the perversions in our society today, there's no telling what film like that could be used for. I ask you to think about how you'd feel if you were the one standing in that shower or locker room, not knowing who else might see you without any clothes on.

This isn't a matter of equal rights. It's a matter of privacy — the most basic privacy you can imagine. All the women I've talked to about this policy are just as outraged about it as I am. Talk about taking the notion of "public figure" to an extreme!

It's not as if athletes aren't willing to talk to female reporters. They can interview athletes right outside the locker rooms. Most young guys love to talk to women — for obvious reasons. Maybe the solution is to ban all reporters from locker rooms. Regardless, society shouldn't be forcing nude players to mingle with journalists of the opposite sex. In our locker rooms, we can see how the drive for sexual equality has gone berserk.

How did all this get started? Back in 1977, a female reporter for *Time* magazine sued the New York Yankees and major league baseball officials for barring her from the Yankees' locker room during the World Series. She said the team was discriminating against her based on her sex. *Time* supported her suit.

The next year, a federal judge ruled that teams that banned female reporters from locker rooms violated the Fourteenth Amendment. This amendment, which was passed after the Civil War, gave ex-slaves "equal protection of the laws." Now, the courts have turned the equal protection clause into something else. Ironically, they've ruled that the clause requires sports leagues to let female reporters roam through predominantly black male locker rooms. Get real!

Since that suit, all four major pro sports leagues have opened their locker rooms to women. In 1985, the NFL's policy book was changed to state clearly that locker rooms are open to female reporters. The commissioner threatened to fine players and coaches who didn't go along with the new policies.

The league's policy on female reporters hasn't been smooth sailing. The first major flap over the policy happened in 1990. Lisa Olson, a female sports reporter for the *Boston Herald*, complained that three members of the New England Patriots had deliberately exposed themselves to her. She called it sexual harassment. The league fined the three players, and Olson sued the team. Eventually, she won a settlement and moved to Australia.

Open-and-shut case for the reporter, right? Not quite. It turns out that the three players said Olson was notorious for staring at players when they were naked. They called her a "looker" because of her staring. That's why they took it upon themselves to teach her a lesson.

I don't condone what they did. But any sensible person would sympathize with them. I've seen a lot of female reporters and camerawomen ogling guys in the locker room. It's only natural when you throw members of the opposite sex together like that. I can see why those guys with the Patriots felt they had to resort to that kind of vigilante action.

A few weeks after this incident with the Patriots, there was another controversy. Sam Wyche, who was then the head coach of the Cincinnati Bengals, barred a female *USA Today* reporter from the Bengals' locker room. The league fined him almost $28,000.

Coach Wyche didn't back down. He spoke out against this ridiculous policy—the last time anyone really has challenged it. "Men and women don't conduct business in the nude in the real world," he pointed out. "Why should the locker room be any different?" He also noted that it's not practical to take a towel to the shower because most showers don't have a place to hang a towel.

A few months after the incident, Coach Wyche announced that he'd received $30,000 in donations from thirty-seven states and twelve countries to help him pay his fine.

You don't hear much about the policy on female reporters anymore. But that doesn't mean all the problems and hard feelings have gone away. In 1995, for example, two teenage girls taking part in a journalism program went with reporters into the locker room of the Denver Nuggets, an NBA team. Players were showering and dressing after a game. One player complained that the two students and a female photographer stood just a few feet away from him while he got dressed.

This rule isn't right. It is just as wrong for male reporters to go into the locker rooms of the Women's National Basketball Association (WNBA). That's where this rule has led us. And that's what's happening now: male reporters are allowed into WNBA locker rooms. Women shouldn't have their privacy violated like that. The boorish male reporters who go into those locker rooms should be embarrassed for invading their privacy.

I can tell you that the players hate this rule. Our wives hate it too. We shouldn't surrender to such nonsense based on one court ruling. We should challenge this all the way to the Supreme Court. I just hope that if that happens, one of the exhibits before the court isn't film of Reggie White.

Faith Without Fear

So that's what's wrong with sports today. Now let's talk about what's right.

One hopeful trend in sports deserves special attention. It's the growing number of athletes praising God for their accomplishments.

When I came into the NFL fourteen seasons ago, few players were open about their faith out on the field. That has changed. I've noticed that more and more players are giving credit to God for their success. Whether it's a player kneeling in prayer in the end zone after a touchdown, pointing a finger to heaven, or praying after the game at midfield, there are a lot more demonstrations of faith before, during, and after games.

Things have changed, I think, because the players aren't ashamed to show their faith. It's more acceptable now. I'd like to think that some of the Christian athletes who've been at it for a while helped to pave the way for this change. That kind of legacy, frankly, means a lot more than trophies and records.

The media seem unsure of how to handle all these new signs of faith. They almost never comment on it. A lot of reporters seem uncomfortable bringing it up.

That's okay because we're not doing it for their benefit. We're doing it to give glory and thanks to God.

Let me tell you what my routine was when I was a player. After every game, I'd meet with other players at the 50-yard line for a prayer session. We'd kneel and pray to God. We'd thank Him for getting us through another game without serious injury. We'd also thank Him for giving us the chance to play the game.

And I admit that I'd do a little preaching in that prayer huddle. Often, players who weren't Christians would join us. I wanted them to hear the good news about Jesus.

The media often seem skeptical of religion in athletes. Many journalists don't like it when we share our faith with others. They tell us to be role models, but then want us to be secular. They want us to be good citizens and to spend money to help people, but not to preach our religion.

They can't have it both ways. Christianity means sharing your faith. Christianity is the reason we are good citizens. That's why, after we won the Super Bowl, I made sure to say to the whole world, loudly and proudly, "Thank You, Jesus!"

The media also are skeptical of Christian athletes after they convert. They tend to hold a player's past over his head. It's almost as if the burden of proof is on the athlete to show that he's changed. Non-Christian athletes aren't given nearly that level of scrutiny.

I've noticed this skepticism in the media's treatment of Deion Sanders since he became a Christian. They basically used to give him a free pass on what he did in his private life. Now that he's saved, some people don't want to believe it. They keep looking for the slightest flaw or sin in his lifestyle.

In sports, there are always heroes to be found—if you know where to look. When I was growing up, my hero in football was Roger Staubach—a Christian and a great player. Today, I see heroes in football and other sports. In basketball, for example, David Robinson and A. C. Green stand out as men of God. And around the NFL, guys like Mark Brunell in Jacksonville and Aeneas Williams in Arizona are humbly but firmly practicing their faith.

These guys lay it on the line for God every day, under the very watchful eye of the media. They're the greatest source of hope for sports today.

I'm proud to have played on the same field with them. I'm also proud to have been among those players who worked to bring about a resurgence of faith in sports. I know that when God reviews our career achievements, He'll be paying a lot less attention to the number of quarterbacks we've sacked and a lot more to the number of souls we've touched.

Chapter Nine

V-Chip Morality

One night, I was switching channels on my TV when I saw something that caught my attention. I saw a man who was naked. I couldn't believe it.

I thought, *I canceled HBO. Why am I seeing this?* I kept switching channels, then going back to that one. I thought something was wrong with my cable.

Finally, I figured out what was going on. The program was on a network—during prime time. It was ABC's *NYPD Blue*.

Naked people on free TV? It's unbelievable how far our standards have sunk. Every new TV season lowers already low moral standards for TV programming. We say we don't want violence, adultery, and kids having kids in our society. But every time we turn on the TV or radio, that's what the entertainment industry is encouraging.

"You worry about schools, violence, sex, drugs, tobacco and alcohol, but I never thought television would become such a full-time responsibility," one mother of three in New Jersey told a reporter for the *Los Angeles Times*. "It's supposed to be benign entertainment, yet now it's this overwhelming weight on you, another thing to worry about."

It used to be that television, movies, and music told stories or sang lyrics about love or harmless, everyday things. If they didn't always have a great, uplifting message, at least they weren't encouraging the worst in us.

Now, you have to brace yourself every time you turn on the TV or radio. Movies and TV shows are filled with sex, violence, and profanity. Music encourages our children to shoot one another, sleep around, do drugs, and live immoral lives. As technology improves, popular entertainment is everywhere. There's no way parents can monitor everything their children see or hear from the media. And every year, the moral bar is lowered so that media profits will rise.

I can understand why so many parents feel they're under siege. "Ninety-nine percent of what's on TV these days is trash, in my opinion," a mother of two sons in State College, Pennsylvania, told the same *Los Angeles Times* reporter. Another mother in Orchard, Texas, commented, "What I see is distortion. There's crime, inappropriate sex and language that doesn't reflect the world I know, and I've traveled in large cities and small. On TV, I don't see real people." Amen, sister.

It's not that TV shows used to be ideal entertainment. Shows like *Leave It to Beaver* and *The Brady Bunch* could be pretty corny. Not many shows featured black folk back then. But surely, media executives are creative enough to come up with entertaining, diverse, and wholesome TV programs. I've got to believe there's a way to handle adult themes without pandering to sin. There must be room for virtue as well as vice in today's entertainment.

I don't expect this to happen anytime soon. These days, ratings and profits go up when moral standards go down. Besides, if you look at the lives and beliefs of Hollywood celebrities and entertainment executives, they obviously believe in sex without consequences. Maybe they think their consciences won't bother them as much if they talk the rest of us into living the same way they do.

The black community has especially suffered from the low morals of entertainment. Black ministers preach against "low-down Hollywood producers" because they see the damage these values are doing in the inner city.

Today's entertainment perpetuates gross stereotypes. In movies and on TV, black characters are usually thugs or sex fiends. I hope that white folk who have grown weary of hearing black folk complain about media stereotypes will consider these statistics. In a 1998 poll of 1,200 children, 59 percent said they thought TV criminals were likely to be black. Seventy-one percent saw TV bosses as white. Blacks make up 12 percent of the U.S. population but are portrayed as aggressors in 25 percent of violent music videos. Ninety-five percent of these aggressors are men.

These are the characters young people in the inner city are supposed to look up to? With entertainment like this, how can we expect to purge our society of its harmful stereotypes of blacks and minorities?

Because of the cynical pursuit of profits, the entertainment industry continues to applaud and reinforce the pathologies of the inner city. The next time there's a riot in Los Angeles, entertainment executives will have no moral right to complain if the looters go after Hollywood.

The people running the entertainment industry are smart people. They know what they're doing for corporate profits is wrong. When they see so many young people shooting one another and then saying they were inspired by some movie or song, and yet do nothing, those executives become accomplices to such crimes.

Unsafe in Our Own Homes

Almost all of us have a TV set. Because television is in our homes, it has a great deal of power over our family life and culture. It's especially influential with our kids. With so many parents working and spending less time with their children, TV has become an even more important factor in childhood today.

Sixty-nine percent of Americans, and 71 percent of parents, believe excessive violence and sex on television and the movies are a very serious problem. Seventy-six percent of black parents feel that way. It's no wonder.

Look at the amount of violence we're exposed to. The average American child will watch more than 8,000 murders and 100,000 other violent acts on TV by the time he leaves elementary school. By the time the child turns 18, he will have witnessed 40,000 murders and 200,000 other violent acts. Even before 1971, more than 3,000 studies showed a strong connection between watching TV and acting violently or aggressively in society.

Now, I'll admit I'm a big fan of cop shows and action films. Obviously, these always feature violence. But the good shows and movies—the ones I really like—have a moral to their story. They teach that crime doesn't pay and that evildoers will be punished. These programs don't have to have a happy ending every time. But they also shouldn't just be about killing people and destroying things for the thrill of it.

The problem is gratuitous violence—violence for the sake of violence, with no moral to the story. A major three-year study by researchers at four universities, published in 1998, found that gratuitous violence is becoming more common on TV. They found that good characters instigated nearly 40 percent of violence on TV. About one-third of all violent programs featured bad characters who weren't punished. Roughly half of violent shows showed no physical injury or pain on the victim's part.

Less research has been done into the effects of sex on TV. But if there's a link between TV violence and violence in society, it's hard not to conclude that the same holds true for TV sex. Kids see an estimated fourteen thousand sexual messages on TV each year.

Whether we like it or not, TV is like a coach to America's kids. Saying these messages don't influence our children is like saying a coach has no influence on his players. Lately, in the case of television, the coach has been lewd, crude, and outrageous.

It used to be that the first hour of prime-time television was considered a "family hour." The networks voluntarily limited the first hour of TV at night (8:00 to 9:00 P.M. eastern and Pacific time and 7:00 to 8:00 P.M. central and mountain time) to family shows such as *Little House on the Prairie* and *Happy Days*. That has now changed.

A 1996 study by the Media Research Center found that "today's 8-to-9 viewer is inundated with filthy language, sexual innuendo, and perverse storylines." This is being broadcast to an estimated 13 million prime-time viewers who are seventeen and under. The study found that 72 obscenities were said in 117 hours of "family hour" programming. One out of three programs had obscenities.

In addition, "portrayals of sex outside marriage—premarital, extramarital, and homosexual — outnumbered those of sex within marriage by a ratio of 8 to 1." Almost one out of three shows referred at least once to sexual intercourse. Most were references to premarital sex. Often raunchy shows such as *Beverly Hills, 90210*, and *The Simpsons* on Fox actually target younger audiences.

According to the study, *Beverly Hills, 90210*, was one of the worst offenders. One episode featured three uses of the word *b***h* and two of *b****rd*. Its characters are young people whose sex lives are the main focus of the show. Almost all of these characters have been sexually active since high school.

A study by Children Now and the Kaiser Family Foundation found that 75 percent of family hour programs in 1996 contained some sexual content. That was up from 65 percent in 1986 and 43 percent in 1976. Sixty-one percent contained sexual behavior, an increase from 48 percent in 1986 and 26 percent in 1976.

Young children now are starting to "get" TV jokes about sex. The study found that even in the groups of eight- to ten-year-olds, some of the kids understood a joke in the show *The Nanny* about the main character losing her "virgin . . . airlines ticket."

One of the hottest new shows among children is *South Park*, which is on the cable network Comedy Central. It's a cartoon about third graders who, in the words of a *New York Times* media critic, "use extremely vulgar language, make scatological jokes and commit despicable violence against each other (Kenny is killed in every episode)." A recent show featured a boxing match between Jesus and Satan.

Joyce Knight, a grandmother in Albany, Texas, says that she's seen her eight-year-old grandson getting sassier and more rebellious from watching shows such as MTV's *Beavis and Butt-head* (which was recently canceled). "The kids here are good kids, but they won't be good kids for long if we keep filling their minds with that trash," she said. In 1997, after growing disgusted with MTV's programming, Knight circulated a petition and obtained 650 signatures from neighbors asking the local cable company to drop MTV and replace it with a Christian station. The cable company agreed. "Maybe there's a lot worse than MTV, but you do have to start somewhere," Knight explained.

Daytime TV has been one of the worst culprits in TV's moral slide. Morning and afternoon TV used to be filled with soap operas. These programs weren't profound, but once upon a time they weren't chock full of sex, either. How do I know? I'll share a secret with you: I used to be a fan of certain soap operas.

Now, though, soap operas have become sex pageants. Their plots revolve around couples cheating on each other, premarital sex, and graphic "love scenes."

Most of daytime TV is no longer devoted to soap operas. Even worse programs have taken their place: daytime talk shows. These programs show off and prey upon poor people and kids living sinful lives. These people are so desperate to be on TV that they're willing to share with millions of people the perverted, shameful things they've done.

Daytime shows such as *Jenny Jones* and *Jerry Springer* celebrate the worst in us. These programs also take advantage of minorities and lower-income people in particular. Robert Woodson has pointed out,

> Television talk shows, such as *Sally Jessy Raphael* and *Ricki Lake*, have become virtual circuses in which the deformities and wounds of low-income people are continually put on display. The producers of these shows know that the more shocking the societal aberrations they present, the higher their ratings will be. . . . The only time we hear of deviance among upper-income people is when they have graduated from the Betty Ford clinic and are publicizing their books about their past experiences.

One welcome exception is Oprah Winfrey's show. In recent years, Oprah has steered clear of these perversities. She devotes a lot of her airtime to books and uplifting themes. Because of this sacrifice, some say her profits have dipped. But that's sometimes the price we pay for fighting the good fight. Way to go, Oprah.

Another troubling trend is all the TV shows about the occult. *The X-Files, Buffy the Vampire Slayer, Charmed,* and other shows glamorously portray the dark side. I know a lot of people these days don't give much thought to the devil and evil spirits. But the Bible tells us repeatedly that they exist. The Bible reminds us there are demons and evil spirits in the world trying to lure us into temptation. We shouldn't romanticize these dark forces.

There is some good news coming from TV these days. TV shows are doing a better job of dealing with religion, although there's still a lot of room for improvement. Even though Americans are a deeply spiritual people, for every positive depiction of devout believers on TV, there are ten negative ones. Still, the number of positive treatments of religion has gone up in recent years. By the way, of all the networks, CBS was the most favorable toward religion. Apparently, the researchers didn't talk to the folks at CBS Sports!

At least TV isn't ignoring religion anymore. CBS's *Touched by an Angel* is a top ten hit. It features angels who intervene in the lives of people. The show sometimes even offers valuable lessons for life. In one show, for example, a paroled rapist who has become born again quotes the Bible to his parole officer, "When you walk through the fires, you shall not be burned." The officer, who is one of the show's angels, replies, "Yes, when you walk through that fire, God will be with you. But He never said there wouldn't be fire."

These are good words of advice for anyone fighting the good fight, including those who would like to see more TV programs such as *Touched by an Angel.* Hollywood responds to what we consumers demand. As long as we keep watching and rewarding positive programs, the media eventually will raise their standards.

Movies and Music

One thing that really stood out about the recent school shootings was how many of the shooters said they'd been influenced by movies or songs. The *New York Times* noted, "To varying degrees, each of the attackers seemed to have been obsessed by violent pop culture."

Friends of Barry Loukaitis, the fourteen-year-old honor student in Moses Lake, Washington, who shot his teacher and two students, testified in his trial that one of his favorite music videos was "Jeremy," a song by the group Pearl Jam. "Jeremy" tells of a youth who fantasizes about using violence against classmates who taunt him. Loukaitis also told a friend he thought it would be "pretty cool" to be a mass murderer like the two lead characters in the film *Natural Born Killers*.

Mitchell Johnson, the main instigator in the Jonesboro, Arkansas, shootings, was devoted to gangsta rap. A favorite song was "Crept and We Came," by Bone Thugs-N-Harmony, which is about going on a killing spree. His English teacher, Debbie Pelley, testified on Capitol Hill that he listened to violent rap songs "over and over" in the months before the shooting. "Mitchell brought this music to school with him, listened to it on the bus, tried listening to it in classes," she testified. He often sang along with the lyrics about "coming to school and killing all the kids."

Luke Woodham, who committed the school massacre in Pearl, Mississippi, says he was a fan of Marilyn Manson. Manson's lyrics on his album *Antichrist Superstar* are satanic. Woodham fell into a satanic cult and said that demons taunted him into doing the killings.

Michael Carneal of Paducah, Kentucky, admitted being influenced by the movie *Basketball Diaries*. In the movie, a character has a dream in which he shoots some of his classmates.

Kip Kinkel of Springfield, Oregon, enjoyed violent TV programs and Internet sites. Shortly before his rampage, his parents unplugged the cable television and took away his computer in an attempt to wean him from those influences.

Is this pattern really all that surprising? Movies and music aren't "just entertainment." They literally tell us how to live our lives. Good movies and music can be inspirational. Ronald Reagan, for example, said that the movie *Mr. Smith Goes to Washington* inspired him to run for president years later. By the same token, sinful movies and music can be extremely damaging to impressionable souls, especially young people.

Hardly any entertainment company these days is above encouraging immorality or making sinful movies. Look at what's happened to Disney. Disney was founded by Walt Disney, by all accounts a very decent man. For decades, Disney made wholesome, high-quality movies. Many of those early movies are classics.

Now, Disney is at the forefront of promoting the homosexual lifestyle. Michael Eisner, chairman of the board for Disney, and Joe Roth, chairman of Walt Disney Motion Pictures, sit on the board of Hollywood Supports, a homosexual rights group. Hollywood Supports has persuaded every major U.S. film studio to offer domestic partner benefits to its employees—including Disney.

Many leading Disney executives are openly homosexual. According to Eisner himself, the number is 40 percent. Disney now has an annual Gay and Lesbian Day at Walt Disney World.

Disney hired a convicted child molester, Victor Salva, to direct its 1995 movie *Powder*. It tells the story of a young albino man who teaches tolerance to people who think he's strange and won't accept him. In 1988, when he was thirty-one, Salva was convicted of five felony counts of child molestation after police found videotapes of him having sex with a twelve-year-old boy who appeared in his first professional film, *Clownhouse*.

A laser disc version of the Disney film *Who Framed Roger Rabbit?* shows Jessica Rabbit wearing no underwear. In the same movie, background graffiti displays Michael Eisner's home phone number advertised as a brothel run by Allyson Wonderland. Other movies by Disney and its companies promote phone sex (*The Santa Clause*), extreme violence (*Pulp Fiction*), and negative portrayals of priests (*Priest*, which is about Catholic priests who are homosexual, alcoholic, or sexually immoral).

Recent movies about black folk, especially black men, haven't offered very positive images. Obviously, not all movies portray blacks unfavorably. Denzel Washington has made some terrific films. So has Cuba Gooding, Jr. But these, I say, are the exceptions. If you look at many of the recent releases, movies such as *Booty Call* and *How to Be a Player*, I think you'll agree that they reinforce negative stereotypes.

Even some otherwise wonderful movies are unfair to black people. The 1997 movie *Amistad* is a good example. It tells the powerful story of African slaves who overthrow their Spanish slavers, take control of the slave ship, and eventually land in the United States. A trial is held to determine whether they should be set free.

There's one really moving scene that I thought was the best in the movie. One slave is holding a Bible, which he took from an abolitionist protesting outside the courthouse. The slave points out the pictures showing the life and death of Jesus to Cinque, the lead character.

But the makers of *Amistad* also added something that really marred the film for me. Near the film's end, the U.S. Supreme Court announces its decision on the slaves' court case. The famous person chosen to play the chief justice is none other than former Justice Harry Blackmun—the author of *Roe v. Wade*, which has led to the deaths of more than ten million black babies.

Much of popular music carries a sinful message. I've noticed that in black music, the sins are more sexual in nature. The videos on Black Entertainment Television (BET), for example, have a heavy sexual content. With white music, there's more outright satanism. For all their faults, you never see black entertainers directly promoting Satan.

That certainly doesn't mean that all popular black music is inspirational. The lyrics of gangsta rap, for example, frequently promote violence, sex, and drugs. We've heard the excuses from the music industry. I know that young black men sing this music. But I also know that young black men commit too many crimes, and that doesn't make their crimes any more excusable. Predominantly white music executives shouldn't reward these misguided young men by producing music that damages their community and society.

Rap doesn't have to be angry and degrading to women. Positive rappers such as Hammer and Run DMC have shown this. We need to reward these and other similar acts by listening to them and buying their CDs.

I've tried to take things a step farther. A few years ago, I started Big Doggie records. My goal was to promote high-quality Christian music. I also wanted to help out some new acts that had caught my attention and that I thought showed talent.

I found out, though, that it's hard to compete with the big labels. Christian music companies can be just as brutal in squeezing out their competition as secular companies. Eventually, we had to throw in the towel and close the company. But I believed enough in the project that I invested more than seven figures to try to get it going.

Yet, I'm not one to give up easily on a dream. That's why in 1998, I started a new venture to produce inspirational entertainment, a venture that I hope will yield better fruit. It's called Reggie White Studios. My plan is to produce family-oriented films and music that parents will feel comfortable sharing with their kids. I call it "family-safe entertainment."

My hope is to set up studios that will produce high-quality family movies and positive music. That includes uplifting and fun secular music. I think it's important to reach out to non-Christians too. The studios would create good jobs for a lot of people other than actors and actresses.

A friend of mine in Hollywood tells me that many directors, actors, and actresses would love to work on more family-oriented projects. The problem is that the top executives aren't willing to fund them. I have to believe we've never heard of many terrific actors and actresses because their consciences won't allow them to do movies with sex scenes and anti-Christian messages. These artists in God's service shouldn't have to sell their souls to be successful. Reggie White Studios, I hope, will give them a new outlet for their talents.

So far, things look promising. I'm pleased to report that some well-connected people with substantial resources have gotten behind the studios. Regardless, we should support entertainment that puts families first. The power of the dollar seems to be the only thing that really gets Hollywood's attention.

Reggie's Recommendations

How do we hold the media accountable for their actions? Let me suggest, first of all, what we shouldn't do. The V-chip, for example, is not a solution. In 1996, Congress and the president passed a law requiring all new TV sets to have a V-chip. The chip receives encoded information about each show as part of the broadcast transmission. Parents can then program their TV to block out shows that the networks have coded as violent or sexually explicit.

Yet we can't rely on the networks to label their shows honestly. In 1997, executives at all the major networks except NBC agreed to start using voluntary ratings. They would note with various symbols whether shows had a V for violence, S for sex, or L for suggestive language. But a 1998 study discovered that 79 percent of shows with violence and 92 percent of shows with sexual activity didn't carry the V or S "content descriptors." Even if the networks were more honest, studies have shown that labeling a program or movie violent or sexually explicit makes kids more interested in watching it.

For that matter, commercials aren't safe these days. One frustrated Denver mother explained how hard it is to monitor the TV. "Even if you are watching a decent show or a radio station you have chosen, then you get the commercials coming in and, 'Oh, I thought I was safe for fifteen minutes.'"

Besides, we shouldn't rely on new technology as a substitute for parents. One man in Seattle said it well when he noted in a recent letter to the local newspaper, "If parents do not take an active interest in their children's activities, whether it is television viewing, Internet access or anything else, not all the technology in the world can make a difference." He added that parents can't entrust their children to a "silicon wafer" in a TV.

Media executives who fill the airwaves with irresponsible programs, and think they can wash their hands of the consequences by forcing us to install V-chips, have embraced a very low morality. In the face of this threat to our families, we can't afford to be apathetic. The most effective way to send media executives a message is to support entertainment that's good for kids and society.

Sometimes, it's hard to know what entertainment meets this test. For what it's worth, I thought I'd share with you my favorite TV shows, movies, and music. If you haven't already seen or heard some of these programs or songs, you might want to check them out.

When it comes to TV, as I said, I'm a big fan of cop shows. *New York Undercover* is one of my favorites. At times, the show has too much sexual content. Overall, though, I have to say the show is very entertaining. Compared to other programs on TV, it's a winner.

I enjoy watching sports, of course. I watch football and basketball games regularly. At least with those shows, you know what to expect. They also teach kids the value of teamwork, self-discipline, and hard work.

I'm a big fan of professional wrestling. Wrestling is very popular with other pro athletes, I might add. It's good, old fashioned entertainment that you know won't really hurt anyone. I was one of the many wrestling fans rooting for Jesse "the Body" Ventura in his recent campaign in Minnesota.

Some of the most fun I've ever had came from my one pro wrestling match. A few years ago, I squared off in Charlotte, North Carolina, against Steve McMichael, who played with the Chicago Bears and the Packers. I admit that I lost. But for the record, he cheated!

Pro wrestling is fun to watch and usually shows a stark battle between good and evil. I enjoy watching wrestling matches with my son, Jeremy.

When it comes to movies, I like action. My two favorite movies are *Terminator* and *Terminator 2*. I like just about every Arnold Schwarzenegger movie. Except for *Conan the Barbarian*, I'm not aware of any movie in which he has been part of a sex scene (a couple of other actors shared a sex scene in the original *Terminator*). He makes good movies with a lot of action and plots centered on good versus evil.

I love *Rocky*. That movie really gets the blood going. Some of my other favorites are a wide variety of films with a positive message. They include *Crimson Tide*, *The Wizard of Oz*, *Glory*, *Chariots of Fire*, and *Coming to America* (one of the funniest movies I've ever seen).

A movie I saw recently that I really liked was *Bulworth*. I thought it had too much profanity but still carried a good message. It's about a white politician who runs for office by rapping his campaign slogans. He points out how cynical politics has become and how politicians often forget about the poor. I thought it was a very funny movie.

I enjoy upbeat music. Jazz and black gospel music are my favorites. For artists, I turn to Kirk Franklin, Rance Allen (he has an awesome voice), and John P. Kee. There's also a new female group out, Trinity, which I really like. And I love the Winans family, especially Angie and Debbie.

Those are my favorites, anyway. I can't guarantee that you'll like them, or that you won't find anything objectionable about them. But based on what we have to pick from, they are, in my opinion, the best of the best. I believe the artists and moneymen who produce this entertainment deserve our vote of confidence.

Chapter Ten

Raising Good Children in Tough Times

How many of us parents would want to be a kid today? Incredible pressures are tugging our kids in the wrong direction — pressures that we didn't have to deal with. Kids have always faced peer pressure, of course. When I was a kid, the other kids called me a square because I read the Bible and didn't do drugs. But now, peer pressure is only one of a whole slew of bad influences on a child. I minister to many kids who tell me these pressures can feel overwhelming.

It's natural for kids to rebel against parents and society. It's their way of flexing their muscles in the big world. Today, though, kids are bombarded with all the wrong signals about how to live their lives. When society piles on its own pressures — broken families, raunchy movies and music, and so forth — it's a wonder any kids turn out all right.

The statistics tell us all we need to know about how we're letting our children down. Juvenile crime is near a record high. Between 1987 and 1994, the juvenile crime rate rose 70 percent (in 1995, it dropped 3 percent). From 1950 to 1993, the murder rate for kids younger than fifteen tripled. Between 1985 and 1995, the number of juveniles murdered rose 116 percent. Almost half of the victims were black. Twenty-two percent of adolescents say they come across gangs every day.

Teen birth rates and sexual activity rates have gone down slightly among older teens, but that's not the case with younger girls. Between 1988 and 1995, the percentage of girls who say they had sexual intercourse before they turned fifteen rose from 11 percent to 19 percent. One recently retired middle-school counselor in Louisville, Kentucky, was quoted as saying, "We're beginning to see a few pregnant sixth-graders."

Kids are also terribly depressed these days. The lack of a father or both parents, parents on drugs, peer pressure — these are the main things that kids tell me depress them. The statistics themselves are depressing. From 1950 to 1993, the suicide rate for kids under age fifteen quadrupled. American children are twice as likely to commit suicide as children in other industrialized countries. Almost one out of four high-school students admits having "thought seriously about attempting suicide."

And that's not all that our kids are up against. Kids aren't taking care of their health the way they should. The number of Americans under eighteen who smoke daily rose 73 percent between 1996 and 1998. Fewer than one out of four kids in grades four through twelve exercise every day.

What's causing all these problems? A study by the polling group Public Agenda, called *Kids These Days: What Americans Really Think About the Next Generation*, polled some parents and kids to try to find out their opinions on the matter. They polled focus groups of adults in New Jersey, Colorado, and California, and youngsters between the ages of twelve and seventeen by telephone. When asked the first thing that comes to mind in describing today's children, 53 percent of adults said something negative. Many characterized children as undisciplined, rude, or spoiled. Nearly half thought it was very common for children to be spoiled.

But a lot of these parents were honest enough to admit why kids are turning out this way. They said that parents often aren't there for their kids. One mother in Denver explained why she thought we're having so many difficulties with our children:

> A lot of my friends feel insecure in their role as parents, and they don't let the child know, "I am the boss, you are the child." They want to be friends with them. I think they don't want to relive their parents' [style of parenting] where it was too structured and disciplined. And they have guilt for leaving the kid in day care all day and running off to

work. So it's "We can't tell them no, we must buy them everything they want."

The kids, for their part, complained that they didn't see enough of their parents. One-third of the young people polled said that no adult was at home when they returned from school. Fifty-three percent said that no parent was at home when they were answering the telephone survey—which lasted about twenty-three minutes and asked about private matters. As one California teenager put it, "My friend's parents just don't care—they are never home. There is food in the house, but they are never there to talk or confide in, so he turns to friends. It's not a question of a poverty stricken home—he just has no one to confide in."

Kids also see parents who are afraid to discipline them or their friends. One California teenager said, "We have this one friend who has this mom who is so devoted to him, he just fools around with her. He calls her by her first name: 'I need this, come give it to me.' And she does it." When 49 percent of young people say they think most people their age need more guidance and attention from adults—when self-interest tells them to say the opposite—it's obvious we're not doing right by them.

I think too many parents just aren't engaged enough in their children's lives. We're so busy trying to earn money and buy things that we sometimes forget about our duties to our families. Think about how we deal with kids who run around all hours of the night, up to no good. We tell the police to enforce curfews and the government to pay for midnight basketball programs. Those kids should be home in bed, and we should be there to make sure they are.

But now, let me say something in defense of parents. There's a great deal of confusion these days about *how* to raise children. We're not sure how to discipline them. We're not sure how to give them the right values. I think that's because we've forgotten God's rules for raising children.

When it comes to parenting, guilt and ignorance are two of our biggest enemies. Some of us aren't sure how to handle our past mistakes when dealing with our kids. A *New York Times* reporter talked to parents who had lived rebellious lives growing up in the 1960s. One parent in Irvington, New York, says that when she disciplines her children, they "have a tendency to throw things up in my face from my own past." The article called these parents the "Do as I Say, Not as I Did" generation.

With my kids, I have to deal with the fact that when I was younger, I used to sleep with women I wasn't married to. What's even worse, right after I became a minister as a young man, I'd sleep with a woman one night and get up and give a sermon the next morning. Now that's hypocrisy for you!

The only way I think we can deal with our past is to be up front about it. Just because we've sinned as kids doesn't mean that our kids have to follow in our footsteps. God's rules never change. By being committed to God's rules, you can point to them when you're raising your children. They put an end to any cries of, "But you did it, too, Dad!" Rules are rules.

Ignorance is also a stumbling block to parenting. A lot of us have forgotten or aren't sure of how to discipline our children. We think we're being dictators if we tell our children what to do. Sometimes, it seems that society and the laws support this kind of parenting. One teacher in New York talked about a common attitude:

So now, as a teacher, if I say, "Shut up and sit down," I am the one in trouble because I used the word "shut up," after the kid has been telling me to commit unnatural acts upon myself. . . . It is like we are both equals. Who am I to tell him to sit down and pay attention? This is nonsense!

He's right. It is nonsense. Parents are the boss—and for good reason. We have more experience and maturity than our kids. Not to exert our authority over our children is a dereliction of our duties as parents. God's rules make it clear that we can't trust our children to raise themselves and expect them to turn out okay.

I think it's time for the parents of America to reassert ourselves. It's time to reclaim our proper role in our kids' lives. That means understanding better what we can do, and what God expects us to do, as parents.

Why I Believe in Whuppings

I believe that spankings—or whuppings, as I call them—are important for raising kids the right way. I say this after having learned from the receiving end. When I misbehaved, my mother whupped me with anything she could grab at the time. She used extension cords, sticks, you name it.

I was hardly the only one who grew up this way. Kids all up and down our street got the same treatment from their parents when they acted up. We could expect the same from the teachers at our school.

I can assure you I'm no worse for the wear. In fact, I know I'm a better person because my mother cared enough to do that for me. You see, it's hard to discipline kids. It takes time and attention. More importantly, it's hard to inflict the pain on kids that's necessary to teach them a lesson. I think it's one of the hardest things we do as parents. To tell you the truth, the last two times I whupped my kids, I cried. But I knew I'd done the right thing by them.

I believe that corporal punishment is critical for raising a good child. God's rules on this are clear. Proverbs 13:24 says, "He who spares the rod hates his son, but he who loves him is careful to discipline him." Parents who aren't willing to discipline their children fail them in a big way.

Of course, whuppings should be a last resort, and parents must always control their temper when giving them. I've found that once you've earned a child's respect, a firm way with words almost always will get the job done. This even applies to children who aren't your own. I experienced this when I was speaking at a Promise Keepers rally at a stadium in Greenville, South Carolina, in 1997. When I was standing at the podium, I saw fifteen or twenty kids running around on the football field. I felt they were distracting and should be seated.

All I had to do was to use a commanding voice when I spoke into the microphone. I said, "Every one of you on the field, set your tails down." And every one of them did just that.

Every parent is entitled to that kind of response. Every one of us can gain it too. But first, we have to earn it.

I work every day to earn that respect from my two kids, Jeremy and Jecolia. I don't hesitate to pull off my size forty-two belt and use it when necessary. But I make it a last resort. I'm proud of my kids because I haven't had to use my belt that way for the last two years. In their entire lives, I've only done it probably twenty times between the two of them. But when I've done it, it's made an impression on them.

When I whup them, I don't just walk away afterward. After they've calmed down, I have them explain to me why I whupped them. When they fess up to what they did wrong, and it comes from their mouths, they'll remember why they were punished.

After they've admitted what they did to get into trouble, I'm still not finished with them. Then I hug and kiss them. I think it's important for them to be reminded right then and there that I still love them.

Every child understands pain. That's how we all learn. Children may look like little angels, but we all know they aren't. If left to their own devices, they'll turn into little terrors. I believe we're born with original sin. We have a naturally selfish nature. The only way to teach a child not to be that way is for parents to constantly be on them, watching and correcting them. And once in a while, we have to spank or whup them to get their obedience.

I know this is an old-fashioned point of view. In 1968, 94 percent of Americans said they approved of spanking; today, only 65 percent say so. An interesting statistic is that 90 percent of Americans admit to having spanked their children on occasion. Clearly, though, they know that's not the politically correct thing to admit.

I also think that a lot of parents who want to whup their children are afraid to. They think the police might arrest them. One California parent complained in a focus group, "The law is against the parents on discipline. That gives the kid the mind that, 'I can do what I want to. My mother and father had better not hit me — if they do, I'll call 911.'" Some law enforcement officials and social service agencies do interpret child welfare laws as prohibiting corporal punishment. These government employees are undermining parental authority at its very foundation.

Instead of whuppings, many parents use so-called time-outs. Basically, this means telling a child to go to a room or sit and "chill out." But time-outs are time-consuming. And for parents with little time, they can mean, in reality, no punishment.

Corporal punishment has deep roots in the black community. It's not surprising to me that even today, 83 percent of blacks say they favor whupping children. Also, by a 58 percent to 50 percent margin, blacks are more likely than whites to say it's "very common" to see parents who fail to discipline their children these days. Black social scientists Elijah Anderson and Charles Willie have noted that corporal punishment is a long-standing and respected practice among black folk.

What's more, immigrants from predominantly black countries can't understand why Americans don't believe in corporal punishment. One mother of three from Dominica said almost exactly what that California parent said: "The first thing a child learns here is, 'If you spank me, I'll call 911.'"

Mary C. Waters, a Harvard University sociologist, interviewed West Indian immigrants to New York City from 1991 to 1993. She found that corporal punishment was a very important issue to them. "When I asked what's different about the United States," she reported, "they said: 'The state comes between you and your children. Americans don't discipline their children well, and when you do it the right way, there's the danger your kids can call social services on you.'"

That very thing has happened. Waters said, "The kids all knew they could call D.S.S. on their parents. When new kids arrived from the West Indies, that was one of the first things they'd tell each other. They saw it as a lever to use against their parents."

The *New York Times* reported the case of a fourteen-year-old Haitian boy who had been neglecting his homework and stealing money from his parents. His father, a cab driver, gave him a whupping. The son called 911. The father was arrested and led away in handcuffs. The case was resolved through court-ordered family counseling.

The father pretended that he wasn't mad—until the next summer, when the family returned to Haiti on vacation. At the airport, the father pulled out a leather strap and whupped his son on the spot. Two days later, the family flew back to New York and left the teenager there in Haiti with relatives.

One Jamaican-born city council member from Queens recalled trying to persuade immigrant parents not to spank. She'd suggest they tell the kids they wouldn't get a new pair of sneakers if they didn't behave. "Many families saw that as bribery," the councilwoman said.

I happen to agree with the immigrants. It was bribery. We can learn a lot from these immigrants, I think. They come from countries where the so-called experts haven't confused parents and talked them into letting their kids run the show.

Here in America, most child-rearing "experts" oppose corporal punishment. A leading critic of spanking, Murray A. Straus of the University of New Hampshire, has argued that spanking is an "assault" on children. He goes so far as to call the family the "cradle of violence." Straus believes that having two parents instead of one is bad because it "increases the probability of an adolescent being hit." He even says that spanking leads to a higher murder rate for society.

That's crazy. If that were true, then countries where whuppings are even more popular than in America would have higher murder rates than we do. Besides, research has shown that whuppings help us to rear children the right way. One researcher, Robert E. Larzelere, found in a 1993 review of four major studies that the correlation between corporal punishment and violence was "about .00." His own study in 1991 found that corporal punishment, when combined with reasoning, was a more effective method of discipline than reasoning alone.

Rev. Manuel L. Scott says in *The Gospel for the Ghetto*, "Much of the debacle that drenches our major institutions—schools, homes, churches, and governments—stems from an unwillingness in some youth to be tutored, challenged, or influenced by older people." This is just as true now as it was twenty years ago when he said it. We can't be afraid to do what's best for our children. We also need to change the laws to make it clear to parents that they have the right to spank or whup their kids within reason. The government has no business telling parents how to discipline their children.

Recently, I received a really flattering letter about my son, Jeremy. He attended band camp in Green Bay in the summer of 1998. Afterward, the father of another boy who attended the camp wrote me a letter. The father said that when his son found out who Jeremy was, he expected him to be uppity. You know, "Reggie White's son." But instead, the boy found that Jeremy was a normal kid. The letter said that Jeremy even had gone out of his way to scold the other kids when they got out of line.

I can't tell you how proud I was to hear this. When Sara and I hear that our kids are growing up to be the young adults we've always wanted them to be, it's incredibly rewarding. It beats winning the Super Bowl hands down.

We need to reconsider our attitudes toward kids and child rearing. Think about how confused our thinking is. Why is it that we've come to think it's okay to prosecute juvenile offenders as adults, and even execute them for murder, but it's considered child abuse to spank or whup a child? That whupping could teach the child *not* to do the very things that might get him in trouble with the law. To me, the current thinking doesn't make any sense.

Kids crave discipline. When I speak to kids, I demand that they sit up straight and listen. I'll call them out, even in a crowded school auditorium, if I don't get that respect. And let me tell you, they respond well to that discipline. By the same token, I'm also not afraid to hug and kiss little boys who come to my speeches and behave themselves. Now, whether they'd prefer an autograph, I can't say!

A parent who mixes discipline with love can't go wrong. The child will respond, and the parent will reap the rewards—forever.

Drugging Our Kids

Some parents have given up on disciplining their kids. They're turning to another approach: drugs. More and more parents are giving drugs to their children to calm them down. Drugs such as Ritalin and Prozac are some of the more common ones. I find this trend very sad and disturbing.

Supposedly, these drugs are needed because their kids are suffering from attention deficit disorder (ADD) or attention deficit/hyperactivity disorder (ADHD). These drugs are used on kids who are supposedly hyperactive or who won't listen to or obey their parents. But since the so-called experts can't agree on how to diagnose this disorder, it's all a guess. Dr. Laurence Diller, author of *Running on Ritalin*, notes that doctors can't even agree on "how many children and adults are affected by [ADD], what its chief causes are, the best methods of evaluation and treatment and even how it should be described." All this guessing is erring on the side of drugging our children.

If I were a kid today, I bet many doctors would say I had ADD. When I was a boy, I was extremely hyperactive. I loved playing hard with other kids and being active. I spent a lot of my time playing football or basketball outside. Fortunately for my mother, hard play tired me out. By the time I got home, I wasn't such a handful anymore.

Today, kids don't play as much outside. With crime rates being what they are, parents are probably afraid to let their kids run around the neighborhood the way we used to. Still, I think that far too many boys are being labeled as "hyper" just because they have a lot of energy. I thank God that my mother didn't take the easy way out and stick me with a needle or give me pills.

The number of ADD cases has gone through the roof just as more and more parents can't find the time to discipline their children. Since 1990, the number of children diagnosed with ADD has risen from about

900,000 to nearly five million. During the same time, the number of prescriptions for Ritalin has risen 700 percent. Between one million and three million children in the United States are receiving stimulant drugs for ADD.

Preschool kids are receiving Ritalin in record numbers. A study by the University of Maryland found that from 1991 to 1995, the number of prescriptions for stimulant drugs such as Ritalin for children five years old and younger increased 180 percent. And get this: Ritalin is being used on children as young as one year old. It's no wonder that some are calling the new generation of children "Generation Rx."

About 1.3 million children, or 5 to 6 percent of elementary school children, take Ritalin. Some schools report having one out of four students on Ritalin. Dr. Diller described a suburban school where he saw pictures of children taped to medication cups to keep the lunchtime doses of Ritalin straight. At another nearby school, the kids on Ritalin come into the school office in ten-minute shifts because there are so many of them.

Most toddlers are very active. They also test authority constantly. Robert A. King, an associate professor of child psychiatry at the Yale Child Study Center, noted in discussing the growing use of these drugs, "If you ask most parents with a toddler, 'Is your toddler too active?' they'll say yes." Dr. Diller believes the culture and increased use of day care are the main reasons Ritalin sales have soared. He notes that most Ritalin users come from white, suburban families. "Ritalin will remain very popular in this country as long as the culture believes the way to acquiring emotional satisfaction is through acquiring material goods," he says.

Mary Jane Reed, chairman of the English department at Solon High School in Ohio, believes that "more and more children are being trapped in the acronyms defining hyperactivity—ADD/ADHD—which, for some, can become an excuse for shirking responsibility, failing to work to one's potential or engaging in inappropriate behavior." She recalled a get-together at a house that illustrated her point. As the parents prepared hamburgers and hot dogs, the children played in the house because of bad weather outside.

The hostess noticed one six-year-old who was walking along the back of her new sofa. The father of the child pulled her aside and told her, "He's A-D-D." Unsatisfied with the explanation, the hostess walked over to the sofa and removed the youngster. "Now he's O-F-F," she said.

The full effects of Ritalin aren't yet known. In the short run, the side effects include loss of appetite, nervousness, dizziness, insomnia, and even growth suppression. Dr. Richard Broomfield of Harvard Medical School has said,

> Too many children, and more and more adults, are being given Ritalin inappropriately. In my experience, Ritalin use seems to depend largely on parents' and teachers' ability to tolerate children's behavior. I know of kids who have been given it more to subdue them than to meet their needs, a practice that recalls the opium-rich syrups used to soothe noisy infants in London of the 1890s.

Dr. Peter Breggin of the University of Maryland believes that these drugs suppress and control children and don't really treat biological problems: "In the short term, Ritalin suppresses creative, spontaneous and autonomous activity in children, making them more docile and obedient. In the long run we are giving our children a very bad lesson, that drugs are the answer to emotional problems."

Boys are being singled out for this treatment. Eighty to 90 percent of all kids diagnosed as having ADD are boys. Too many parents and teachers think that when boys act up or are assertive in school, they have a mental problem. Michael Gurian, author of *The Wonder of Boys*, said, "If Huck Finn or Tom Sawyer were alive today, we'd say they had ADD or a conduct disorder."

I know they'd say that about me too. It's bad enough that we find it hard to make time for our kids. For us to sedate our children to make up for our own shortcomings only makes things worse. I say, let boys be boys.

If we parents can't say no to drugs, we can't expect our kids to do any better.

Equal Education for All

Schools play a crucial supporting role to parents. Schools have to teach kids the knowledge they need to succeed in a competitive world. Obviously, it's important that children receive the best education possible during the hours they're in school. Lately, however, it's become clear that many of our schools aren't up to that challenge.

Forty-nine percent of Americans think the public schools fail to give kids a good education. Yet, 67 percent say that improving the public schools would be a very effective way to help young people. The problem is that spending more money doesn't guarantee good results. Total school spending rose almost 600 percent from 1972 to 1997. But at the same time, SAT scores dropped 2 percent. Students in the top five states in per-student expenditures (Alaska, New Jersey, New York, Connecticut, and Rhode Island) don't do as well as students in the bottom five states (Utah, Arizona, Arkansas, Oklahoma, and Mississippi).

Let me stress that I still have a lot of respect for the public schools. I was educated in them, as was Sara. I think I received a high-quality education, and I was blessed with some wonderful teachers. My coaches in middle school and high school, in particular, had a profound effect on my development as an athlete and a person. I know that many terrific teachers in the public schools strive every day to provide an excellent education to their students.

Yet, I've also found that on the football field, the best way to get the best out of every player is competition. When you know someone else is competing to win your place on the team, you give it your all. In an ideal world, we wouldn't need competition. We'd all do our best regardless. But we're all human, and we all work harder when we're forced to. Competition gives us that extra push.

I think the best way to improve our schools is to create more competition with the public school system. In Wisconsin, the state started a program to provide this. It's called school choice. I've seen the benefits of this important reform.

Thanks to the leadership of Annette "Polly" Williams, a black legislator in Wisconsin, the state passed the nation's first school choice law. In 1990, she worked with Governor Tommy Thompson to pass a pilot school choice program. It allowed one thousand students to attend secular private schools with public help. The program gave a voucher of about five thousand dollars to any child whose family's income was near the poverty level.

In 1995, the law was expanded to allow children to use the voucher to go to parochial schools. Opponents of the law, including the American Civil Liberties Union (ACLU) and the National Education Association (NEA), the main teachers' union, filed suit. But in 1998, the Wisconsin Supreme Court and the U.S. Supreme Court upheld the law. Now, fifteen thousand Milwaukee children, or 15 percent of all students, qualify for this assistance.

Parents haven't wasted any time taking advantage of this new opportunity. At Messmer High School, a Catholic school, enrollment went up 20 percent in the school year after the decision. For the first time in its seventy-two-year history, the school has a waiting list.

Aisha James is one of the new wave of kids benefiting from school choice. She says she's glad her mother suggested she attend Messmer: "You can learn better here. People listen to the teacher. At Madison [a public high school], they don't teach you [anything]." Deseree Gordon says she wouldn't send her two daughters to a public school now that vouchers are available. "There's just too many kids in gang trouble or involved with violence," she observes. "The kids can actually learn something when they don't have to deal with all that."

School choice is very popular among black folk. In a poll of Milwaukee residents in 1998, more than three out of four blacks said they supported school choice. Only 53 percent of whites supported it. This is similar to what national polls have shown.

In 1998, I visited the Believers in Christ Academy in Milwaukee. It gave me a good idea of why school choice is so popular with these parents. Believers in Christ is a private, parochial school in the inner city. The parents I spoke to were extremely grateful for the chance to send their kids there. They talked about how wonderful it was that a female pastor ran the school. They also liked the way she ran it. Every morning, the teachers have to give their kids a hug. Because of legal concerns, teachers in the public schools are afraid to touch their students. I think this little routine really helps the kids to connect with their teachers and the school.

That connection is obvious with the older kids. The high-school kids are so attached to the school that many of them volunteer to help with the younger kids after school. They play with the kids, supervise games with them, and help teach them.

The parents have other reasons for liking the school. Joy Allen is able to send her three children to the Believers in Christ Academy because of private support from a charity called Partners Advancing Values in Education. "My children learn more. I think it's a better education," Allen says. She thinks that the school has "a better system, because it allows the parents and teachers to share values together" through prayer and faith. The school is also better able to discipline children. "School choice kids are more calm," she observes.

Studies are starting to show that students in school choice programs do better in their classes. A 1998 study by researchers at Harvard University and Mathematica Policy Research found that low-income students who used vouchers to attend private schools in New York performed better on math and reading tests than their peers in public elementary schools. Paul Peterson, the Harvard professor who led the study, said something that should get the attention of every black parent in America: "If you can get these same effects over the next five years, you can eliminate the differences between blacks and whites."

In Milwaukee, the research has shown the same thing. We've seen third- and fourth-grade low-income kids who, after several years in the choice program, have reading scores three to five percentage points higher than low-income students in the public schools. Math scores are five to twelve points higher. In California, three out of ten Hispanics don't finish high school. But less than 1 percent of Catholic high-school students there drop out—and 29 percent of the student population is Hispanic.

For our part, Sara and I home-schooled Jeremy and Jecolia up until this last year. We home-schooled them because our schedule—between football and our ministry—was so busy. Now, they're in a private Christian school in Green Bay and are doing well. I'm grateful that we have the resources to choose the school we think best fits their needs.

We should all be free to send our children to the school of our choice. It's not right for leaders in government to deny us this choice because they owe favors to teachers' unions or bureaucrats. Frankly, I'm tired of predominantly white elite organizations such as the ACLU and the NEA telling black folk which schools our children can attend. The best way to give children of all races a level playing field is to give them the same educational opportunities.

Advice for Fellow Parents

If I could offer any advice for parents in combating the problems our kids face, it would be to avoid paying too much attention to the so-called experts. These days, a lot of experts know they can get on talk shows and make a lot of money by saying what many parents want to hear. If you've ever watched daytime talk shows, you know what I mean. The so-called experts tell us that we really don't have to spend much time with our kids, or whup them, or discipline them at all if we want to use Ritalin.

These people are leading parents astray. By and large, our kids are what we put into them. They need our firm leadership, now more than ever. They're overwhelmed with the stress of trying to live up to all the pressures around them. These pressures are trying to turn them into adults before they're ready. It's no wonder they're killing each other and themselves. Death is a relief for many kids.

I also think we shouldn't be embarrassed to show our love for our kids. Boys need to see that true manhood means a man isn't ashamed to kiss and hug his son. I'm convinced that so many kids in the inner city are so hardened because they never had a father to let down his guard and show that soft side to them.

In Romans 1, Paul talked about those who've come to have a "depraved mind" (v. 28). These people are "disobedient to parents" and are "without natural affection" (vv. 30–31 KJV). I noticed in my Bible that this phrase "without natural affection" comes from the Greek word *astorgos*. Translated, it means "without family love."

Like many other sins, disrespect for parents comes from a lack of love. If we're to deal with all the new problems confronting kids these days, we have to remedy this first. If we desire the love of our children, we must first show them love ourselves. So much of what kids learn, big and small, comes from us, their parents. Let's make love their first lesson. That will cure any problem that comes their way later. It'll also give us peace of mind because then we'll know we've done our best by them—and that the rest is in God's hands.

Chapter Eleven

The Souls of Black Folk Today

Over the years, the NFL has offered the fans many spectacular moments in football history. But one beautiful sight that occurs in every game, on both sides of the field, is almost never talked about. It's the sight of black and white men hugging and high-fiving one another in celebration—as a team.

After fourteen seasons in the NFL, I can honestly say I've never heard a player make a racist statement. Why is that? I think it's because a team can win only if everyone gets along. Success demands racial harmony. Whatever grievances we might have about other people or groups off the field, we put them aside and play like brothers when we're battling in the trenches. To put it another way, the will to win outweighs the lure of sin.

I can also honestly say that loving and getting along with white folk have never been hard for me. For one thing, I'm a Christian. The God I serve tells me I must love my neighbor, no matter what color he is. My greatest heroes in football—Roger Staubach of the Dallas Cowboys and Howie Long of the Oakland Raiders—are white. I've been blessed with great white mentors and coaches throughout my career, including Buddy Ryan in Philadelphia and Mike Holmgren in Green Bay. Some of my white teammates over the years—Mike Golic in Philadelphia and Brett Favre in Green Bay come to mind—have been among my best friends on the team.

In Green Bay, which is almost all white, the people have been extremely friendly. They've wholeheartedly welcomed my family and me into their community. They've treated us as neighbors—which, of course, is what we are. We've never felt more welcome in any place we've lived.

Because I love my white brothers and sisters, I feel I can level with them. I've tried, for instance, to be frank in this book about some of the differences I see in the races. Doing this got me into trouble in my speech to the legislators. I haven't backed off, though, because I think God wants us to deal honestly with our differences.

Obviously, nobody's perfect, and no race is perfect, either. The problems in the black community—high crime rates, drug abuse, out-of-wedlock births—are well known. A lot of books and articles have been written to document these problems, and some of them have been very blunt. What I don't see, however, is the same willingness by whites to take a hard look at their own problems.

For one thing, look at the way we label these problems. Granted, blacks have high crime and illegitimacy rates. We don't follow God's rules as well as we should. But at least we don't try to explain these sins as nonsins or as ways of keeping up with the times.

With whites, I see something different. The quest for dollars among white folk has become so strong that many old virtues are disappearing. Materialism and hedonism—or *greed* and *lust*, to use the old-fashioned words—have become kings. White psychologists and "experts" say this is all natural and no big deal. That's bunk. I think this mind-set is making it easy for the problems of the inner city to invade the suburbs and heartland.

As white folk have become caught up in the money chase, we've seen a decline in spirituality. Since whites are the majority in this country, the nation has suffered severely from this decline. To be candid, I think a lot of white folk have concluded that they don't need God.

To turn things around, I believe that black folk have to lead the way. If I could make one idea stand out from this book and be remembered more than any other, it would be this: *black Americans should stop chasing the white man's dream of material prosperity and return to their dream—the dream of faith.* That's what we're about as a people. It's our strength, our great reward. As I said before, there's no better gift from God than the gift of spirituality.

Writing in the 1800s, Edward Wilmot Blyden saw that the West, including America, was becoming materialistic. He saw how people in predominantly white countries were abandoning their heritage of faith for the love of money. He was farsighted enough to predict that Africa, his adopted continent, and the African people would become the last hold-out against materialism. He wrote,

> Africa may yet prove to be the spiritual conservatory of the world. Just as in past times, Egypt proved the stronghold of Christianity after Jerusalem fell, and just as the noblest and greatest of the Fathers of the Christian Church came out of Egypt, so it may be, when the civilised nations, in consequence of their wonderful material development, shall have had their spiritual perceptions darkened and their spiritual susceptibilities blunted through the agency of a captivating and absorbing materialism, it may be, that they may have to resort to Africa to recover some of the simple elements of faith; for the promise of that land is that she shall stretch forth her hands unto God.

A few decades after Blyden made these observations about Africans, W. E. B. Du Bois applied them to African-Americans. Du Bois, too, saw that as whites became richer, they became caught up in the money chase. Almost a century ago, he laid out his vision of the differences in the races in his classic book *The Souls of Black Folk*.

Du Bois said of Americans, "We almost fear to question if the end of racing is not gold, if the aim of man is not rightly to be rich." He spoke out against the "deification of Bread" in society. And he feared what would happen if this materialism infected the black community. "In the Black World," he said,

> the Preacher and Teacher embodied once the ideals of this people—the

strife for another and a juster world, the vague dream of righteousness, the mystery of knowing; but today the danger is that these ideals, with their simple beauty and weird inspiration, will suddenly sink to a question of cash and a lust for gold.

Blyden and Du Bois saw blacks as a deeply spiritual people who were making the world's last stand against materialism and the decline of religion. Maybe they overstated their case. Obviously, black folk have a lot of problems that we need to attend to. Still, we black folk should give ourselves some credit. We've clung to our faith. We still believe in the right things. In this age, that's half the battle.

I think it's time for black folk to step up and lead the way out of the darkness. God has given us this great gift of spirituality for a reason. I believe that reason is to lead the people of this nation—and maybe even the rest of the world—back to the God who loves them.

The Gift of Spirituality in Action

Polls reveal just how spiritual black folk are. A 1997 ABC News poll asked Americans whether or not they believed in God. Ninety-five percent of Americans, and 95 percent of white Americans, said yes. Fully 100 percent of blacks said yes. Now, I challenge you to find another poll where you'll get a 100 percent response to any question. It's a very rare thing.

A poll in 1996 asked Americans if they believed in God but had some doubts or no doubts at all. Eighty percent of whites said they had no doubts. Ninety-six percent of blacks had no doubts. A CNN/USA *Today* poll in 1998 asked how important "religion is in your own life." Fifty-six percent of whites said "very important." Eighty-five percent of blacks said the same. In another poll, 37 percent of blacks named religion as the most important thing in their lives—twice the national average. Blacks also have higher rates of church attendance than whites.

My point here isn't that blacks are better people or that we'll all be going to heaven. That's obviously not the case. Besides, only God knows what's truly in people's hearts. My point is that, for all the shortcomings of the black community, blacks clearly have something important to offer America. That something is the gift of spirituality. It's the gift that Blyden, Du Bois, and so many other great black thinkers have talked about.

In *Message to the People: The Course of African Philosophy*, Marcus Garvey outlines what he thinks are the common beliefs of the African people and their descendants around the world. Two chapters are devoted to religion. They're titled "God" and "Christ." The chapter titled "God" begins with a simple but bold proclamation to Garvey's fellow blacks. The first sentence says, "There is a God and we believe in Him."

African-Americans have always been a spiritual people. Du Bois said that the black man is "a religious animal—a being of that deep emotional nature which turns instinctively toward the supernatural." Du Bois also noted that our religious beliefs have been a source of bodily as well as spiritual liberation.

When, in 1831, Nat Turner of Virginia led the most famous slave rebellion in American history, he did so believing he was avenging his people in the name of almighty God. Turner's mother recalled hearing him, when he was three or four years old, describe events that had occurred before his birth. She believed he would be a great prophet like the prophets in the Bible. Turner's grandmother, master, and many others repeatedly said that his extraordinary intelligence made him "unfit to be a slave." Turner had many natural gifts as a leader. But his spirituality was the source of his inspiration.

Southern white folk recognized it too. After Nat Turner's rebellion, many southern states passed laws prohibiting slaves from learning to read and write, forbidding them to preach, and regulating slaves' religious meetings so that they would be under the watchful eyes of whites. They saw that Turner gained his following by appealing to their Christian beliefs.

The special spirituality of blacks was just as apparent after the Civil War. Booker T. Washington remarked, "In proportion to their numbers, I question whether so large a proportion of any other race are members of some Christian Church as is true of the American Negro." Du Bois added, "The Negro church of today is the social centre of Negro life in the United States, and the most characteristic expression of African character." He stated that "a little investigation reveals the curious fact that, in the South, at least, practically every American Negro is a church member."

Of course, that's not the case today. However, polls show that blacks still are deeply spiritual. I believe this spirituality is a blessing that can greatly strengthen and enrich our society.

Throughout this book, I've tried to show that blacks are more traditional in their views than whites on almost every major social issue: homosexual rights, abortion, child rearing, sex and violence in the media, and religion. The reason for these differences, I believe, is blacks' spirituality. When we believe in God's rules, our answers on all these issues don't change over time.

Again, I hope I can be frank with my white brothers and sisters. I think that, to some degree, success has spoiled whites and America as a whole. Rev. Sandy Ray talked about this in his sermon "The Perils of Plenty." He recalled,

> There are many people in the world who were much more godly and devout when they had less. I am from a rural background. The people of my community were poor, backward, unlearned, but they were generous, kind, neighborly, and had the fear of God. Most families were very close and devoted to each other when they had less.

Rev. Ray emphasized he wasn't "advocating poverty, but [he was] suggesting a Godly use of plenty."

Blacks need to remind our society that it's all right to be rich as long as we remain godly. Jesus told us that "it is easier for a camel to go through the eye of a needle than for a rich man to enter the kingdom of God." Faith is our only solid defense to materialism, sin, and death. And while blacks remain poorer than other Americans when it comes to money, our faith is a treasure greater than all others. It is a treasure stored up in heaven, "where moth and rust do not destroy, and where thieves do not break in and steal."

If America is to experience a moral rebirth, I believe blacks must serve as the catalyst. We need leaders to step up from the black community and accept this challenge.

Black ministers must help lead this transformation. Promise Keepers, for example, has tried to bring blacks and whites together by working closely with black ministers. The problem is that many blacks, especially black young people, don't really know these ministers because they don't go to church.

The people who can command the attention of young black folk, especially gangsters and hard-core sinners, are black celebrities. That's why I've long thought that black athletes and entertainers have a special duty to lead this movement. In my speeches and public appearances, I've seen how my association with pro football has attracted young people to my message.

Recently, some of my friends in the NFL and I formed a new organization. It's called CAUSE—Christian Athletes United for Spiritual Empowerment. It's composed mostly of pro football players who are black. Our goal is to spearhead these spiritual changes in America and to invigorate the black faithful. Some of the leading members of CAUSE are Cris Carter, Randall Cunningham, Hardy Nickerson, Merton Hanks, Aeneas Williams, and Michael Dean Perry.

God tells us to invest the talents He gives us. If we black folk fail to invest our gift of spirituality at this time of spiritual crisis, when America is crying out for moral leadership, we will have let God down.

The Need for a New Vision

How should black folk start this revolution? First of all, we have to get our own affairs in order. We've got to work harder to solve the crime, drug, and parenting problems in our community.

When you're trying to make things better for yourself, there's no help like self-help. Two stories illustrate the immense power of self-help. Each comes from one of the two leading African-American thinkers of the early twentieth century.

Booker T. Washington recalled a speech he had heard an older black farmer give to an agricultural association. The farmer talked about how he'd experimented on his cotton until he discovered a way to make a single stalk produce twelve or fourteen bolls of cotton. He figured it out all by himself, by trial and error.

After the farmer had finished his speech, the audience was intrigued. Somebody spoke up and asked the farmer what his name was. He replied, "When I didn't own no home and was in debt, they used to call me old Jim Hill. But now that I own a home and am out of debt, they call me 'Mr. James Hill.'"

Du Bois offered a very different story to make the same point. He disagreed with Washington on how to best lift blacks out of poverty. He believed that blacks needed a level playing field. That meant government intervention, especially strong civil rights laws. But he also knew that the whites of his time were in no hurry to pass such laws.

Du Bois agreed that blacks had to rely on their own grit to climb out of the hole that slavery and segregation had dug for them. In a speech in Atlanta at the turn of the century, Du Bois recalled a riot that had recently taken place there in the city. In 1906, a white mob, angry over the growing prosperity of blacks, targeted blacks and their property in the city.

Du Bois noted with obvious satisfaction how Atlanta's blacks had beaten back the mob. He said, "The day when mobs can successfully cow the Negro to willing slavery is past. The Atlanta Negroes shot back and shot to kill, and that stopped the riot with a certain suddenness." Du Bois didn't mention that he had rushed back to Atlanta when the rioting began to stand guard over his property. He defended his home by sitting on his porch with a shotgun in his hand.

Where Washington and Du Bois agreed was in the unique spirituality of blacks, and the need to rely on that heritage to win justice for their people. Du Bois drove his point home mercilessly. He challenged the whites of his time by saying things like this: "Who can doubt that if Christ came to Georgia today one of His first deeds would be to sit down and take supper with black men, and who can doubt the outcome if He did?" Both challenged whites of their time to live up to their Christian convictions.

Black folk should insist that government promote spirituality in public life. I'm not talking about the government endorsing a particular church or denomination. I'm saying that black elected officials, above all other politicians, have a responsibility to promote our spiritual beliefs.

Unfortunately, black politicians often don't honor this responsibility. Too many black elected officials go along with the predominantly white agenda for abortion rights, homosexual rights, and other laws that are against God's rules. I can think of only one black politician who came to my defense after my speech—Congressman J. C. Watts.

Why don't blacks vote for people who'll support their spiritual agenda? It's simple. Blacks vote for Democrats because we're loyal. We remember who was there for us when the votes were cast in Washington for civil rights. And we stick with our friends.

However, as the saying goes, power corrupts and absolute power corrupts absolutely. More and more, the Democratic Party has been taking us for granted. That doesn't mean, of course, the Democrats are awful people. It's just human nature. They know they have our vote, so they focus on trying to get votes from whites. The trouble is that the whites and white organizations they're courting, by and large, are committed to overthrowing God's rules.

In his book *Black Labor, White Wealth*, Claud Anderson talks about a case in point—feminism. White feminists are a major force in the Democratic Party. To be elected, a Democrat basically has to kneel before that group. But as Anderson points out, feminists historically have "attempted to drive wedges between black women and black men."

Anderson quotes one prominent white feminist from the suffrage movement, Elizabeth Cady Stanton, and her comments about blacks. After the Civil War, Congress passed the Fifteenth Amendment. It gave blacks a constitutional right to vote (which southern states later ignored).

Stanton thought Congress should have extended the right to vote to women as well. In trying to make her point, she resorted to blatantly racist arguments: "Think of Sambo . . . who [does] not know the difference between a Monarchy and a Republic, who never read the Declaration of Independence, making laws for Lydia Maria Child, Lucretia Mott, or Fanny Kemble." Stanton also said, "The black women would be better off as the slave of an educated white man, than of a degraded, ignorant black one."

Anderson then explains why feminist and black concerns are so different:

> Equating discrimination against women to discrimination against blacks is like comparing a headache with cancer. Being a woman in the mainstream society may have its challenges, but it can in no manner be compared to being black in America. Yet, in the 1970s, the two struggles were linked.

It's wrong for homosexual activists to compare their cause to the civil rights movement, and I agree with Claud Anderson that feminism also shouldn't be linked to civil rights. Anderson points out that feminism now "serves as a major impediment to black family unity and racial solidarity. It is no accident that every time blacks are on the verge of receiving relief from their oppressive conditions, the women's issue emerges. . . . Feminists continue to compete against blacks."

This is definitely the case when it comes to morality and God's rules. Feminists are in favor of overturning God's rules on sex and family life. Blacks, polls show, are strongly against this. Our opposition arises primarily from our spirituality. Yet Democrats almost always side with feminists.

Black folk should judge politicians by their message, not their party. As Charles Mischeaux, president of the St. Louis chapter of the NAACP, said recently, "We should be educated enough politically to listen to the issues and pay attention to the candidates, not the parties. It's time for us to stop running to the polls like slaves and automatically voting for Democrats just because they're Democrats."

Now, don't get me wrong. I'm not a liberal or a conservative, a Democrat or a Republican. I just believe in God's rules. For that matter, I'm also disappointed in the Republican Party.

I know that Republicans are trying to reach out to blacks and other minorities. But my experience is that they can be opportunistic. I can't tell you how many Republicans in Wisconsin have asked me to run for public office. But when a black friend of mine recently ran for office as a Republican, almost none of these people helped him.

I realized that these Republicans wanted me to run just because I was well known. That's wrong. Republicans should reach out and support blacks who are qualified regardless of how famous they are.

As it is, Republicans have enough obstacles to overcome to win back the trust of black voters. Blacks' mistrust of Republicans over civil rights is still very strong. Another obstacle is the perception that Republicans care only about making money for themselves. That may play all right for people in the suburbs, but it won't play with black folk.

One grandmother who attends an African Methodist Episcopal church in Arkansas talked about this to a reporter. "These Republicans don't know what religion is," she said. She then quoted Matthew 25, in which Jesus talked about how the Lord rewards those who feed the hungry and clothe the naked. She added, "They just seem so mean. . . . Being religious means taking responsibility for the weak and poor."

I hope that whatever party they belong to, black elected officials will stand up more often for God's rules. One of the best ways for them to be true to their people and the interests of the country is to take a courageous stand against powerful feminist interests. Wouldn't it be something to hear black politicians tell white feminists to take a hike—because God's rules take precedence?

I also think the black community needs to field a new generation of leaders. We need more leaders like Dr. King and Malcolm X. Why do I hold them up as examples? I'll admit they're my heroes.

Dr. King and Malcolm X had certain characteristics in common that allowed them to serve their people with special distinction. Both were young and aggressive, for one thing. Dr. King was twenty-six when he led the Montgomery bus boycott. Both had tremendous force of character. Both were radical and courageous in their message.

But most importantly, both Dr. King and Malcolm X had a genuine love for their people. It showed in how they lived their lives. It defined who they were.

Also, both leaders reached out to whites. Dr. King realized that black folk and the rest of the nation needed integration. That didn't mean that blacks couldn't be proud of who they were. He felt that God wanted all His children to live together in peace and unity.

Dr. King also wasn't afraid to go against the tide of public opinion. Four days before he was assassinated, in his last Sunday sermon, he said:

On some positions, cowardice asks the question, Is it expedient? Vanity asks the question, Is it popular? Conscience asks the question, Is it right? And there comes a time when one must take a position that is neither safe, nor polite, nor popular — but one must take it because it's right.

Malcolm X was very tough on whites throughout almost his entire adult life. His attitudes changed only after he went to Mecca and saw whites and blacks mingling together in service of Allah. Both Dr. King and Malcolm X died untimely deaths because of their love for their people.

I believe that many black elected officials and celebrities today are too caught up in politics. We've forgotten how important it is just to love and serve our people — and the rest of the nation. We can't be so consumed with getting elected and passing new laws that we forget about our hearts. If our hearts are in the right place, the laws will follow.

A Call for Unity

Because of our gift of spirituality, black folk have a special mission. It's to lead America out of its spiritual swamp. Once we've picked the right leaders to fulfill this mission, we still have to look within our own hearts and make sure that everything's in order.

Whites have done a lot to show they're sorry for their past persecution of blacks. They've passed civil rights laws and enacted programs to give blacks and other minorities a hand up. Whites didn't have to do these things. They outnumber blacks. But they did do them, and they were generous acts.

On the other hand, whites can't expect blacks to suddenly "get over" our past persecution. I remember a white teammate of mine once said, "Reggie, blacks should just leave their problems in the past." He meant we shouldn't complain about our history.

But it's not that simple. History shows that racial feuds can go on for hundreds, even thousands of years. It's been only thirty-five years since the Civil Rights Act passed. Whites practiced slavery, segregation, and discrimination for almost four hundred years. I really hope that whites will be patient and let time heal some of these wounds.

I can assure my white brothers and sisters that racism and prejudice still exist. To me, there's a difference between racism and prejudice. Racism is a belief that one's race is superior to another. This belief implies that one's race is in a position of power. Otherwise, a belief in racial superiority makes no sense. Prejudice or bias, in contrast, can be practiced by members of any race. Blacks and other minorities can be prejudiced, biased, or hateful toward whites. But they can't really be racists, in the true sense of the word, unless they're in a position superior to whites. In America, at least, they're not.

From what I can tell, every black person in America, at some point, has received an unfriendly reminder of our continuing inferiority of power. You may have heard the phrase "Driving While Black." It refers to times when police pull over black motorists for no reason except the color of their skin. It's a known fact that police and other law enforcement officials "profile" offenders. If you fit a certain "profile"—if you're black driving a luxury car or wearing fancy clothes or jewelry—police will pull you over, pat you down, check your bags, that sort of thing. White cops have admitted to me that they profile.

In 1997, I gave a speech to a high school in Knoxville and talked about how the police sometimes single out young black men for rough treatment. I'm not saying all police or even most of them do this. A lot of good cops protect us from criminals. But I stand by my remarks.

When it came to light in 1995 that an annual Good Ol' Boy Roundup was being held in Tennessee not far from Knoxville, and was attended by agents from the FBI, Drug Enforcement Administration, and Bureau of Alcohol, Tobacco, and Firearms (ATF), I saw some of my worst fears materialize. It turned out that these federal law enforcement agents were meeting in rural Tennessee at a place where T-shirts with racist themes were sold; a poster at the entrance read, "Nigger Check Point"; and a skit was put on in which one participant dressed as a Ku Klux Klan member and pretended to sodomize another participant in black face. It's impossible to express how damaging such incidents are to race relations and how much they reinforce blacks' suspicion toward law enforcement officers.

If you think this is just black folk being paranoid, let me offer you a couple of examples of injustice from my life. A few years ago, when I played for Philadelphia, I was driving my Mercedes, and a police officer in the city pulled me over. I hadn't seen a sign saying not to make a right on red.

But when the cop walked up to the car, he didn't ask me about that. He asked, "Why are you driving a car like this?" I guess he thought I was a car thief or drug dealer. When I told him, "I'm Reggie White," he apologized. But if I hadn't been a celebrity, things might not have worked out so well.

Then there was the time I was driving my family back home from Florida. We were driving to Vidalia, Georgia, to see a boys' home that was run by Mel Blount, former cornerback and Hall of Famer for the

Pittsburgh Steelers. I was driving our forty-five-foot bus, which is what we take on vacations.

I was driving along—observing the speed limit, I might add—when I saw a white state trooper pull up alongside the bus. He looked in the window to see who was driving. Then he fell back and started tailing me.

After about half an hour, the trooper put on his lights and pulled us over. I got out of the bus and asked, "Officer, what did I do?" I knew I hadn't been speeding.

He said that my speed had been "going up and down." I told him that it had been going up and down because the speed limits kept changing as we drove through small towns along the way. I knew what his agenda was. He just wanted to see who was driving a bus like that, and why.

Sara then got off the bus and asked to see the radar. "I think you really stopped us because we're black," she said.

The trooper refused to let us see the radar.

"By law, you have to let us see it," she insisted. She's right. That is the law. Still, the cop said no.

I told Sara to get on the bus. I knew it was a black man's word against a southern cop's. Sara then picked up the camcorder and filmed every-thing—just in case.

Finally, after looking over my license and registration, the trooper told us we could go. "Just slow down," he warned us.

As long as incidents like this happen in America, they'll continue to aggravate race relations. I know from talking to other black celebrities that my experiences are hardly unique.

Even so, I think we can break through racial barriers by coming to more of an understanding between the races. Let me lay it all out to you. Whites have to understand that they have to overcome a legacy of mistrust. This is going to take time.

Blacks have to understand that we have to completely forgive whites for the injustices we've suffered. This can happen only when black folk feel that racism is completely in decline, and that whites have made restitution for the sins that have placed black folk in such an economic dis-advantage.

Remember, this country grew rich off the backs of free black labor. One way for whites to make restitution is for affirmative action programs to stop benefiting white females the same as they do minorities. This senseless policy is driven by politics instead of justice.

Edward Wilmot Blyden always found a way to eloquently get to the heart of race relations. He recalled Acts, chapter 8, the passage in which Philip preached to the Ethiopian eunuch. Philip read to him a passage from Isaiah that foretold of Christ's persecution. Blyden noted:

> And there was something symbolic, also, of the future sad experience of his race — and at the same time full of consolation — in the passage which he read. It was holding up Christ as the "man of sorrows and acquainted with grief," as if in anticipation of the great and unsur-passed trials of the African. These were to be the words of comfort and uplifting to these people in their exile and captivity. They were to remember that if they were despised and scorned, a far greater [person] than themselves had had a similar experience. Christ was to be held up to the suffering African not only as a propitiation for sin, and as a Mediator between God and man, but as a blessed illustration of the glorious fact that persecution and suffering and contempt are no proof that God is not the loving Father of a people — but may be rather an evidence of nearness to God, seeing that they have been chosen to tread in the footsteps of the first-born of the creation, suffering for the welfare of others.

If our suffering has been for the glory of God, is there any greater tri-umph than that? By treating our white brothers and sisters like teammates, black folk can show the whole world how humbly we serve our God and how mighty a God He is.

Chapter Twelve

Defenders of the Faith

In March 1998, a few weeks before I gave my speech, Sara and I led a pilgrimage of 317 people to Israel. We went to the Holy Land to visit the sites where Jesus walked among us before laying down His life. To see those places with my own eyes was deeply moving.

I'll admit I went to the Holy Land thinking I might see or feel something supernatural. After all, that's no ordinary place. But that wasn't what I experienced. What really stands out about the trip were the people who went with us.

I'd say seven out of ten of our fellow pilgrims were elderly. Quite a few had lost their spouses. Many seemed lonely. But there was something about being there, on those holy grounds, that gave us all new life. One older woman who had come in a wheelchair walked the whole trip. Another woman told me she and her husband had been married for fifty-one years, and for the first time, she'd finally seen him cry.

Their faith had led them to those sacred sites. They came to pay their respects to their Savior and the fathers of their faith. I think that's why they went back to America spiritually refreshed, with greater joy for life. Maybe that was even God's way of rewarding them for coming to His holy grounds.

Jesus told us in Matthew 17:20 that with the faith of a tiny mustard seed, we can literally move mountains. I believe that faith is the single best solution to all our personal and social problems.

When I use the word *faith*, however, my definition is different from most people's. To make faith more meaningful, we first must understand

and agree on what faith really is. Only then will we truly be defenders of the faith.

It seems to me that too many Christians and non-Christians believe that faith means merely belief in God. That's the definition we hear from many pulpits today. Faith, these preachers or spiritual leaders say, means believing in God — nothing more.

Obviously, belief in God is essential. In my case, I can't remember a time when I didn't believe in God. Through God's grace, I've never doubted His existence. I know that for some people, believing in God is a challenge. I think it's hard for them to accept the fact that God expects us to believe in Him unquestioningly, like little children. To some of us, believing in something we can't see or touch makes us feel we're losing control of our lives. And, in fact, we are. That's all part of God's plan.

Other preachers and spiritual leaders tell us that faith means believing God will do things to help us. For instance, God will give us possessions or perform a miracle in our lives or straighten out our finances. Even those of us who've messed up our own finances think that if we have enough faith, God will bail us out.

I believe these definitions of faith are incorrect. Faith defined in these ways doesn't demand much from us. Faith, I believe, means something more. That something is the hardest thing that people are ever asked to give anyone or anything: obedience.

Faith Is Obedience

There's no question, based on the polls, that the American people believe in God. Ninety-five percent of Americans say they do. Six out of ten Americans say that religion is very important in their everyday lives. Judging from these numbers, some might conclude that America is a very faithful nation.

Yet we have to dig deeper to find out how faithful we really are. Other facts show how shallow our spirituality has become. For example, just four out of ten Americans attend religious services once a week. And through-out this book, we've looked at the wide variety of social problems we're experiencing that are directly related to a lack of spirituality in our lives.

By any fair measure, we're not a faithful people. Why do I say that? Because faith means more than belief in God or miracles. It means action. It means making a commitment to God and sticking to it, no matter what.

Why do I believe this? For one thing, the Bible makes it clear that servants of God are expected to do more than just acknowledge God's existence. Jesus told us, "Not everyone who says to me, 'Lord, Lord,' will enter the kingdom of heaven, but only he who does the will of my Father who is in heaven." True faith is belief plus obedience.

There's another reason why I believe in this definition of faith. I believe God shared this concept of faith with me when He spoke to me a few years ago.

In 1996, the Packers had finished the regular season with home-field advantage for the play-offs. We appeared to be in a dominant position to make a run for the Super Bowl. After twelve years of playing in the NFL, I was finally on a team that looked to be headed toward winning a championship.

It was then, before the playoffs began, that I believe God spoke to me. He asked me, *Why do you think I'm giving you a chance to win a championship?*

"I don't know," I answered. "I know it's not because of my faith."

You're right, God said. *It's not because of your faith, because your definition of faith is wrong. The same is true for the rest of My children.*

So I asked Him, "What is faith?"

God said, *Go read Hebrews, chapter 11.*

I did what He told me to do.

The chapter begins, "Now faith is being sure of what we hope for and certain of what we do not see." Paul talked about many of the great patriarchs and prophets who served God "by faith": Abel, Noah, Abraham, Joseph, Moses, and so on. Instead of being rewarded on earth for their service,

Paul pointed out that they were "destitute, persecuted and mistreated — the world was not worthy of them."

Then God explained to me why my definition of faith was wrong. *You treat Me like a spiritual genie,* He said. *You think you can rub a bottle, and Poof! I'll give you what you want. That's not faith. That's desire.*

God went on: *Do you know why I'm letting you win now?*

"Why?" I asked.

I'm letting you win because four years ago, when I told you to go to Green Bay and everyone said you were crazy to go, you went anyhow.

Of course, He was right. Four years earlier, I'd left Philadelphia and moved to Green Bay. To be honest, it was a hard decision for me. I'd heard Green Bay was a cold, small city in the upper Midwest that was almost all white. The Packers had had a tough time recruiting black players. After spending extensive time in prayer, and after concluding that God wanted me to go to Green Bay, I signed with the Packers and moved my family to Wisconsin.

In the end, everything worked out beautifully. Green Bay was extremely friendly toward my family and me. I spread the word around the league that black folk were welcome, and I think that was important in our attracting high-quality black free agents. Four years later, we ended up winning the Super Bowl.

When God spoke to me before the 1996 playoffs, I finally came to understand what faith really means. God was explaining that obedience is part of the definition of faith. That's what Paul was saying in Hebrews, chapter 11. God was also letting me know that He was allowing me to be on a championship team because I'd believed in Him *and* I'd obeyed Him.

You may not believe the events I've just related to you. But if you don't believe me, I hope you'll at least read Hebrews 11. There, God spells out what He expects from us in terms of faith.

I now realize that faith means more than belief. True faith means that we do what the Master tells us to do. We obey Him and His rules. We do it no matter how much persecution comes our way. To be truly faithful, we have to leave this earth knowing that others will say of us what Paul said of the patriarchs and prophets of old—"the world was not worthy of them."

Restoring Faith in America

A few months after I gave my speech, I was asked to appear on CNN's *Crossfire* to talk about—what else?—homosexuality. At one point in the show, a host of the program, who was defending homosexual rights, said, "Reggie, you and I are men of faith."

Now, I'm not experienced at those rapid-fire talk shows, so I didn't give him the response I should've. I should've challenged his definition of faith. He's not a true "man of faith" because he doesn't obey God's rules. If he did, he wouldn't be defending homosexuality in direct violation of Scripture.

The same goes for America. If we were a faithful nation, we wouldn't be saying we believe in God and value religion, yet keep on breaking so many of God's rules. God would know us from our obedience. I think He would honor us by washing away many of the personal and social problems that are plaguing us—problems rooted in sin.

God has been gracious enough to teach us how to read, write, and record history. From history, we know how nations rise and fall. All the great nations of history have fallen when they moved away from faith. Even when their faith was in gods that didn't exist—Greek and Roman gods, for example—their faith at least made them obey rules that weren't just the values of the day.

One of the main lessons of the Bible is that nations that turn away from God risk His wrath. By disobeying His rules, we lose His favor. Rev. Sandy F. Ray offered some powerful sermons that took up these themes. He compared America to the Israelites under Joshua shortly after they had come out of the wilderness. Rev. Ray observed of the Israelites:

As their powers and prestige grew, they had a tendency to forget their spiritual history. They wanted the fatherly protection of God without a childhood obedience to him. They wished to be the chosen people of God, but they wanted the privilege of choosing their own course of life. Like a wayward child, they wanted the protection and security of a good home, but resented the discipline of the parents.

Our response to those who deny or break God's rules must be the same defiant response that Joshua gave to the Israelites who turned away from God: "But as for me and my household, we will serve the Lord."

In his sermon "The Testimony of a Towel," Rev. Ray shared other important, related lessons. What our society really needs, Dr. Ray believed, is humility. He thought one story really summed up what humility is all about. Rev. Ray reminded his audience of how at the Last Supper, Jesus picked up a towel, wrapped it around His waist, and proceeded to wash the feet of His disciples. The message Jesus was sending, Rev. Ray concluded, was this: "The greatest in my kingdom shall be the towel takers. In my kingdom, seats will be won by service. . . . The towel is the test of true greatness."

Rev. Ray admitted, "The tale of the towel is not popular in our world of pushing and pride." Yet "a towel team is the hope of our arrogant, domineering, pompous, haughty world. The Lord is trying to say something to us, girded in a towel. . . . If we would be great in the kingdom of God, we must take a towel. A towel is the route to glory." Rev. Ray closed by noting, "When Jesus returns, he will not be seeking titles; he will be checking towels."

Humility is the first step toward obedience. Once we accept God's sovereignty and superiority over us, we're well on the way to faith.

How do we, as a nation, become faithful again? Some may think it's impossible at this point. We've slid so far away from God's rules.

I say we have to take it a step at a time. We have to begin by looking at our own hearts and souls to see how we can purify our own lives. No one is so pure that he can't stand a little improvement. America can use all the reduction in sin we can muster.

We must then learn to love God with all our heart, soul, and mind, as

Jesus commanded us. That is the "first and greatest commandment." The second commandment is, "Love your neighbor as yourself." In James 2:8, we're told that this is the "royal law." Think of how quickly all our suffering, as individuals and as a nation, would disappear if we humbly and completely obeyed these two supreme rules of life.

We can't expect to do this all by ourselves, either. The world tells us that we're the masters of our fate. That's not true. We can do only so much to change ourselves. Remember, Jesus died to change us. It's through God's grace that we do anything worthwhile, that we ever turn away from sin.

To truly change, we must have faith like little children, as Jesus told us. That means belief plus obedience. For the same reasons that many of us resist submitting to God, new Christians sometimes prefer not to believe that only God can change them. I think some of them resist because, like atheists, they're afraid of losing control. But we must remember that even the greatest saints among us do what they do only through God's grace and under His leadership.

Let me put it another way. Once we commit our lives to God, the hardest part is over. We know what we have to do. God has left us His rules so that we all have a clear action plan for life. Once we're on our knees, the Lord will take it from there.

Conclusion:

The Soldier Versus the Cadet

It's tempting to become discouraged over America's flight from God. Standing up for God's rules these days is kind of like making a goal-line stand in football. That's the hardest situation for a defense to be in. It's when a team finds itself backed up to its own end zone, only a few yards away from giving up a touchdown.

If we're going to prevent the other side from winning, we have to dig in our heels and push back—as hard as we can.

Our backs are to the wall. But we have a lot to be grateful for and hopeful about. Throughout America, there are incredible stories of hope and liberation that we run across every day we fight the good fight. I've seen people freed from homosexuality, promiscuous youngsters turned into family men, and gangsters who've become model citizens. The stories I've shared in this book are only a tiny sample of the miracles God works for those who meet Him even halfway.

Jesus reminded us, "With God all things are possible." What more encouragement do we need?

Still, all of us must be active in fighting the good fight. Enthusiastic new recruits are always needed. As long as there is sin, there'll always be plenty of work for men and women of God. The Christian life is not a spectator sport.

That point came home to me in a conversation I had with Keith Jackson, one of my former teammates and best friends. One night, he called and told me that the Lord had sent him a message to relay to me.

"Big Dog"—that's my nickname—"the Lord told me to give you the word," Keith said. "The Lord told me to tell you that you're a soldier."

I wasn't sure where he was going. So Keith explained.

"You know the difference between soldiers and cadets? Soldiers are trained for battle. But cadets are still in training. They need to be challenged while they're being trained.

"You're a soldier, Big Dog. You've got to help train the cadets."

I could see where he was going. Our nation is full of people who reject God's rules. But among those who accept His rules, there are two kinds of people: those who fight for them, and those who aren't yet ready to.

Then Keith mentioned something else that really got to me. "A soldier fights until the last trumpet blows. Remember, when the trumpet blows—when Jesus comes back—it's all over."

I knew what Keith meant. Any service we're going to offer to God has to be rendered before Jesus comes back. When the trumpet blows and Jesus returns in His glory to judge us, it's like the horn blowing at the end of a ball game. The game is over. The winners and the losers are already determined.

"Keith," I told him, "that is the Word."

If we're going to serve God, we must do it now. We don't know when we're going to be called to account for how we've lived our lives. And there are so many people hurting, so many souls searching for hope in a world full of sin and suffering, that we can't afford to remain cadets. Once we bow before God and accept His rules, we have to join the fight. God's rules are all the training we need. In the words of the old spiritual, we must sign up to be soldiers in the army of the Lord.

When that trumpet blows and the battle is over, let's make sure we're not cadets still trying to figure out whether we really want to serve God and our neighbors. Let's plunge into the battle. Let's fight the good fight. And through God's grace, let's make sure we walk off the field the winners.

Notes

Chapter One: I Didn't Make the Rules

Associated Press: Sharon Theimer, "TV Wannabe Reggie White Blasts Gays in Speech," *Arizona Republic*, March 26, 1998, C1.

"Extremist and outdated": David Kopay, "Dear Reggie White: You Just Don't Get It," *New York Times*, August 2, 1998, sec. 8, p. 13.

"Stereotypical": Jarrett Bell, "White Can't Sack Controversy," *USA Today*, July 24, 1998, 1C.

"Odious" and "vicious": Cynthia Tucker, "Black Anti-Gay Prejudice Adds to AIDS' Toll," *Atlanta Journal and Constitution*, May 24, 1998, B7.

"Crass": Jonathan Rand, "White's Controversial Remarks Aren't Surprising," *Kansas City Star*, March 29, 1998, C8.

"Reprehensible": Milton Kent, "White's Brand of Furor Not Favorite of Networks," *Baltimore Sun*, April 30, 1998, D2.

James T. Campbell: James T. Campbell, "When a Good Guy Puts His Foot in His Mouth," *Houston Chronicle*, March 30, 1998, A16.

Jennifer Frey: Jennifer Frey, "Opinion Laced with Ignorance, Arrogance," *Washington Post*, March 27, 1998, D1.

Campbell Soup spokesman: Robert Imrie, "White's Comments May Hurt CBS Hopes," Associated Press, March 27, 1998.

Leslie Ann Wade: Bob Wolfley, "Remarks May Cost White Job in TV," *Milwaukee Journal-Sentinel*, March 26, 1998.

"Honor Thy Contract": Editorial, "Honor Thy Contract," *Wall Street Journal*, April 24, 1998, W13.

Chapter Two: The New Slavery

San Francisco Chronicle: Elaine Herscher, "Controversial Conversions," *San Francisco Chronicle*, August 19, 1998, A17.

Harvard Law School: Mac Daniel, "At Harvard, Debate Flies Over 'Ex-Gay' Ministry," *Boston Globe*, October 11, 1997, B1.

U.S. News: Wray Herbert, "Politics of Biology," *U.S. News & World Report*, April 21, 1997, 74.

Paul in Romans: Romans 6:18; 6:14.

Anita Bryant: Paul Power Jr., "Anita 'Orange Juice Lady' Bryant Still Appeals to Florida Citrus Growers," *Tampa Tribune*, May 11, 1998, Business & Finance, 6; Mitchell Smyth, "Whatever Happened to . . . Anita Bryant?" *Toronto Star*, May 15, 1994, B11.

Angie and Debbie Winans: Interviews with A. P. Thomas, July 15, 1998.

Lott and Armey: Alison Mitchell, "Controversy Over Lott's Views of Homosexuality," *New York Times*, June 17, 1998, A24; Nancy E. Roman, "Condemnation of Sin Sparks Fierce Debate," *Washington Times*, June 17, 1998, A1.

1 Percent of Population: Priscilla Painton, "The Shrinking Ten Percent," *Time*, April 26, 1998, 27–29.

Socarides and Kaufman: Charles Socarides, Benjamin Kaufman, Joseph Nicolosi, Jeffrey Satinover, and Richard Fitzgibbons, "Don't Forsake Homosexuals Who Want Help," *Wall Street Journal*, January 9, 1997, A10.

Socarides: Charles Socarides, M.D., "A Survey of Treatment Results," National Association for Research and Therapy of Homosexuality (NARTH) Web site (www.narth.com).

Masters and Johnson: Studies discussed in Robert Dickes, "Observations on the Treatment of Homosexual Patients," in *The Homosexualities and the Therapeutic Process*, edited by Charles W. Socarides and Vamik D. Volkan (Madison, Conn.: International Universities Press, 1991), 9.

1998 NARTH study: NARTH, "New Study Confirms Homosexuality Can Be Overcome," May 17, 1997, NARTH Web site.

Joseph Nicolosi: Joseph Nicolosi, "Fathers of Male Homosexuals: A Collective Clinical Profile," NARTH Web site.

Dreikorn: William L. Dreikorn, "Sexual Orientation Conversion Therapy: Help or Hindrance," summary of doctoral dissertation, NARTH Web Site.

George Morales: John Blake, "The 'Ex-Gay Movement' Sets Off Intense Debate," *Atlanta Journal and Constitution*, June 6, 1998, F4.

John Paulk: Karen Kleinwort, "Couple Touts Gay-Conversion Therapy," *Denver Post*, August 30, 1998, B1.

Socarides on sexual abuse: Charles W. Socarides, *Homosexuality: A Freedom Too Far* (Phoenix: Adam Margrave, 1995), 87.

Dreikorn on sexual abuse: Dreikorn, "Sexual Orientation."

Child Abuse and Neglect: Lynda S. Doll, Dan Joy, et al., "Self-Reported Childhood and Adolescent Sexual Abuse Among Adult Homosexual and Bisexual Men," *Child Abuse and Neglect* 16 (1992): 855–64, 858, 862.

Two prominent geneticists (re LeVay): Paul Billings and Jonathan Beckwith, "Born Gay?" *Technology Review*, July 1993, 60–62, 60.

Socarides on Hamer and Bailey: Socarides, *Homosexuality: A Freedom Too Far*, 94–99.

Washington Post: Hanna Rosin, "Crusade Turns Gays to the Straight and Narrow," *Washington Post*, July 31, 1998, A1.

Bob Davies: Kim Painter, "Can Gays Be Converted, Body and Soul?" *USA Today*, August 4, 1998, D4.

Dennis Jernigan: Interview with A. P. Thomas, November 17, 1998; Marsha Gallardo, "The Song of a Wounded Heart," *Charisma*, July 1995, 38–42.

Westbrook-Davis and Washington Wizards fights: Ric Bucher, "Remark Led to the Fight Between Murray, Strickland," *Washington Post*, December 24, 1997, E1.

USA Today poll: *USA Today*, June 1998, obtained from Roper Center for Public Opinion Research, University of Connecticut (hereinafter Roper Center).

Los Angeles Times poll: *Los Angeles Times*, October 1995, Roper Center.

Time magazine poll: Painton, "The Shrinking Ten Percent." 1993.

Lambeth Conference: Editorial, "Bruising Bishops," *Wall Street Journal*, August 14, 1998, W11.

Mugabe: Lynne Duke, "Mugabe Makes Homosexuals Public Enemies," *Washington Post*, September 9, 1995, A19.

Homosexual charter ships: Serge F. Kovaleski, "Gay Cruises Anger Island Residents," *Washington Post*, April 26, 1998, A25.

Colin Powell: Jason L. Riley, "Not a Civil Rights Issue," *Wall Street Journal*, August 13, 1998, A14.

Jason Riley: Ibid.

Romer v. Evans: 116 Sup. Ct. 1620 (1996).

Lawsuits re homosexual teens: Lena H. Sun, "Gay Students Get Little Help with Harrassment," *Washington Post*, July 20, 1998, A1.

Poll on homosexual employment: Gallup Poll, November 1996, Gallup Poll Archives (www.gallup.com).

New York Times: Katharine Q. Seelye, "House Votes Another Antigay Measure," *New York Times*, August 8, 1998, A11.

Rep. Steve Largent: Ibid.

Chapter Three: Going Our Separate Ways

One out of three babies: National Center for Health Statistics, "Out-of-Wedlock Births," 1996, NCHS Web site (www.cdc.gov/nchswww).

Out-of-wedlock birth statistics: Ramon G. McLeod, "The Changing Profile of Unwed Mothers," *San Francisco Chronicle*, June 7, 1995, A1.

Out-of-wedlock birth rates for white professional women: Jennifer Lenhart, "Single Motherhood Rising Steeply, Census Bureau Reports," *Houston Chronicle*, November 8, 1995, A3.

Divorce rate: National Center for Health Statistics, "Divorce," 1996, NCHS Web site.

60 percent of children will live with single parent: "Rise in Single-Parent Families," *Washington Post*, April 9, 1996, Z5.

Whitehead: Barbara Dafoe Whitehead, "Dan Quayle Was Right," *Atlantic Monthly*, April 1993, 47–84.

Candice Bergen: Lisa Schiffren, "Candice Bergen vs. Murphy Brown," *New York Times*, June 12, 1998, A21.

Poll re sex outside marriage: Gallup Poll, December 1997, Gallup Poll Archives.

Only one in five teenagers: Alan Guttmacher Institute, "Facts in Brief—Teen Sex and Pregnancy," AGI Web site (www.agi-usa.org/home).

Teenage pregnancy rates compared to other countries: Jane E. Brody, "Teen-Agers and Sex: Younger and More at Risk," *New York Times*, September 15, 1998, F7.

Grosse Pointe scandal: Ron French, "Pain, Tears, Plea End Pointe's Sex Scandal," *Detroit News*, September 23, 1998, A1; "Former Class President Given Jail Term in Underage-Sex Case," *Chicago Tribune*, October 15, 1998, 6.

Spur Posse: Jill Smolowe, "Sex with a Scorecard," *Time*, April 5, 1993, 41.

Glen Ridge, N.J.: Sally Jenkins, "An All-American Nightmare," *Washington Post*, July 21, 1997, C8.

Forty-seven percent of teenagers: "Teenage Sex: Many Feel Pressured to Have Encounter Before Being Ready," *Chicago Tribune*, March 31, 1998, 7.

One out of four teenage girls: Guttmacher Institute, "Facts in Brief—Teen Sex," AGI Web site.

Parents in Lakewood: Smolowe, "Sex with a Scorecard."

Cohabitation poll: Gallup Poll, December 1997, Gallup Poll Archives.

Divorce rates for cohabiting couples: Editorial, "Couples More Apt to Stay Together If Marriage Precedes Moving In," *Omaha World Herald*, June 21, 1995, 22.

1992 poll on divorce: James Patterson and Peter Kim, *The Day America Told the Truth* (New York: Plume Books, 1992), 93.

Divorce "touches a nerve": Dana Milbank, "Blame Game: No-Fault Divorce Law Is Assailed in Michigan, and Debate Heats Up," *Wall Street Journal*, January 5, 1996, A1.

David Michael: Ibid.

Christine Kurth: Dirk Johnson, "No-Fault Divorce Is Under Attack," *New York Times*, February 12, 1996, A8.

Cloning: An excellent summary of anticloning arguments is John Cardinal O'Connor's contribution to "Will Cloning Beget Disaster?" *Wall Street Journal*, May 2, 1997, A14.

"Although 50 percent": Walter Kirn, "The Ties That Bind," *Time*, August 18, 1997, 48–50.

Covenant marriage: Christine H. Whelan, "No Honeymoon for Covenant Marriage," *Wall Street Journal*, August 17, 1998, A14.

Statistics on teenage birth, adult divorce rate: Barbara Vobejda, "Traditional Families Hold On," *Washington Post*, May 29, 1998, A2.

Statistics on high-school students: Barbara Vobejda, "Study: More Teens Refrain from Sex," *Washington Post*, September 18, 1998, A2.

"If anyone would come after me": Mark 8:34.

Chapter Four: The Complete Image of God

"Love your neighbor as yourself": Matthew 22:39.

"I raised you up": Romans 9:17 (quoting Ex. 9:16).

Thomas Sowell on stereotypes: Thomas Sowell, *Race and Culture: A World View* (New York: Basic, 1994), 11.

Marcus Garvey: Marcus Garvey, *Message to the People: The Course of African Philosophy* (Dover, Mass.: Majority Press, 1986), 42.

Pastor Stewart on black churches: Warren H. Stewart Sr., *Interpreting God's Word in Black Preaching* (Valley Forge, Pa.: Judson Press, 1984), 62–63.

Jonetta Rose Barras: Andrew Peyton Thomas, "Independents' Day," *The American Enterprise*, November-December 1998, 42.

Edward Wilmot Blyden on "every race": Edward Wilmot Blyden, *Christianity, Islam, and the Negro Race* (Baltimore: Black Classic Press, 1994), 318.

Blyden on "When the African" and "There is not a tribe": Ibid., 133, 132.

Blyden on Africa's importance in the Bible: Ibid., 177.

Census Bureau: U.S. Bureau of the Census, *Current Population Reports*, Household and Family Characteristics, Table on Extended Families by Race/Hispanic Origin, 1997 (obtained from Ken Bryson, Census Bureau, Population Division).

Birth rate of Mexican women: Lenhart, "Single Motherhood."

Mexican divorce rate: Alexis Vargas, "For Many Immigrants, Marriage Is Too Much of an Endurance Test," *Wall Street Journal*, November 18, 1998, A1.

Polls of Hispanics on abortion: Cable News Network/*USA Today* poll, January 1998, Roper Center.

"Once a Latino girl gets pregnant": Barbara Vobejda and Pamela Constable, "Hispanic Teens Rank 1st in Birthrate," *Washington Post*, February 13, 1998, A10.

Polls of Hispanics on family values: *Los Angeles Times*, October 1995 (homosexuality); *Washington Post*, July 1997 (importance of getting married and close relationships with relatives); data obtained from Roper Center.

Japan's resources: Thomas Sowell, *Migrations and Cultures: A World View* (New York: Basic, 1996), 108.

China's economy: Karl Zinsmeister, "Why China Doesn't Scare Me," *The American Enterprise*, July-August 1998, 4.

Sowell on how Japanese "seized upon Western technology": Sowell, *Race and Culture*, 8.

Sowell on "The behavior and performance": Sowell, *Migrations and Cultures*, 139.

Blyden on contributions of races: Blyden, *Christianity, Islam, and the Negro Race*, 138–39, 186.

Chapter Five: A Covetous People

John Wesley: Erwin Paul Rudolph, ed., *The John Wesley Treasury* (Wheaton, Ill.: Victor Books, 1979), 44–48.

Tenth commandment: Exodus 20:17.

Dr. Sandy F. Ray: Sandy F. Ray, *Journeying Through a Jungle* (Nashville: Broadman, 1979), 41.

Polling data on *the good life*: Shannon Brownlee and Matthew Miller, "5 Lies Parents Tell Themselves About Why They Work," *U.S. News & World Report*, May 12, 1997, 60.

"For where your treasure is": Matthew 6:21.

Consumer spending and new home sales: Clay Chandler and Stephanie Stoughton, "Ignoring the Economy's Doomsayers," *Washington Post*, August 4, 1998, E1.

"Buy things to fill them up": Ibid.

All-time records for consumer debt and personal savings: John M. Berry, "Consumers Keep Their Borrowing in Check," *Washington Post*, August 19, 1998, C9.

All-time record for bankruptcies: Robert A. Rosenblatt, "Congress Pushes for Bankruptcy Overhaul," *Los Angeles Times*, June 1, 1998, A1.

Rep. James P. Moran: Ibid.

Credit card companies: Ibid.

Bankruptcies' cost to businesses: Katharine Q. Seelye, "Senate Votes to Curb Bankruptcy Abuse by Consumers," *New York Times*, September 24, 1998, A1.

Property crime rate: U.S. Department of Justice, Bureau of Justice Statistics, *Sourcebook of Criminal Justice Statistics* (Washington, D.C.: U.S. Government Printing Office); and U.S. Department of Justice, Federal Bureau of Investigation, *Crime in the United States* (Washington, D.C.: U.S. Government Printing Office); calculations performed by Daryl Fischer, Policy and Research Bureau, Arizona Department of Corrections, in graph entitled "U.S. Property Crime Rate 1960–1996" (hereinafter Fischer Report, Arizona Department of Corrections, 1998).

Robbery, larceny, motor vehicle theft rates: Ibid.

Rev. Manuel L. Scott: Manuel L. Scott, *The Gospel for the Ghetto: Sermons from a Black Pulpit* (Nashville: Broadman, 1973), ix.

Association of Certified Fraud Examiners: Harrison Rainie with Margaret Loftus and Mark Madden, "The State of Greed," *U.S. News & World Report*, June 17, 1996, 64.

Cheating on taxes: M. Hirsh Goldberg, *The Complete Book of Greed: The Strange and Amazing History of Human Excess* (New York: William Morrow, 1994), 200.

"About six in ten parents": Gallup Poll, February 1997, Gallup Poll Archives.

"Fifty-five percent of new mothers": Faye Fiore, "Full-Time Moms a Minority Now," *Los Angeles Times*, November 26, 1997, A1.

"From 1965 to 1997": Melissa Healy, "A Less Taxing Approach to Day Care?" *Los Angeles Times*, May 11, 1998, A1.

"74 percent of Americans": Ibid.

1974 study: J. Conrad Schwarz, Robert G. Strickland, and George Krolick, "Infant Day Care: Behavioral Effects at Preschool Age," *Developmental Psychology* 10 (1974): 502–6.

1985 study: Ron Haskins, "Public School Aggression Among Children with Varying Day Care Experience," *Child Development* 56 (1985): 689–703.

Jeree Pawl: Karl Zinsmeister, "The Problem with Day Care," *The American Enterprise*, May-June 1998, 32.

NICHHD study: National Institute of Child Health and Human Development, *Mother-Child Interaction and Cognitive Outcomes Associated with Early Child Care* (Washington, D.C.: NICHHD, 1998), overall summary, 2.

American Pediatric Association: Zinsmeister, "The Problem with Day Care," 41–42.

Dreskins: Quoted in ibid., 29–31.

Armand M. Nicholi: Healy, "A Less Taxing Approach."

Median income and size of new homes: Brownlee and Miller, "5 Lies Parents Tell," 60.

David Broder: David S. Broder, "No Mystery to Clinton's Popularity," *Washington Post*, September 30, 1998, A17.

Poll data on President Clinton's popularity: James Bennet with Janet Elder, "Despite Intern, President Stays in Good Graces," *New York Times*, February 24, 1998, A1; Ceci Connolly and Thomas B. Edsall, "Political Pros Looking for Explanations," *Washington Post*, February 9, 1998, A6.

Polls after Kathleen Willey and Starr Report: Dan Balz, "Willey's Story Gets a Shrug from Public," *Washington Post*, March 19, 1998, A1; Richard Morin and David S. Broder, "Worries About Nation's Morals Test a Reluctance to Judge," *Washington Post*, September 11, 1998, A1.

Paul Gigot: Paul A. Gigot, "Woodward and Bernstein Lose Their Fastball," *Wall Street Journal*, August 14, 1998, A14.

Wall Street Journal reporter: Dennis Farney, "Clinton's Support Remains Strong Because Voters View Him as Successful CEO, not Moral Example," *Wall Street Journal*, February 6, 1998, A24.

"One woman in New York": Richard L. Berke with Janet Elder, "Keep Clinton in Office, Most Say in Poll, but His Image Is Eroding," *New York Times*, September 16, 1998, A1.

Charles Krauthammer, "History's Verdict," *Washington Post*, March 20, 1998, A25.

Military leaders: Bradley Graham, "Military Leaders Worry Privately About Impact," *Washington Post*, September 15, 1998, A10.

"Kids in New York City": Jane Gross," Make the President Sit in the Corner, or Even 'Slap Him Silly,'" *New York Times*, September 5, 1998, A9.

"I praise you, Father": Luke 10:21.

"Godliness with contentment": 1 Timothy 6:6.

Jeffrey K. Salkin: Jeffrey K. Salkin, "Smash the False Gods of Careerism," *Wall Street Journal*, December 29, 1994, A10.

"Come to me": Matthew 11:28–30.

Chapter Six: Crime, Drugs, and Salvation

Ten-year-old boy in Janesville: Kathleen Ostrander, "A Killer at Age 10, Boy, Now 15, Is Freed," *Milwaukee Journal-Sentinel*, August 13, 1998, 1.

Evan Ramsey: Steve Fainaru, "Alaska School Murders: A Window on Teen Rage," *Boston Globe*, October 18, 1998, A1; "Teen Warned He'd Kill at School," *Seattle Times*, February 21, 1997, B2.

Luke Woodham: Carol Morello, "Pearl, Miss., Sees Chance for Closure," *USA Today*, June 8, 1998, 4A; Carol Morello, "Woodham Gets Life," *USA Today*, June 15, 1998, 4A.

Michael Carneal: Timothy Egan, "Where Rampages Begin," *New York Times*, June 14, 1998, A1; Tom Zucco, "Shooters in the School Yard," *St. Petersburg Times*, June 14, 1998, 1F.

Mitchell Johnson: William Booth, John Schwartz, and Stephanie Mencimer, "Ark. Teen's Troubles: Some Usual, Some Not," *Washington Post*, April 5, 1998, A1.

Kip Kinkel: Patricia King and Andrew Murr, "A Son Who Spun Out of Control," *Time*, June 1, 1998, 32–33; Jeff Jacoby, "The Classroom Culture That Spawned Kip Kinkel," *Boston Globe*, May 28, 1998, A23.

Luke Woodham re his mother: Morello, "Pearl, Miss."; "Boy's Video Confession Shown at Trial in Death of Mom, 2 Teens," *Chicago Tribune*, June 3, 1998, 16.

Mitchell Johnson's family: Booth, Schwartz, and Mencimer, "Ark. Teen's Troubles."

Barry Loukaitis's family: Egan, "Where Rampages Begin."

"Worst school year": Ibid.

Statistics on rates of overall crime, violent crime, property crime: Daryl Fischer, graph entitled "Crime and Incarceration Rates: Percentage Change from 1991 to 1996," Fischer Report, Arizona Department of Corrections.

Statistics on homicide rate: Ibid.; U.S. Department of Justice, Bureau of Justice Statistics Web site (www.ojp.usdoj.gov/bjs)(homicide statistics from 1900 to 1995; homicide rates "remain near historic highs").

Twenty-five years to return to 1960 crime rate: Daryl Fischer, graph entitled "U.S. Crime Rate: Years Until Return to 1960 Rates," Fischer Report, Arizona Department of Corrections.

"Between 1965 and 1991": Ellis Cose, "Breaking the 'Code of Silence,'" *Newsweek*, January 10, 1994, 23.

White incarceration rate: Joe Davidson, "Caged Cargo," *Emerge*, October 1997, 36.

"The FBI has reported": Federal Bureau of Investigation, *Uniform Crime Reports 1991* (Washington, D.C.: U.S. Government Printing Office, 1991), 279.

White high-school students stealing something over fifty dollars: Bureau of Justice Statistics, *Sourcebook 1996*, 244–45.

False crime statistics: Fox Butterfield, "As Crime Falls, Pressure Rises to Alter Data," *New York Times*, August 3, 1998, A1.

Statistics on number of Americans in prison or jail or on probation or parole: Bureau of Justice Statistics Web site.

"Incarceration rate has risen 209 percent": Daryl Fischer, graph entitled "Crime and Incarceration Rates: Percentage Change from 1980 to 1996," Fischer Report, Arizona Department of Corrections.

"Fifty-two percent": Fox Butterfield, "Prison Population Growing Although Crime Rate Drops," *New York Times*, August 9, 1998, sec. 1, p. 18.

"One out of four black men": William Glaberson, "One in 4 Young Black Men Is in Custody, a Study Says," *New York Times*, October 4, 1990, B6.

"1.4 million black men": Roberto Suro, "Felonies to Bar 1.4 Million Black Men from Voting, Study Says," *Washington Post*, October 23, 1998, A12.

Jesse Jackson: Davidson, "Caged Cargo"; see also James Brooke, "Prisons: A Growth Industry for Some," *New York Times*, November 2, 1997; Steven R. Donziger, "Fear, Crime, and Punishment in the United States," *Tikkun* 12, no. 6, pp. 24–27, 77.

Homicide rate since 1960: Daryl Fischer, graph entitled "U.S. Homicide Rate: 1960–1996," Fischer Report, Arizona Department of Corrections.

Number of prisoners on death row: Bureau of Justice Statistics Web site.

Statistics on drug arrests for adults, juveniles: Ibid.

Tougher laws for juveniles: "40 States Have Adopted Tougher Youth Crime Laws," *Pittsburgh Post-Gazette*, November 19, 1996, C6.

Boot camps: Charles Oliver, "Drop and Give Me 20 Push-Ups," *Investor's Business Daily*, March 22, 1994, A1.

John J. DiIulio and Glenn Loury: Glenn C. Loury, *One by One from the Inside Out: Essays and Reviews on Race and Responsibility in America* (New York: Free Press, 1995), 298–303.

"Seventy percent of juvenile offenders": Federal Bureau of Investigation, *Uniform Crime Reports 1991*, 279.

"Boys from divorced families": Myron Magnet, "The American Family, 1992," *Fortune*, August 10, 1992, 42.

"One out of three boys": Judith S. Wallerstein and Sandra Blakeslee, *Second Chances: Men, Women, and Children a Decade After Divorce* (New York: Ticknor & Fields, 1989), xvi.

"One out of ten girls": Ibid.

"Surprisingly high incidence of alcoholism": Ibid., 153–54.

McLanahan and Harper study: "Boys with Absentee Dads Twice as Likely to Be Jailed," *Washington Post*, August 21, 1998, A3.

Babies damaged by methamphetamine: Judy Pasternak, "Meth Kids: Heartland's Tragic Tale," *Los Angeles Times*, May 29, 1998, A1.

Manuel L. Scott: Scott, *Gospel for the Ghetto*, 35.

Crime rates in depression: Max Boot, *Out of Order: Arrogance, Corruption, and Incompetence on the Bench* (New York: Basic, 1998), 36.

Crime rates in the 1960s: James Q. Wilson, *Thinking About Crime* (New York: Vintage, 1985), 13–25.

Thorlief Pettersson: Thorlief Pettersson, "Religion and Criminality: Structural Relationships Between Church Involvement and Crime Rates in Contemporary Sweden," *Journal for the Scientific Study of Religion* 30 (1991): 279–91, 279–280.

Tittle and Welch: Charles Tittle and Michael Welch, "Religiosity and Deviance: Toward a Contingency Theory of Constraining Effects," *Social Forces* 61 (1983): 653–82, 654.

Youth & Society: Stephen J. Bahr, Ricky D. Hawks, and Gabe Wang, "Family and Religious Influences on Adolescent Substance Abuse," *Youth & Society* 24 (1993): 443–65, 446.

Deviant Behavior: David Brownfield and Ann Marie Sorenson, "Religion and Drug Use Among Adolescents: A Social Support Conceptualization and Interpretation," *Deviant Behavior* 12 (1991): 259–76.

Rutgers study of prisoners: Todd R. Clear, Bruce D. Stout, Harry R. Dammer, Linda Kelly, Patricia L. Hardyman, and Carol Shapiro, "Does Involvement in Religion Help Prisoners Adjust to Prisons?" *NCCD Focus*, November 1992, 1–7.

Jesus' reading of Isaiah: Luke 4:16–19.

Newsweek: Cover on June 1, 1998, issue.

Rev. Eugene Rivers: John Leland, "Savior of the Streets," *Newsweek*, June 1, 1998, 20–25.

Robert L. Woodson Sr.: Robert L. Woodson Sr., *The Triumphs of Joseph: How Today's Community Healers Are Reviving Our Streets and Neighborhoods* (New York: Free Press, 1998), 78–79, 80–81.

Nicky Cruz biographical material: Nicky Cruz with Jamie Buckingham, *Run, Baby, Run* (Green Forest, Ark.: New Leaf Press, 1992).

Teen Challenge cure rate: Peter K. Johnson, "Forty Years on the Streets," *Charisma*, February 1998, 42.

Sonny Arguinzoni: Interview by A. P. Thomas of Vaso Bjegovich, November 21, 1998; Victory Outreach Web site (www.victoryoutreach.org).

Creative street ministries: Allison Samuels, David Gordon, and Steve Rhodes, "The Lord's Foot Soldiers," *Newsweek*, June 1, 1998, 26–28.

Leonard W. Levy: Leonard W. Levy, *Original Intent and the Framers' Constitution* (New York: Macmillan, 1988), 192–93.

Los Angeles Times investigation of Safe and Drug-Free Schools funds: Ralph Frammolino, "Failing Grade for Safe Schools Plan," *Los Angeles Times*, September 6, 1998, A1.

"The full armor of God": Ephesians 6:11.

Chapter Seven: Deaths in the Family

Roe v. Wade: 410 U.S. 113 (1973).

"31 million American babies" and "one out of four babies": Guttmacher Institute Web site, "Facts in Brief—Induced Abortion."

"Brain cells multiply": Rick Weiss, "Brain Cell That Multiplies Is Isolated," *Washington Post*, October 31, 1998, A3.

Polling data on abortion: Carey Goldberg with Janet Elder, "Public Still Backs Abortion, But Wants Limits, Poll Says," *New York Times*, January 16, 1998, A1.

Reasons given for abortion: Guttmacher Institute, "Facts in Brief—Induced Abortion."

Pastor Stewart: Warren H. Stewart Sr., *How to Handle Giants: Sermons to African American Youth and Their Mentors* (Nashville: Townsend Press, 1995), 133.

Infanticide in Milwaukee: David Doege, "Woman Charged with Homicide in Death of Her Newborn Baby," *Milwaukee Journal-Sentinel*, October 21, 1998, 3.

Delaware "Prom Mom": Blaine Harden, "N.J. 'Prom Mom' Accepts Plea Agreement," *Washington Post*, August 21, 1998, A4.

Pastor Stewart on right to life, baby Jesus: Stewart, *How to Handle Giants*, 88–89.

United Nations Convention: Quoted in Dorothy Roberts, *Killing the Black Body: Race, Reproduction, and the Meaning of Liberty* (New York: Pantheon, 1997), 102.

Biographical information on Margaret Sanger: George Grant, *Grand Illusions: The Legacy of Planned Parenthood* (Brentwood, Tenn.: Wolgemuth & Hyatt, 1988), 43–58.

Sanger and eugenics: David M. Kennedy, *Birth Control in America: The Career of Margaret Sanger* (New Haven: Yale University Press, 1970), 116–23; Grant, *Grand Illusions*, 87–94.

Sanger's writings on eugenics: Margaret Sanger, ed., *Birth Control Review*, November 1921, 1 ("To create a race of thoroughbreds"); Margaret Sanger, "A Plan for Peace," *Birth Control Review*, April 1932, 107–8; Grant, *Grand Illusions*, 91. Copies of Sanger articles obtained from Akua Furlow of LEARN.

Brooklyn clinic: Grant, *Grand Illusions*, 92.

Papers at Second International Congress of Eugenics: Roberts, *Killing the Black Body*, 71.

Ku Klux Klan: Ibid., 72.

Creation of Negro Project: Ibid., 76–79; Grant, *Grand Illusions*, 92–94.

"The mass of Negroes": Roberts, *Killing the Black Body*, 76–77.

Sanger's letter to Clarence J. Gamble: Letter from Margaret Sanger to C. J. Gamble, December 10, 1939. Copy obtained from Akua Furlow of LEARN.

Gamble memorandum: Roberts, *Killing the Black Body*, 78.

George Grant on southern health officials: Grant, *Grand Illusions*, 93.

Roberts on white-controlled birth control programs, Harlem clinic: Roberts, *Killing the Black Body*, 78, 87.

1972 and 1973 surveys: Ibid., 98.

Leaders of Planned Parenthood: Grant, *Grand Illusions*, 59.

Abortion rates among the races: Guttmacher Institute, "Facts in Brief—Induced Abortion"; Betsy Wagner, "Who Has Abortions," *U.S. News & World Report*, August 19, 1996, 8.

Number of black babies aborted: Juluette Bartlett Pack, "A Historical View of Eugenics and Its Role in Abortion in Black America," Life Education and Resource Network (LEARN) Web site (www.learnusa.org/articles).

"78 percent of abortion clinics": Pack, "A Historical View of Eugenics," 2.

"In the 1980s": Grant, *Grand Illusions*, 94.

Poll of blacks and whites on abortion: Cable News Network/USA *Today*, January 1998, Roper Center.

Studies cited by Akua Furlow: Akua Furlow, "African-American Women Are Exploited by Abortion," LEARN Web site.

Jared Taylor: Jared Taylor, *Paved with Good Intentions: The Failure of Race Relations in Contemporary America* (New York: Carroll & Graf, 1992), 349. Taylor's book received a favorable review in *National Review* magazine and from Patrick Buchanan on CNN's *Crossfire*.

George Grant on the media: Grant, *Grand Illusions*, 167–85.

Stephen Hess: Eleanor Randolph, "GOP Finds That Media-Bashing Is the Right Path," *Los Angeles Times*, July 22, 1996, A12.

Planned Parenthood funding from U.S. foreign aid, United Way, and March of Dimes: Grant, *Grand Illusions*, 28–30, 149–64.

Number of adoptions: Esther B. Fein, "Secrecy and Stigma No Longer Clouding Adoptions," *New York Times*, October 25, 1998, A1.

Homes for black children: Woodson, *Triumphs of Joseph*, 31–32.

"State adoption agencies": Ibid., 32.

Decline in abortion rate: Barbara Vobejda, "Abortion Rate in U.S. Off Sharply," *Washington Post*, December 5, 1997, A1.

Chapter Eight: Personal Fouls

Gary Payton: Stephen A. Smith, "Iverson's NBA Colleagues Talk of His Troubles," *Seattle Times*, July 26, 1998, D1.

Pros and Cons: Jeff Benedict and Don Yaeger, *Pros and Cons: The Criminals Who Play in the NFL* (New York: Warner, 1998), viii.

Sports Illustrated: Grant Wahl and L. Jon Wertheim, "Paternity Ward," *Sports Illustrated*, May 4, 1998, 62–71.

"25 major-college athletic programs": Bill Brubaker and Mark Asher, "A Building Boom in College Sports," *Washington Post*, November 3, 1998, A1.

Doug Dickey's denial: "White: Tennessee AD Barters for Donation," *Rocky Mountain News*, October 2, 1998, 5C.

1977 locker room suit: Molly Woulfe, "Suit Won Entry to Locker Room," *Chicago Tribune*, September 18, 1988, C4.

"All four major pro sports leagues": Jane Gross, "Female Sportswriters Make Their Mark," *New York Times*, May 26, 1988, D23.

NFL policy book: Rob Gloster, "Female Sports Reporters Still Have to Fight Prejudice on Beats," *Los Angeles Times*, September 8, 1985, part 3, p. 2.

Lisa Olson: Timothy W. Smith, "Tagliabue Waffles on Lisa Olson File," *New York Times*, May 31, 1992, sec. 8, p. 7; Melvin Durslag, "She Would Be Wiser to Forget the Lawsuit," *Los Angeles Times*, April 29, 1991, C3.

Sam Wyche: "Wyche Receives Support in Locker Room Crusade," *Chicago Tribune*, January 3, 1991, C3; Timothy W. Smith, "Wyche Still Fighting on Locker Rooms," *New York Times*, March 17, 1991, sec. 8, p. 8.

Denver Nuggets: Curtis Eichelberger, "Teenage Girls in School Program Enter Nuggets Locker Room," *Rocky Mountain News*, November 24, 1995, 4A.

WNBA: Jennifer Frey, "A Look Inside the Women's Locker Room," *Washington Post*, July 27, 1997, D11.

Chapter Nine: V-Chip Morality

"You worry about schools": Josh Getlin, "Parents Liken TV to Night Patrol in Hostile Territory," *Los Angeles Times*, June 13, 1997, A1.

Poll of 1,200 children: Stephen Magagnini, "TV Gives Distorted Picture of Real Life, Kids Complain," *Sacramento Bee*, May 9, 1998, A1.

Violent music videos: Lisa M. Krieger, "Video Violence," *Chicago Sun-Times*, April 10, 1998, 41.

8,000 murders on TV: Scott Stossel, "The Man Who Counts the Killings," *Atlantic Monthly*, May 1997, 90.

"More than 3,000 studies": Ibid., 87.

"Major three-year study": Findings reported in John Stamper, "Pounded by TV Violence," *Houston Chronicle*, April 17, 1998, A22.

Analysis of TV "family hour": Thomas Johnson, "The 'Family Hour': No Place for Your Kids," Media Research Center Web site (www.mrc.org/specialreports/ent/).

Children Now study: Children Now and the Kaiser Family Foundation, "Sex, Kids and the Family Hour: A Three-Part Study of Sexual Content on Television," Children Now Web site (www.childrennow.org/media/familyhour/FAMHOUR.html).

South Park: Lawrie Mifflin, "Curfew in 'South Park'?" *New York Times*, March 11, 1998, E7.

Joyce Knight: Michael Precker, "MTV Dispute: Protection of Youth vs. Freedom of Choice," *San Diego Union-Tribune*, August 2, 1997, E4.

Robert Woodson: Woodson, *Triumphs of Joseph*, 11–12.

Religion on TV: Thomas Johnson, "Faith in a Box: Entertainment Television on Religion—1997," Media Research Center Web site.

New York Times on violent pop culture: Egan, "Where Rampages Begin."

Barry Loukaitis: Ibid.

Mitchell Johnson: Ibid.; "Arkansas Shooting Renews Debate over Music-Violence Link," *Washington Times*, June 17, 1998, A9.

Luke Woodham: Egan, "Where Rampages Begin."

Michael Carneal and Kip Kinkel: Ibid.

Disney: "Walt Disney's Legacy Has Been Trashed Today," *Rocky Mountain News*, July 29, 1997, 31A; American Family Association, "Why Americans Should Boycott Disney," AFA Texas Web site (www.afatexas.org/document/boycotts/disney.html).

Victor Salva: Joe Baltake, "A Hollywood Powder Keg," *Sacramento Bee*, November 6, 1995, C1.

False labeling of programs: Don Aucoin, "Despite Vow, Many TV Shows Lack Rating Labels, Study Says," *Boston Globe*, September 25, 1998, A1.

Labeling May Attract Kids: Tara Parker-Pope, "Danger: Warning Labels May Backfire," *Wall Street Journal*, April 28, 1997, B1.

"Frustrated Denver mother": Steve Farkas and Jean Johnson, *Kids These Days: What Americans Really Think About the Next Generation*, (New York: Public Agenda), 1997, 18.

Seattle man: Ian S. King, letter to the editor, "Video Technology—Parents Should Watch TV with Children, or Turn It Off," *Seattle Times*, August 18, 1998, B5.

Chapter Ten: Raising Good Children in Tough Times

"Juvenile crime rate rose 70 percent": Melissa Sickmund, Howard N. Snyder, and Eileen Poe-Yamagata, U.S. Department of Justice, Office of Juvenile Justice and Delinquency Prevention, *Juvenile Offenders and Victims: 1997 Update on Violence*, August 1997, National Criminal Justice Reference Service (NCJRS) Web site (www.ncjrs.org/ojjdp/juvoff).

"From 1950 to 1993": "Murder, Suicide Claiming More Victims," *Orlando Sentinel*, February 7, 1997, A7.

"Between 1985 and 1995": Sickmund, Snyder, and Poe-Yamagata, *Juvenile Offenders and Victims*, NCJRS Web site.

"Twenty-two percent of adolescents": Farkas and Johnson, *Kids These Days*, 34.

Percentage of young girls having sex and middle-school counselor in Louisville: Kay S. Mymowitz, "Kids Today Are Growing Up Way Too Fast," *Wall Street Journal*, October 28, 1998, A22.

Suicide rate from 1950 to 1993: "Murder, Suicide," *Orlando Sentinel*.

"American children are twice as likely": Ibid.

"Almost one out of four high-school students": Bureau of Justice Statistics, *Sourcebook 1996*, p. 256, table 3.55.

"Number of Americans under eighteen who smoke": "Daily Smoking by Teens Has Risen Sharply," *Washington Post*, October 9, 1998, A3.

"Fewer than one out of four kids": "Whether It's Homework or TV, Fewer Children Are Exercising," *Los Angeles Times*, July 16, 1997.

"53 percent of adults" and "spoiled" children: Farkas and Johnson, *Kids These Days*, 11.

"One mother in Denver": Ibid., 14.

Young people complained they didn't see enough of their parents: Ibid., 33.

"One California teenager": Ibid.

Parent in Irvington, N.Y.: Trip Gabriel, "Boomers: 'Not as I Did' Parents," *New York Times*, November 30, 1995, B1.

Teacher in New York: Farkas and Johnson, *Kids These Days*, 14.

"94 percent of Americans" approved of spanking: Brigid Schulte, "Sparing the Rod Helps Behavior, AMA Indicates," *Arizona Republic*, August 15, 1997, A1.

"The law is against parents": Farkas and Johnson, *Kids These Days*, 15.

"83 percent of blacks": Schulte, "Sparing the Rod."

"58 percent to 50 percent": Farkas and Johnson, *Kids These Days*, p. 39, table 3.

Elijah Anderson and Charles Willie: Discussed in Murray A. Straus with Denise A. Donnelly, *Beating the Devil Out of Them: Corporal Punishment in American Families* (New York: Lexington, 1994), 116–17.

Immigrants and corporal punishment: Celia W. Dugger, "Immigrant Cultures Raising Issues of Child Punishment," *New York Times*, February 29, 1996, A1.

Murray A. Straus: Straus and Donnelly, *Beating the Devil Out of Them*, xiii ("cradle of violence"), 112–13 (higher murder rate); Murray A. Straus and Denise A. Donnelly, "Corporal Punishment of Adolescents by American Parents," *Youth & Society* 24 (1993): 419–42, 437–38 (risk from two parents and "assault"); Murray A. Straus, David B. Sugarman, and Jean Giles-Sims, "Spanking by Parents and Subsequent Antisocial Behavior of Children," *Archives of Pediatrics & Adolescent Medicine* 151 (1997): 761–67 (spanking related to antisocial behavior).

Robert E. Larzelere, "Response to Oosterhuis: Empirically Justified Uses of Spanking: Toward a Discriminating View of Corporal Punishment," *Journal of Psychology and Theology* 21 (1993): 142–47.

Manuel L. Scott: Scott, *Gospel for the Ghetto*, 114.

Dr. Diller on "doctors can't agree": Sharon Kirkey, "Doctor Fears Ritalin Is Overprescribed," *Ottawa Citizen*, September 29, 1998, A2.

"Number of children diagnosed with ADD": Lisa Jennings, "The Ritalin Generation," *Orange County Register*, October 14, 1998, E1.

700 percent increase in Ritalin prescriptions: Ibid.

"University of Maryland study" and "children as young as one year old": Susan Okie, "Hyperactivity Drugs Given to Very Young," *Washington Post*, June 2, 1998, Z7.

"Generation Rx": Jennings, "The Ritalin Generation."

"About 1.3 million children": Larry Atkins, "Ritalin, Once a Godsend, Now a Real Danger," *Cleveland Plain Dealer*, May 3, 1998, 1D.

"5 to 6 percent of elementary school children": Okie, "Hyperactivity Drugs."

"One out of four students on Ritalin": Roger Dobson, "Give Them Understanding, Not Just Drugs," *The Independent (London)*, September 15, 1998, 11.

Dr. Diller describes suburban schools: Kirkey, "Doctor Fears Ritalin."

Robert A. King: Okie, "Hyperactivity Drugs."

Dr. Diller on white, suburban families: Gayle Vassar Melvin, "Pediatrician Takes a Tough Stance on the Increasing Use of Ritalin," *Houston Chronicle*, October 15, 1998, 2.

Mary Jane Reed: Mary Jane Reed, "Ritalin No Substitute for Responsibility," *Cleveland Plain Dealer*, July 21, 1998, 8B.

Dr. Richard Broomfield: Atkins, "Once a Godsend."

Dr. Peter Breggin: Dobson, "Give Them Understanding."

Michael Gurian: Quoted in Barbara Kantrowitz and Claudia Kalb, "Boys Will Be Boys," *Newsweek*, May 11, 1998, 56.

"Forty-nine percent of Americans" think public schools fail: Farkas and Johnson, *Kids These Days*, 18.

"67 percent say that improving the public schools": Ibid., 23.

"Total school spending rose" and SAT scores: Andrew Peyton Thomas, "Equal Time," *National Review*, September 14, 1998, 28–30.

School vouchers in Wisconsin: Joan Biskupic, "Wisconsin Wins School Vouchers Case," *Washington Post*, June 11, 1998, A1; Editorial, "Choice Thunderclap," *Wall Street Journal*, June 11, 1998, A22.

Enrollment at Messmer High: Jon Jeter, "As Test of Vouchers, Milwaukee Parochial School Exceeds Expectations," *Washington Post*, September 1, 1998, A3.

Aisha James and Deseree Gordon: Ibid.

Three out of four blacks support school choice: Daniel Bice, "Blacks More Likely to Favor Expanded Choice," *Milwaukee Journal-Sentinel*, August 9, 1998, 15.

National polls on school choice: Terry M. Neal, "School Choice a Key Issue for GOP," *Washington Post*, September 7, 1997, A14.

Study by Harvard University and Mathematica: Linda Perlstein, "School Voucher Supporters Get a Boost," *Washington Post*, October 28, 1998, A15.

Hispanic students in California schools: Anne-Marie O'Connor, "Many Latinos Fare Better in Catholic Schools," *Los Angeles Times*, August 3, 1998, A1.

Chapter Eleven: The Souls of Black Folk Today

Blyden on materialism: Blyden, *Christianity, Islam, and the Negro Race*, 143.

Du Bois on materialism: W. E. B. Du Bois, *The Souls of Black Folk* (New York: Bantam, 1989), 55, 57.

1997 ABC News poll: ABC News, March 1997, Roper Center.

Poll re doubts on God: Poll by Yankelovich Partners for *Time*/Cable News Network, June 1996, Roper Center.

CNN/*USA Today* poll: Gallup Poll for CNN/*USA Today*, January 1998, Roper Center.

"Thirty-seven percent of blacks": Hanna Rosin, "Competing Views of Faith Resonate with Flexible Electorate," *Washington Post*, October 29, 1998, A1.

Rates of church attendance: Gallup Poll for CNN/*USA Today*, June 1998, Roper Center. Thirty-one percent of whites, as compared to 38 percent of blacks, attend church or synagogue at least once a week.

Marcus Garvey: Garvey, *Message to the People*, 45.

Du Bois on "religious animal": Du Bois, *Souls of Black Folk*, 139.

Nat Turner: Kenneth S. Greenberg, ed., *The Confessions of Nat Turner and Related Documents* (Boston: Bedford Books, 1996), 1–3; W. E. B. Du Bois, "Religion in the South," in *The Negro in the South: His Economic Progress in Relation to His Moral and Religious Development* by Booker T. Washington and W. E. B. Du Bois (New York: Citadel, 1970), 161–65.

Southern state laws after Nat Turner's rebellion: Du Bois, "Religion in the South," in *The Negro in the South*, 165–67.

Booker T. Washington on black spirituality: Washington, "The Economic Development of the Negro Race in Slavery," in *The Negro in the South*, 29.

Du Bois on the Negro church: Du Bois, *Souls of Black Folk*, 136–37.

Sandy Ray: Ray, *Journeying Through a Jungle*, 41–42.

"Easier for a camel": Matthew 19:24.

"Where moth and rust do not destroy": Matthew 6:20.

Washington re James Hill: Washington, "The Economic Development of the Negro Race Since Its Emancipation," in *The Negro in the South*, 52–54.

Du Bois re Atlanta riots: Du Bois, "The Economic Revolution in the South," in *The Negro in the South*, 115.

Du Bois holding his shotgun: Introduction to *The Negro in the South*, x.

Du Bois on Jesus coming to Georgia: Du Bois, "Religion in the South," 177.

Claud Anderson on feminists: Claud Anderson, *Black Labor, White Wealth: The Search for Power and Economic Justice* (Edgewood, Md.: Duncan & Duncan, 1994), 58–62.

Charles Mischeaux: Ronald Walters, "Is the Party Over?" *Emerge*, November 1998, 54.

Grandmother at Arkansas A.M.E. church: Rosin, "Competing Views."

Dr. King's last Sunday Sermon: Quoted in James Dobson, *Family News from Dr. James Dobson* (Colorado Springs: Focus on the Family), November 1998.

Good Ol' Boy Roundup: Ginger Orr, "ATF Agents Blamed After Racist Fetes," *Chicago Tribune*, July 22, 1995, 3.

Trip to Vidalia, Georgia, also discussed in Reggie White with Steve Hubbard, *God's Play Book* (Nashville: Thomas Nelson, 1998), 110–11.

Blyden re Ethiopian eunuch: Blyden, *Christianity, Islam, and the Negro Race*, 185–86.

Chapter Twelve: Defenders of the Faith

"Ninety-five percent of Americans": ABC News poll, March 1997, Roper Center.

"Six out of ten Americans": Gallup Poll for CNN/*USA Today*, June 1998, Roper Center.

"Four out of ten": Rosin, "Competing Views."

"Not everyone who says to me, 'Lord, Lord,'": Matthew 7:21.

Sandy Ray on the Israelites: Ray, *Journeying Through a Jungle*, 40.

"As for me and my household": Joshua 24:15.

"The Testimony of a Towel": Ray, *Journeying Through a Jungle*, 31–38.

The first and second commandments: Matthew 22:37–40.

Conclusion: The Soldier Versus the Cadet

"With God all things are possible": Matthew 19:26.

About the Authors

Reggie White

Reggie White recently retired from the NFL as one of the greatest football players of all time. A former defensive end with the Green Bay Packers, he is the NFL's all-time career leader in sacks. He was selected for thirteen consecutive Pro Bowls, also an NFL record. In 1997, White helped lead the Green Bay Packers to their first Super Bowl victory in three decades.

An ordained minister since the age of seventeen, White preaches throughout the country and has been honored numerous times for his humanitarian efforts. He has received a Tolerance Award from the Simon Wiesenthal Center and the Jackie Robinson Humanitarian Award. He and his wife, Sara, founded Urban Hope, an inner-city ministry. White lives in Green Bay, Wisconsin, with Sara and their two children.

Andrew Peyton Thomas

Andrew Peyton Thomas is a graduate of the University of Missouri and Harvard Law School, where he was a legal assistant for the Boston NAACP. He is the author of the critically acclaimed book *Crime and the Sacking of America*, and he has written articles for the *Wall Street Journal*, *National Review*, *Weekly Standard*, and many other publications. He currently practices law in Phoenix, where he lives with his wife, Ann, and their three children.